SPORT BRANDS

Sport brands are a central element of modern sport business and a ubiquitous component of contemporary global culture. This groundbreaking book offers a complete analysis of the topic of sport brands from both a marketing management approach (strategy and implementation) and a psycho-sociological approach (consumption and wider society). In doing so it explores both supply and demand sides, offering a complete introduction to the nature, purpose and value of sport brands not found in any other sports marketing text.

The book covers the whole heterogeneity of sport brands, going much further than the sport team and league brands covered in most other books. As well as teams and leagues, the book considers the brands of sports celebrities, events, media, computer games and governing bodies, as well as the ethical, professional and technological 'label brands' associated with sport. Richly illustrated with cases, examples and data, the book explores the tangible and intangible influence of sport brands, their economic and social value, and the subcultures and communities that grow up around them. It also introduces common strategies for growing brands, and growing through brands, and examines the challenges and threats that sport brands face, from boycotts and ambush marketing to counterfeiting.

An understanding of sport brands is essential for a fully rounded understanding of contemporary sport marketing. As a result, this book is important reading for any student or practitioner working in sport marketing, sport business, or mainstream marketing management.

Patrick Bouchet is Professor of Sport Management and Marketing within the Sport Sciences Faculty at the University of Burgundy, France, and is a member of the Socio-Psychology and Sport Management research group. His research is interested in actors' behaviours (consumers, groups and organisations) linked to sport consumption (event, tourism and retailing). He has co-edited several books on Sport Management and Marketing and two books on Sport Brands (Economica, 2008; De Boeck, 2009) in French.

Dieter Hillairet is Lecturer in Sport Management and Marketing within the University of Clermont-Ferrand, France, and is a member of the Clermont centre of research in management (CRCGM). He is also the director of the Masters course in Sport Entrepreneurship, Strategy and Innovation. His research mainly deals with innovation management, entrepreneurship and branding. He has authored two books about sport and innovation, one book about sport economy and entrepreneurship, and co-authored two books about sport brands in French.

Guillaume Bodet is Lecturer of Sport Marketing and Management within the Institute of Sport and Leisure Policy and the Centre for Olympic Studies and Research, School of Sport, Exercise and Health Sciences at the University of Loughborough, UK. His research primarily deals with consumer behaviour regarding sport organisations, events and brands. He has co-edited the *Routledge Handbook of Sport Management* (2012).

ROUTLEDGE SPORTS MARKETING

Series Editor: Simon Chadwick – Director of the Birkbeck Sport Business Centre, and Programme Director for the MSc Sport Management and the Business of Football at the University of London, UK.

The Routledge Sport Marketing Series provides a superb range of texts for students and practitioners covering all aspects of marketing within sports. Structured in three tiers the series addresses:

*   sub-disciplines within sports marketing: for example, branding, marketing communications, consumer behaviour
*   sports and sporting properties to which marketing is applied: for example, the marketing of football, the marketing of motor sports, marketing of the Olympic Games
*   philosophy, method and research in sports marketing; for example, research methods for sports marketing students, theoretical perspectives in sports marketing, undertaking successful research in sports marketing.

The Routledge Sport Marketing Series is the first of its kind, and as such is recognised as being of consistent high quality and will quickly become the series of first choice for academics, students and managers.

Available in this series:

Marketing and Football
Michel Desbordes

Consumer Behaviour in Sport and Events
Daniel Funk

Relationship Marketing in Sports
Andre Buhler, Gerd Nufer

Sport Public Relations and Communication
Maria Hopwood, James Skinner, Paul Kitchin

Sport Brands
Patrick Bouchet, Dieter Hillairet and Guillaume Bodet

Ambush Marketing in Sports
Gerd Nufer

SPORT BRANDS

Patrick Bouchet, Dieter Hillairet and Guillaume Bodet

Routledge
Taylor & Francis Group

LONDON AND NEW YORK

First published 2013
by Routledge
2 Park Square, Milton Park, Abingdon, Oxon OX14 4RN

Simultaneously published in the USA and Canada
by Routledge
711 Third Avenue, New York, NY 10017

Routledge is an imprint of the Taylor & Francis Group, an informa business

British Library Cataloguing in Publication Data
A catalogue record for this book is available from the British Library

Library of Congress Cataloging in Publication Data
Bouchet, Patrick.
Sport brands / Patrick Bouchet, Dieter Hillairet and Guillaume Bodet.
pages cm
1. Sports—Marketing. 2. Professional sports—Economic aspects. 3. Sports—
Economic aspects. 4. Sports—Social aspects. 5. Sports administration. I. Title.
GV716.B664 2013
796.06—dc23
2012033184

ISBN: 978-0-415-53284-6 (hbk)
ISBN: 978-0-415-53285-3 (pbk)
ISBN: 978-0-203-11466-7 (ebk)

Typeset in Bembo and Stone Sans
by FiSH Books Ltd, Enfield

MIX
Paper from
responsible sources
FSC
www.fsc.org   FSC® C018575

Printed and bound in Great Britain by MPG Printgroup

CONTENTS

LIST OF FIGURES AND TABLES

Figures

Tables

PREFACE

Brands are at the heart of economic activities as they attract massive financial transactions and streams. While some of them were born at the beginning of the industrial era, the post-world war period and what Baudrillard (1998) named the consumer society saw the emergence and growth of numerous brands which are estimated to be about 1.2 billion worldwide. They contribute to the performance and prosperity of national economies and this is not surprising as economically-rich countries, where purchase power is high, abound with international megabrands. A free-market economy without brands is unthinkable as their primary function is to differentiate offer origins and competitors. Nowadays numerous products and services are commercialised worldwide under the same brand. This commercial notoriety has become a strong asset for companies alongside their particular know-how and expertise, production processes and human resources. Moreover, the globalisation of societies and economies has created an intensification of competition between economic actors which has made certain observers talk about a shift from market economies toward brand economies.

As for other sectors of the economy, the growth of sports and recreation markets is strongly driven by the development of brands. The acquisition of an international brand can strongly reshape an entire market and its segments by modifying the competitive balance and leadership positions, increasing the stock exchange value of the company, strongly affecting human resources through for example production process changes, redundancies and relocation, and changing final users' consumption practices. It seems that the creation of new industrial and tertiary sectors and the competition increase between firms and nations have put brands in such a central position. However, this position is also strongly influenced by the roles consumers play in the process. They have indeed become major actors who influence both firms and distributors and are at the heart of brands' marketing strategies aiming to attract and seduce them, satisfy them and make them loyal to maintain companies' and brands' profitability. In the same time, the consumers' environment has been massively influenced and changed by marketing actions. Furthermore, it is not only about the real world, but also hyper-real (those which reproduce and/or simulate real worlds, such as Las Vegas' hotels) and virtual worlds as well. Brands and their marketing have indeed created a tangible consumption culture which plays a considerable role in the way people interact with commercial offers, and other aspects of their lives. This cultural impact concerns the way people think and behave, their tastes as well as the cultures, subcultures and communities they belong to. Therefore, consumers and marketers coexist in a reciprocal influential and complex relationship which makes it difficult to say if we should support a *No Logo* (Klein, 2001) or a *Pro Logo* (Chevalier and Mazzalovo, 2004) stance. Drawing the line between reality and marketing narratives is more difficult than in the past and this confusion affects people in their everyday and leisure behaviours. This is particularly true as brands develop social, green and responsible marketing strategies while they try to make consumers purchase spontaneously and sometimes compulsively.

Sport markets do not escape these trends where sport brands are developing new strategies and tactics to create and encourage demands, and where consumers use, re-appropriate, divert and sometimes boycott them to express their individual and social identities. In 2000 Adidas and Nike were ranked, respectively, sixth and fifteenth worldwide, among the brands which contributed the most to well-being, improvement and quality of life in the last century (Pernès, 2000). Consequently, the analysis of the relationships between sport brands and their consumers cannot be accurately conducted without taking into consideration the cultural influences on consumer perceptions, attitudes, ideas and behaviours. Their impact on sport products and services' purchase and usage is clearly noticeable when making intercultural and international comparison. Nevertheless, from workshops to superstores, from publicity to public spaces, from marketers' minds to consumers' behaviours, the cultural influence of sport brands produce both contextual and universal consequences which are worth studying. In providing an original and diverse framework of analysis, this book aims to bring a new, holistic and critical look at sport brands which have become, in just a few years, icons for the younger generations and significant life partners for people at large.

The authors

Patrick Bouchet PhD is Professor of Sport Management and Marketing within the Sport Sciences Faculty at the University of Burgundy (France) and a member of the Socio-Psychology and Sport Management (SPMS) research group. He is the director of the Master in Social Psychology and Sport Management within the University of Burgundy. He is widely interested in actors' behaviours (consumers, groups and organisations) linked to sport consumption (event, tourism and retailing). He co-edited *Management et marketing du sport: du Local au global* (PUS, 2005) and *Afrique Francophone et développement du sport: du mythe à la réalité* (Harmattan,

2004), and co-authored one book about sport tourism management (PUR, 2009) and two books about sport brands (Economica, 2008; De Boeck University, 2009) in French language. He has published numerous articles in peer-reviewed journals such as *Journal of Sport and Tourism, Group Processes and Intergroup Relations, Loisir et Société/ Society and Leisure, Journal of Sport and Social Issues* and *Sport Management Review.*

Dieter Hillairet PhD is Lecturer in Sport Management and Marketing within the University of Clermont-Ferrand (France) and is a member of the Clermont centre of research in management (CRCGM). He is the director of the Master in Sport Entrepreneurship, Strategy and Innovation. His research interests mainly deal with innovation management, entrepreneurship and branding. He authored two books about sport and innovation, *L'innovation sportive – entreprendre pour gagner* (L'Harmattan, 1999) and *Sport et innovation – stratégies, techniques et produits* (Hermes Lavoisier, 2005), one book about sport economy and entrepreneurship (Harmattan, 2003), and co-authored two books about sport brands (Economica, 2008; De Boeck University, 2009) in French. He has published numerous articles in peer-reviewed journals such as *Journal of Innovation Economics, Revue Française de Gestion* and *Revue Européenne de Management du Sport.*

Guillaume Bodet, PhD is Lecturer of Sport Marketing and Management within the School of Sport, Exercise and Health Sciences at the University of Loughborough (UK). His research primarily deals with consumer behaviour regarding sport organisations, sporting events and sport brands. He has co-edited the Routledge Handbook of Sport Management (2012) and has published numerous articles in peer-reviewed journals such as *European Sport Management Quarterly, International Journal of Sports Marketing & Sponsorship, Journal of Retailing and Consumer Services, Sport Management Review, Journal of Sport Management,* and *Psychology & Marketing.*

INTRODUCTION

Concepts, values and contextual framing

In most countries and for most people, brands have become symbols of a consumer society. They build their strength by expressing awareness (advertising) and a commitment pledge to consumers. Nowadays, a close proximity connects brands with people. In this almost affective and existential relationship, sport brands have a special role. For many consumers, sport brands contribute to their means of expression and ways of being; they convey values for intergenerational objects. For instance, sportswear brands have become a means of expressing an identity and belonging to a lifestyle or to a specific community, such as the communities of skateboarders and free-riders. Quiksilver and Rip Curl have been able to associate themselves with feelings such as cool, fun and freedom which are now identity symbols for young generations. In this regard, to increase its international and global awareness, Quiksilver has also widely used street marketing, a promotion and communication strategy which is in line with its identity and its urban youth target, increasing the brand's presence in everyday life.

Sport brands are in the inner circle of favourite consumer brands. In this sense, they represent a true universal language with their own words, codes, values, references and representations. Like some brands of home appliances (for example Philips), food products (for example Danone), or multimedia material (for example Samsung), sports brands have fully integrated with people's lives. Almost achieving a mythical status, Nike is one of the few brands in the world that records the highest recognition rate among teenagers. Ultimately, Nike is seen both as a trademark associated with the functional and technical performance of its products, and a brand with symbolic values promoting self achievement and transcendence. Across the world, Nike is the subject of a genuine worship. Like Adidas all around the world or Lacoste in Europe and many others, sport brands have demonstrated that beyond all economic and industrial considerations, they have become real consumption objects. Many individuals devote an unlimited adoration to some sport brands, either for corporate or club brands. Sport brands constitute for some consumers a distinctive social and lifestyle marker, they often have a power of social projection, and are synonymous with escape, vitality and strength.

Sport brands have an enviable feature: the best known very often represent the entire sector because they have grown up in parallel with the market they belong to. Their name is enough to designate their industry: Rossignol (ski), Prince (tennis rackets), Wimbledon (tennis competition), Reebok (footwear), TaylorMade (golf), Speedo (swimming), McLaren (Formula 1) Air Jordan (shoes), Foot Locker (retail), NASCAR (car racing), Manchester United (football), Cannondale (mountain bike), NBA (basketball), Patagonia (outdoor sports) to name a few. Whether you support them or not, whether you like them or not, you cannot ignore them. Many of them presume to make us happy for what they represent or convey. In many ways, brands are very close to people, interfering in their lives and affecting their physical appearance. In developed and developing societies, sport brands have a real meaning which conveys a symbolic function exceeding their legitimacy and their original territory, the sport territory, because they have very strong cultural and social meanings which contribute to consumers' tagging process). For instance, there are elitist brands and 'neighbourhood/ghetto' brands, American brands and European brands, Australian surfing brands and English rugby brands, global and regional brands . . . 'Being Nike, Adidas or Lacoste has not the same symbolic [meaning], even if the sport shoes do not seem so different' (Lewi, 2006, p. 67). Much more than their non-sport counterparts, sports brands have powerful allusive contents. If they represent a guarantee of authenticity, a promise of performance, a steady satisfaction or a significant attachment, they also create strong cultural and social landmarks.

Inherently, sport brands have an ability to construct and convey meanings through narratives and discourses. The semiotic power of sport brands is very strong. Unlike brands which are often embedded in a specific use, a meaning or an industry, sport brands are cross-functional, which is one of their greatest strengths. Beyond their original purpose, which can be providing clothes and equipment to athletes, sport participation or spectacle, sport brands are seen as signifiers with multiple properties that transcend everyday life. For young people, they even escort them far away from stadiums and sports venues for which they were originally designed. If Quiksilver is a sport brand, it is also the emblem of an entire philosophy of life, a surfing culture. Therefore, authenticity is certainly the most salient characteristic of sport brands which could explain their success (Ohl, 2003). Wearing surf brands carries a message, displaying the ideals of freedom, fun, escape and nature which are at the roots of the surfing and snowboarding cultures (Heino, 2000).

Although their commercial success is undeniable, and despite the fact that they are certainly not the only ones to blame, some iconic brands such McDonalds, Coca-Cola and Wal-Mart stigmatise the excesses and drifts of the consumer society. These megabrands are accused today of imposing, against all odds, a monotheistic dogma through their conception of the consumer society. Some critical observers have started wondering whether these brands are able to offer consumers other things, other values than those of a standardised and globalised lifestyle and dream, often seen as the American dream, and whether they are able to convey messages, speeches and images, out of fast food, sodas, retailers and what Ritzer (2010) named the cathedrals of consumption. It seems, however, that these interrogations less concern, if not at all, sport brands which are perceived to be built on transversal and plural modes and whose success lies precisely in this capacity to embody a set of values that most non-sport brands fail to symbolise. In this sense, sport brands are probably what brands want to be: suppliers of meaning and life principles. More than just kit suppliers and entertainment providers, sport brands perfectly reflect deeper societal trends that are closely linked to current consumption patterns.

Sport brands are now a reality which goes beyond the partitioned universes of sports and sportsmen and women. Sport fashion is now a state of mind or being which corresponds with many consumers' aspirations and expressions of identity. A different clothing style portrays the image that this person has of him/herself and probably reflects the different stages of his/her life. A clothing style is located at the interface between oneself and others, at the junction between the intimate and the social public spheres. Wearing this specific sweatshirt, this specific colour and this specific brand is, especially for many young people, perceived as a necessity if people want to be fashionable and be accepted by their peers. Finally, the clothing styles promoted by sport brands are ultimately identity markers for both individuals and the groups which they belong to. Sport brands participate a lot in social mimicry phenomena, particularly for shoes. Nevertheless, the ways to wear shoes, associated with other branded products (for example trousers, shirt, sweatshirt, accessories) tend to show the diverse abilities of 'arts de faire' (de Certeau, 1988) to integrate, appropriate, customise as well as reject fashion and society.

Today, sports brands have become powerful, some even mythical, and get great benefits from their successful products, their images and the values they hold (for example for Nike, transcendence, teamwork, mutual respect and differences; for Adidas, authenticity, loyalty, respect for the rules; for Manchester United, success, performance and glory). They have been able to strongly exploit the power of images through media exposure and advertising which have become the key links with consumers. Moreover, their successes are based on their ability to enhance the perception and the recognition of symbols associated with them. To this end, advertising promotes brands by allowing them to tell a story, deliver a message, but also to maintain a relationship of complicity and loyalty with consumers. Therefore, we can understand why a good name, a good logo and a good slogan give another dimension to the brand. Who does not remember 'Become what you are' (Lacoste), 'Impossible is nothing' (Adidas) or 'Just do it' and 'I Can' (Nike)?

Beyond the implicit contract with their consumers, sport brands often advocate an idea and a cause. They claim, with varying degrees of determination, a vision (what they want or stand for), a mission (their purpose), a vocation (their commitments), an ambition (what they aim for) and a system of values which are tied to an area of expertise and legitimate know-how (originality, performance and quality). If the technical and functional dimensions of sport brands are well understood and appreciated for the value and the intrinsic qualities of their products and services, it is not the same for their intangible dimension. Brands carry, for example, ideological and/or political (Patagonia claims a designing process that respects the environment), psychological (Nike invites athletes to excel), sociological (Lacoste displays social success) or cultural (Michael Jordan and Tiger Woods have become icons of Black Americans' success in society).

In this book, we have purposely decided to set a framework for reflection using multiple and complementary (socio-cultural, economic, managerial, ethnological and psychosocial) approaches. The concept of sport brands has many senses and interpretations which should allow the reader to fully grasp its whole richness and complexity. Indeed, talking about sport brands is also talking about their products and services (that is products/services that are wanted, purchased and used), their businesses (manufacturers, owners, suppliers and employees who are responsible for defining and providing the offer), and the complex phenomena of sport's consumption in society.

The difficult objectification of sport brands

From a theoretical point of view, talking about brands cannot be done before properly defining the object and this is not a simple task. Indeed, it seems that more and more brands try to be associated with the sport tag while many sport organisations and companies are diversifying and extending their offers in non-sport sectors, such as finance with the Manchester United credit card and fashion with Adidas Originals. Discussing sport brands then requires defining the territory, the perimeter in which they can be bound, and this task appears extremely difficult. Under the term 'sport brand' can be found international sporting events, famous athletes, famous clubs, franchises and leagues, corporate brands, retail brands, sport services, etc. For most of them, their main currency is gained through their status and their uniqueness in their consumption sectors. The question is important because it will affect the managerial approaches they adopt. If sport brands are not unique and distinct then generic management solutions and analytical models can be applied; on the contrary if they are specific then contextual managerial responses need to be considered. Unfortunately the response to this question is complex and not binary. Many sport brands' features will appear unique while others will be comparable to other non-sport brands. For this reason a double understanding is necessary: an understanding of the sport brands' specificities to consider tailored and specific approaches but also an understanding of universal principles and similarities which allow analysts, observers and practitioners to consider comparative and benchmarking approaches. A central difficulty in this task is to define and bound what sport means and how brands are related to it. Is sport only associated with sport organisations? Is it related to the nature of the organisation or the nature of the products and services offered? Is it only about the contexts of application?

Should sport be defined objectively by experts and researchers? Or should it be subjective and self-defined, by brand managers and/or consumers and participants? The answer is particularly complex because as previously mentioned sport brands increasingly extend their offers and now provide non-sport products and services and target consumers who do not necessarily participate in sport activities: how many sport shoes have never been used on a sport field or track? Consequently, because of the diversity of sports and sport activities, as well as the diversity of sport organisations, a holistic approach of the term should be followed if a full understanding is sought.

The ambiguity also lies in the brand concept and the different academic fields (for example sociology, management, psychology, and economics) defining it. For instance, for many economists and management experts, sport brands are first of all corporate brands supplying sporting goods, clothes and shoes. In this case, sport brand is defined as the function which distinguishes and differentiates products purchased and used by sport participants. Sport brands should then have a direct and natural link with sports and sport activities. This stance is obviously not incorrect but it is limited as it excludes all sport service providers such as broadcast companies and sporting events. It also excludes professional leagues and clubs and federal sport governing bodies. Conversely, when sport marketers are asked, they seem to mainly focus on league, club and event brands excluding most corporate brands. Another ambiguity concerns the entity which owns the brand. Although, from a legal perspective, a brand belongs to the company which registered it as a trademark, many observers consider that a brand belongs first to its consumer. They do not own the benefits generated through the exploitation of the brand but they still own its branded products and services, they possess them and consume them, consequently they recognise the brand, define, and existentialise it. Moreover, brands also belong to cultures because they represent cultural and social facts. Therefore, ownership in all its diversity seems to be shared by different entities. This corresponds to an expression used by managers: when they are offered to the public, brands do not belong (only) to them anymore. On one hand companies and organisations have a legal, implicit and patrimonial ownership whereas on the other hand, consumers have an explicit, usage, recognition and fate ownership.

Finally, two complementary axes with brands, companies and organisations and markets on one hand and consumers and consumption on the other hand seem relevant to us to define sport brands in light of the various issues previously mentioned. To be qualified as a sport brand, a brand has then to respect all the following conditions:

1. The brand must be valorised to satisfy commercial, industrial or organisational purposes by an entity clearly identified and recognised as capable of such.
2. The brand possesses a name and an identity designating goods and services identified as belonging to the sport industries.
3. The brand is at the core of the industrial and organisational activities or integrated among the primary missions of the owner, which exclude

opportunistic brands which only surf on the sport trend and fashion and are not primarily attached to the sport industries.

4. The brand is registered nationally or internationally in a category of products and services which are directly linked to the sport market and industries; this excludes counterfeiting brands for instance.

5. The brand is recognised as part of a sport sector by socio-professional actors and is then listed in the databases of branches and sector organisations (for example. Kompass Sport, Sport & Social Industry Association, and Sporting Goods Industry Association).

6. The brand has to make the majority of its turnover in the sport industries and sectors.

7. The company or organisation owning the sport brand has to explicitly conduct marketing and promotional activities centred on products and services targeting sports consumers (B to C) or sport sectors' professionals and companies (B to B).

8. Consumers have to be able to easily and sustainably access the products and services designated by the brand within sport markets and sectors.

9. The brand has to possess a sufficient notoriety and reputation in its market sector to clearly define a specific and recognised brand territory.

Regarding all the criteria, many brands which are actively involved in the sport industries such as sponsors would not be considered as sport brands. For instance, even if Coca-Cola has been very active in its sponsorship activities endorsing major sporting events as the Olympic Games and the FIFA World Cup, and has even given its name to races and stadiums such as the Coca-Cola 600 and the Coke Zero 400 for the NASCAR sprint series and the Coca Cola Park, the former Ellis Park Stadium, in Johannesburg, it cannot be considered a sport brand *per se*. Many companies have created sport sponsorship divisions and departments and some have even created distinct sporting entities. This is the case of Michelin Competition and Red Bull which are strongly involved in the sport sectors and car racing in particular. However, can we consider these tyres and soda brands as sport brands? By only looking at the financial side of it, the answer would be certainly positive because their sport budgets are worth millions of euros. However, if the sport side of their activity is compared to the rest of their activities and their financial results, it appears to be marginal or certainly not core. Consequently, these two firms and brands cannot be considered as sport brands.

Similarly, a brand which belongs to a non-sport sector which occasionally offers sport products and services cannot be considered as a sport brand. For instance, if a car brand produces and commercialises mountain bikes or other sporting goods under the same name, it will not be eligible because the offer is not regular, sustainable and part of a long-term strategy within the sport markets. The same reasoning applies for clothing brands which offer, during a season, sportswear items and travel agencies which only provide sport packages during major sporting events. However, video-games and software brands which continuously provide sport related video-games constitute an exception with regard to their importance in the sport sub-category and could be considered sport brands. This is ultimately the tight semantic link that connects brands' products and services with the sporting activities needed to strongly bind the concept. In further applying this rule, all products and services which are only peripherally connected with the sport object (for example transport, banking, and multimedia) are excluded from this denomination, even if their communication territory has close links with one or several sports (for example promoting the value of a product by referring to a sport) and if they can be useful to the realisation of these sport activities. For example Arva, an avalanche transceiver's brand, is widely used by free-riders but cannot be considered as a sport brand. Despite being widely used in hiking and mountaineering boots, Vibram soles fall into the same category.

Nevertheless, despite these specific brand conditions and the link products and services have with sport practice, it would be inaccurate to say that a line is clearly drawn between brands and sport brands and many cases remain uncertain. If a brand has already a strong reputation outside the sport industries (for example electronics or distribution), and creates a new line targeting sport participants and consumers, creating significant commercial activities, should it be automatically excluded? It depends on numerous factors which evolve over time. For instance, if a different name is given after a few years of activity, this new brand could be considered as a sport brand. But in that case what about previous years? It seems that the categorisation might require taking into consideration not only the picture of the brand at a given moment but the whole movie of its evolution. In any case, if a doubt persists, we would recommend being inclusive rather than exclusive as that brand's evolution could provide more richness to and a deeper understanding of the broader analysis.

The diversity of brand theories

Brand can theoretically be defined according to an almost infinite number of ways as illustrated by the quantity of references and authors who have tried to do so. Consequently, this notion takes many forms within the literature (Kapferer, 1998, 2005; Keller, 1998). Nevertheless, a consensus has seemed to emerge around the concept of brand equity as introduced by Aaker (1996) to measure their strength and power. Brand equity embraces all the different active and passive elements linked to a brand name or symbol and which provide an added value to the unbranded item. The merit of this definition is including both brand perspectives: the valorisation of the brand as part of a company's brand portfolio (the firm-based brand equity) and the value representing a system of influence on consumers' purchase decisions (the customer-based brand equity). Originally used in the eighties by investors to express brands' financial value, the concept of brand equity has been adopted by managers and marketers to express brands' competitive power within specific markets. In this context, brand equity shall guide marketing strategies and operations to maximise brands' value in assessing their strengths and weaknesses in comparison with their main competitors. Recently, the concept has been extended to the different mental associations consumers hold about the brand (Keller, 1998). In this case, brand equity does not only refer to a specific value but also to a network of meanings and evocations related to it. This quite recent conceptualisation is important because it has shaped many recent approaches and publications about brands and their strengths. If brands are intangible and volatile as they mainly exist in consumers' minds, they also are tangible in the sense that they possess a physical expression through names, symbols, colours, packaging, communication and promotional supports. The success of many sport brands, such as Nike and Adidas, essentially relies on their capacity to valorise the recognition of their associated symbols. To achieve this, they know how to use the media, publicity and images' power to put forward their own distinctive signs and symbols which are immediately identified by consumers. From a consumer perspective, this power also corresponds to a commitment from the brands to provide products and services guaranteed with a certain level of quality and technicality; a promise and authenticity. But more than that, brands are also synonymous with seduction, dream, pleasure, escape, fashion and identity. Therefore, brands fulfil both an identification role, recognising the origins of the products and services, and a differentiating role, positioning the brand in comparison with the other providers of the same products and services.

During the fifties and sixties, it was easy to recognise the origins of products because of their national and/or regional character. Due to many factors among which industries' development and globalisation play a significant part, this identification is becoming far more difficult. For companies, the challenge is to draw attention and give confidence through the brands. Niall FitzGerald, the former CEO of Unilever, once said that a brand was 'a storehouse of trust' meaning that a trustworthy brand should be efficient and make life easier for consumers (July 2012).[1] The brand is an implicit contract which is an important dimension for consumers. Trust will normally generate an attachment which can take various forms and which can be very intense as demonstrated with the relationships between young consumers and sportswear brands (Ohl, 2003). However, when activist groups accuse brands and sport brands such as Nike and Adidas of not respecting human rights and encouraging child labour in their Asian sweatshops, this moral contract and trust relationship can be broken. This example highlights the fact that a trustworthy relationship implies a dual responsibility for brands towards their consumers: on one hand they are considered as symbol carriers which should be distinctive and on the other hand they are increasingly considered as entities which should be socially responsible. Taking a slightly different perspective, Floch (2001) estimated that the notion of brand should rely on two fundamental dimensions. First, a brand has to be considered as a signifying entity, meaning that it has to be constituted of recognisable and identifiable elements which can be visual (logo, name, signature, design, colour) or not (sound, music, taste). Second, a brand has to be a signified entity meaning that it should refer to mental associations, codes, meanings, references and evocations. It should refer to both a functional universe which is tangible and real and a symbolic universe which is intangible and virtual. The functional universe essentially comprises the physical attributes of products and services, their intrinsic qualities, and the promise which makes them credible and justified to consumers. These two dimensions, tangible and intangible, are the essential elements of the complex process of generating brand equity. They concern everything consumers will experience and involve all the necessary means to communicate about this experience: name, publicity, products or services and distribution channels.

The narrative function of brands expresses well this duality between signifying and signified, tangibility and intangibility, and the challenge of its apprehension. Contrary to products and services' functionality and physical aspect which only evoke their usage value, brands tell a story beyond their own history and these narrative elements constitute the primary sources of brands' identification. The role of narratives is to link consumers to brands which is essentially done though publicity and communication. They constitute the starting point of the brand–consumer relationship which has to be fed, enriched and sustained over time. Creativity, proximity and loyalty represent the master-words of this relationship (Lewi and Rogliano, 2006). The construction of a brand's discourse needs to empathise with the brand's legitimacy (that is, its presence on the market is justified), credibility (that the discourse is honest and trustworthy), consistency (the brand follows its own logic and remains loyal to its perceived image), relevance (its message and promise correspond to consumers' expectations), and uniqueness (the brand establishes a special relationship with its consumers who understand it).

To sum up, a brand holds a complex symbolic dimension which goes beyond its sole name and which refers to a network of meanings. Nevertheless, its primary role is to give a distinctive feature to its products and services within cluttered markets. This added value will tend to reduce the importance of the price element in comparison with the originality and image it provides. Consequently, a brand needs to constantly make sure that it is distinctive and maintains a relationship with its consumers. This can be done by putting forward a clear vision, mission, commitment, ambition and a system of values which bound its field of expertise and legitimacy. Furthermore, a brand has to clarify its intentions and its limits, from a strategic, ideological and ethical point of view. Through its commitments and the values it defends, consumers will be able to clearly understand what the brand is and what it is not. All sport brands carry a system of values existentialising the relationships they have with their consumers. As illustrated by Patagonia in one of its advertising campaigns: 'We have a special conception of extreme sports as a way to get closer to nature. We have to defend this identity'.

Brands have to be considered as social phenomena whose objectification requires various perspectives and points of reference, which unfortunately do not necessarily simplify their understanding. Behind the concepts of brand and brand equity exist a broad range of associated terms which blur researchers', observers', practitioners' and consumers' comprehension. As Merunka (2002) said, the academic literature is full of terms and expressions related to the concept of brand:

brand equity, extension, power, identity, image, centrality, associations, beliefs, essence, stature, discourse, territory, relevance, attachment, detachment, involvement, trust, heritage, multiple relationships (for example friendship, love, nostalgia, addiction), personality, value, link and even gender. How it is then possible to create common and unifying foundations which are not systematically put under question or are the objects of intense debates about the exact nature and meaning of the terms employed? Brands are subject to many comparisons, metaphors and analogies, in particularly with human activities, which can represent a way to enhance reflections, to position and to convince but a brand can also represent a danger if it creates confusion and approximation. Studying and analysing brands necessarily requires a broad and multidisciplinary approach because of the plurality of theoretical definitions and possible orientations; one cannot refer to a single framework or point of view. Many academic fields are involved such as economy, sociology, semiology and management and various stakeholders are concerned (for example consumers, employees, suppliers, distributors, shareholders, public authorities, nations) with particular and often contradictory interests (Davidson, 2001). To avoid a theoretical scattering, it is therefore understandable that numerous researchers and authors prefer following the streams of popular and pioneer authors such as D.A. Aaker, J.N. Kapferer, G. Lewi, P. Kotler, A. Ries and K.L. Keller, but this should not hinder them from following their natural curiosity and embrace other approaches and views.

From an academic point of view, brands constitute a recent object of study. Although limited to a few pages in marketing and advertising handbooks before, the nineties saw the publication of the first dedicated frameworks and textbooks on the topic (Aaker, 1991; Kapferer, 1991), despite the fact that the first articles dealing with brand loyalty were published in the late sixties and the early seventies (Day, 1969; Sheth, 1968). For a long time, and it is still probably the case in various disciplines, brands have not been considered 'serious' enough by economists and not noble enough for many social scientists. For many of them, brands cumulated two strong weaknesses: they were considered futile and associated to the world of money and consumption. The management and marketing disciplines were the first to produce scientific articles specifically about brands and branding (Park *et al.*, 1986; Aaker and Keller, 1990). Finally the academic research has been articulated around major themes such as brand equity (Kapferer, 1997; Keller, 1993; 1998), brand extension (e.g. Aaker and Keller, 1990), brand-consumers relationships through the concepts of attitudes (Kapferer and Laurent, 1998), brand loyalty (Day, 1969; Sheth, 1968), brand involvement (Laurent and Kapferer, 1985) and industrial brand (Malaval, 2001).

Brand and brand equity in terms of business and consumer

Brand equity constitutes the best asset of a firm and for this reason it is at the core of firms' economic and strategic stakes and challenges. Brand equity can be evaluated by its dynamics which gather all elements linked to the brand situation on a market: penetration rate, market shares, awareness, purchase intentions, and empathy (for example 'this is the brand I love'). It can then be evaluated by its brand image which relies on the product and service image, regarding all the benefits associated with products and services, and social image which is linked to the brand consumers' profile. The final step consists of looking at the brand substance which includes its personality, its system of values, and its relational climate characterising the brand–consumer bonds. As previously mentioned, a brand represents the name and the different signs related to a specific offer of goods and services whose purpose is to be recognised, perceived as providing an added value and in turn purchased.

Based on the work of Kotler and Dubois (1997) who analysed the brand concept from its marketing perspective, it seems relevant to analyse it according to six main dimensions. First, a brand evokes a set of attributes and characteristics ('Lacoste is about colourful polo shirts'). Second, a brand puts forward a set of functional, emotional and social benefits ('Wearing Lacoste's polo shirts makes you smart and elegant'). Third, a brand is characterised by a set of values expressing the culture of the firm or the organisation ('Lacoste is authentic'). Fourth, it represents a cultural affiliation ('Lacoste means French tradition'). Finally, a brand is characterised by the profile of its consumers ('Successful and classy people wear Lacoste polo shirts') and a personality ('Lacoste means elegant, relaxed, patient, wealthy and sophisticated'). This personality dimension is relatively important. By being part of people's everyday life because of the relationships consumers establish with them, brands have almost become individuals with their own character and personality. As a person would be, brands would be considered according to their physical, emotional and mental characteristics. The physical aspect is related to the corporality and is an essential dimension. There is a semantic and an etymological link between corporality and the terms corporate and corporation. The body of the brand is represented by its logos, its products, its colours, its characters which incarnate the brand's identity. The emotional aspect characterises the relationship established with a brand, its capacity to create affective and emotional links with its consumers. Companies and organisations have to make sure that this relationship is nurtured and enhanced via constant dialogues and interactions which should create an attachment value. Last, the mental aspect refers to the fantasy and dream the brand is able to arouse. The construction of this escape component goes alongside the universe of representations and signs the brand generates.

From a consumer perspective, products or services and brands form two inseparable components. Park and Srinivasan (1994) have demonstrated that the value of a brand and consumers' behaviour largely depend on this inseparable couple. A preference for a branded product depends on its tangible dimension based on its objective utility, the product attributes as well as its intangible dimension. For consumers, one benefit associated to brands is to reduce the perceived risk associated with purchase and consumption by providing insurance over the origins and the quality of the products (Kapferer, 2003). This perceived risk increases almost proportionally with the technological level of the product and its price and can be financial (that is it does not correspond to expectations), physical (health and body integrity can be at stake), psychological (it does not reflect the person the consumer wants to be) and social (it does not refer and correspond to the community or subculture wanted). Consumers have to be reassured by brands but they also have to be encouraged to try new products, new styles, new services, new technologies, and this can be done thanks to a trust contract.

At the same time, consumption has become increasingly necessary for integration within cultures, subcultures, communities and tribes. For many consumers, purchasing and using sport brands is a way to participate in a socially valorised group. The increase in media exposure of sport activities also creates a stronger social recognition of athletes and sport participants. However, this media exposure cannot explain everything otherwise non-sport celebrities would have replaced athletes and sporting celebrities as role models. Sports are simultaneously more accessible and simple to comprehend than other cultural areas and practices. The modification of consumers' cultural relationships with sport brands is due to their own characteristics and changes such as the affirmation of ethnic, territorial or community identities and modifications of the integration processes within social groups. Moreover, the significant economic valorisation of the sporting culture reinforces the willingness of social actors to get closer to sports. Wearing sport clothes and shoes is being part of a culture valorised in the media through sporting heroes and legends but it is also adopting a clothing style which appears significant and is praised by peers.

This book is structured around seven chapters. In the first chapter, the diversity of sport brands is presented and analysed. In the second chapter, a focus is given to the tangible influence of sport brands, whereas sport brands' intangible influence is analysed in the third chapter. In the fourth chapter, the relationships between sport brands and subcultures and communities are analysed. In the fifth chapter, the economic and social value of sport brands is analysed whereas in the sixth chapter, the focus is brought to sport brands' growth strategies. Finally, the seventh chapter is dedicated to the identification and the analysis of sport brands' threats.

1

THE GREAT VARIETY OF SPORT BRANDS

The sport marketing literature and the sport brand literature in particular provide various brand classifications. According to a classical perspective, authors either position their classification from the creation and production side (offer) or from the behaviours and contexts of consumption side (demand). As an example, in France, Megabrand System is a brand classification elaborated by the firm Taylor Nelson Sofres which identified nine categories of brands across all markets:

- star brands;
- champion brands;
- everyday-friend brands;
- alternative brands;
- landmark brands;
- baron brands;
- contested brands;
- unknown brands; and
- brands with potential.

If all classifications provide a different perspective, their profusion creates confusion and does not give credibility to the 'brand science'. In 2004 Lewi warned that the number of categories of brands and sub-classifications should remain limited in order to keep it clear and simple for managers and consumers. Indeed, according to the contexts and the theoretical fields of analysis, new categories and terms are used such as 'umbrella brands', 'generic brands', 'own brands', 'parent brands', 'source brands', or 'guarantee brands' which generally only add tiny nuances, in comparison with the categories traditionally and widely used by practitioners and experts. They certainly are indicators of an increasing interest and focus on brands but they also tend to blur the identification of brands' roles and functions either from an economic, cultural or social perspective. Therefore, in order to clarify the roles and functions of sport brands it is necessary to identify their main categories. Besides the types of brands usually found in all industries (corporate brands, service brands, constituent brands and e-brands) that we call 'classical brands', two other distinct categories can be identified in relation to sport brands (see Figure 1.1): sport-specific brands and certification and label brands.

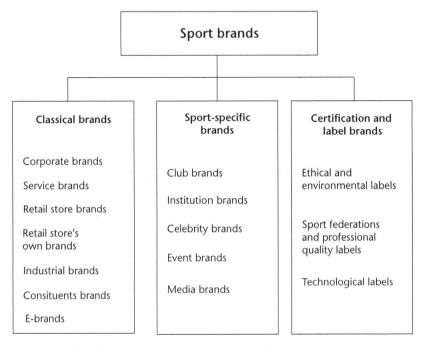

FIGURE 1.1   The three main categories of sport brands

Classical brands

Classical brands have been widely considered and analysed in management and marketing textbooks and comprise corporate brands, service brands, and store and distributor brands. Within this category, industrial brands require a specific treatment because, as suppliers' brands, they can be found and associated with many other brands. Finally, e-brands are also analysed separately.

Corporate brands and trademarks

Historically, the name of a company has constituted the main recognition sign for a brand, and then identifies the corporate brand. Often associated with the manufacture, the founder or the place where a product is made, corporate brands constitute the model for most major contemporary brands. Also frequently linked to a familial enterprise or tradition, they create, manufacture and sell their products which are clearly identified. The development of the service economy however, significantly modified this pattern. Brands in this category are often leaders of their market and are very frequently megabrands with international awareness and reputation. Corporate brands often aim to keep a tradition or a 'home spirit', often characterised as their DNA, which relies on respect for specific values and the protection of a unique expertise or know-how. With these brands, the brand's history very often overlaps the company's history. For many of them, the name of the brand is the name of the company which is also the name of the founder and entrepreneur. All products are then generally branded under the same appellation. In the sport industry, huge corporate brands such as Nike, Salomon, Adidas, Shimano, Wilson or Prince represent classical examples but sport corporate brands of this dimension are, actually, not so common. Dorotennis, a women tennis clothing specialist is another typical example. After being a pioneer in the 70s, this brand has become a leader in women's sportswear and is nowadays managed by the founder's daughter. In another sector, the sport boat industry, Zodiac is a good example of a corporate brand with all its products branded with the company name.

However, besides these well-known and high-profile corporate brands, the hyper-segmentation of the sport markets has allowed the emergence of new corporate brands, either new in their structure or in their philosophy: subculture brands and lovemarks. They generally represent very small companies which have a niche positioning and whose products are limited and sometimes crafted or hand-made. Their appeal and reputation mainly rely on the valorisation of a name, an innovation and an alternative and avant-garde image which also represents the key characteristics of their business model. They are above all brands of passionate people for passionate people which mean that they are often associated with emergent and new sport practices such as the sliding ones (e.g. surfing, snowboarding, skating or kite-surfing) illustrated by Quester, Beverland and Farrelly (2006). The most recent examples of brands from the skiing sector such as Movement and Bumtribe do not directly compete with the major ones and target people interested in new, technical and original offers in line with free-ride and free-style practices. Proof of their efficiency and model: many of the subculture brands' ideas and concepts are copied by the major dominant brands of the sector.

Easy to identify, store brands rely on the reputation of distribution chains and companies. Like corporate brands, they were born in the industrial era but really took off with the advent of the consumer society and the mass distribution of corporate brands' products. Intersport, Decathlon (property of Oxylane Group), Sports Direct International plc, JD Sports Fashion plc (JD), and Foot Locker are all examples of sport specialised retail brands. However, store brands should be distinguished from stores' own brands and not all stores or chain stores distribute their own products. In many aspects, stores' own brands can appear like corporate brands: they are owned by retail stores but their name is different. Sometimes names are even different between the types of products. This is for example the case in Europe with Decathlon and its own sport brands such as Tribord (for nautical sports), Artengo (for racket sports) and Quechua (for outdoor activities). These brands' products can only be found in the owner's stores. These store's own brands are often created to respond to the demand of chain and retail stores that want to increase their profit margins and/or cannot obtain exclusive products and deals from corporate brands to differentiate them from their main competitors. However, it is not necessary for them to have a visible brand logo or identification as they are sure to be distributed and the stores themselves can guarantee a good shelf position (Malaval and Bénaroya, 1998). This is not the case for corporate brands which need to be clearly identified and distinguished to be distributed in retail stores.

Derived from corporate brands, service brands provide services for both consumers and other businesses. They develop a competence, specific values and a distinct positioning: renting, consultancy, catering, hospitality... In the sport industry, service brands seem to have a bright future due to the increasing craze for sport in general and sport participation in particular. Brands of sport and recreation parks, fitness clubs, sport travel agencies, media, and marketing and communication companies are good examples of service brands. The Intersport international network seems to be a good example. For many years, it has been demonstrating the service values it has been bringing to sport participants by offering for instance online skiing equipment hire. Since 2005 the website of the brand (www.intersportrent.com) has had a turnover multiplied by two or three per year. Within the same sector, ski resorts are also service brands because they provide various kinds of sport and non-sport services to visitors, sport participants and tourists.

Industrial and constituent brands

Industrial brands are sometimes named supplier brands. Their main difference from corporate, service and store brands is that they are not well-known by the general public because they are mainly present within business to business markets (B to B). They generally supply manufacturing brands providing different components (for example fabrics and textiles, pieces, material) which are used in the composition of sport goods and equipment, ticketing, club brands' accessories and merchandised products. Industrial brands allow the final brands to provide offers, thanks to techniques, know-how or skills that the final brands do not possess . For instance a tennis racquet brand needs an industrial production process (machines, transport equipment), information and technological systems (computer-aided design, stock and order management system), maintenance and logistic supports, without which it cannot achieve its objectives. Before becoming in 1994 a brand specialised in the production of tennis racquets (currently ranked 2 worldwide) and sport shoes, Babolat, since 1875, had been a supplier of strings for the main international racquet brands.

But as we said before, because industrial brands are not always in direct contact with final consumers they are generally not well-known. According to some observers, these industrial brands are corporate brands which did not go to the end of their logic as they stayed at a technological level and did not reach the consumer-product encounter level. The success of industrial brands is linked to the prescription (positive word-of-mouth) surrounding the brands and companies they supply to. In this sense, the success criterion is quite similar to those of B to C brands. Within industrial brands we can distinguish raw and transformed material brands, constituent brands, small equipment brands, big equipment brands, industrial service brands (catering and ticketing functions) and management and consulting brands. With regard to the specificities of sport markets, the focus will mainly concern constituent brands. Contrary to raw material or industrial service brands, some of these constituent brands are well known to the public because their contribution is widely promoted by corporate brands. For instance, in the sportswear sector, Gore-Tex is a constituent brand with a good reputation and a high level of awareness. Sportswear brands extensively use Gore-Tex's reputation to sell their products because it provides an added value, which is often translated into higher prices too. In the sport goods industry and beyond the brands supplying accessories and specific equipment (for example Shimano and Sach for bikes, Wichard for marine hardware and sailing equipment, Vibram for free climbing rubber compound), are numerous. Among the most famous we can cite Gore-Tex, a brand which belongs to W.L. Gore & Associates, Kevlar, Nylon, and Lycra which belongs to the American giant Du Pont de Nemours. Many others exist but often known only by professionals and specialists (see Table 1.1 for some examples).

These 'hidden brands' as Lewi (2004) called them, can become true technological labels whose quality and reputation can even go beyond the final brands that use these constituents. This is for instance the case with Gore-Tex and other Gore products which allow famous brands such as Patagonia, Columbia, Millet, Rossignol, Nike, Lafuma, Rip Curl, Quiksilver, Eider or less well-known brands such as Mammut, ACG, Schoeffel, Trango, Wild Roses, Lowe Alpine to increase their sales of outdoor equipment. In some cases, sportswear brands do not even need to promote their products because of the reputation and image the constituent brand holds. For this reason, sportswear brands increasingly use famous constituent brands because they provide a clear technical and marketing value (see Table 1.2 for an example of constituent brands and final sport brands using them).

From a strategic point of view, this association can be assimilated to a successful functional co-branding and a co-advertising strategy as consumers have become more and more sensitive to constituent brands and because they simultaneously ensure additional revenues and differentiate products (Cegarra and Michel, 2003).

E-brands

E-brands represent a quite new category of brands which are present on the Internet via a website using the name of the brand. Like Amazon, Google or Yahoo, websites which support these brands have become powerful assets. For Lai (2005), e-brands provide three types of services: (1) transactional services, selling online

TABLE 1.1 Examples of constituent brands in the sport textile sector

Constituent brands	Producer	Characteristics	Equipment
Cordura **CORDURA** Only by DuPont	Invista/ Du Pont de Nemours	A collection of fabrics known for their durability, resistance which follow stringent test criteria and are available in wide range of weights.	Backpacks, luggage, skiing, hiking, outdoor and climbing products, etc.[i]
Gore-Tex **GORE-TEX**	W.L. Gore & Associates	Waterproof and breathable fabrics which are made by laminating membranes to high performance textiles and then sealing them with specific tape technologies.	Skiing, snowboarding, outdoor, mountaineering clothing and shoes, accessories and sleeping bags, etc.[ii]
Kevlar DUPONT **Kevlar.**	Du pont de Nemours	Kevlar aramid fibre is lightweight and highly resistant, with five times the strength of steel on an equal-weight basis.	Skis and snowboards, surf boards, tennis racquets, helmets, body protection equipment, hulls, baseball bats, etc.[iii]
Lycra LYCRA **LYCRA** ONLY BY DUPONT	Invista	Lycra sport fabrics deliver a range of stretch and recovery power. They are lightweight, breathable and fit with qualification standards in terms of performance and comfort.	Swimwear, T-shirts, sport socks, cycling shorts, clothing, etc.[iv]
Polartec **POLARTEC** FORWARD FABRIC	Malden	Polartec is a collection of fabrics which are breathable, durable, comfortable. There are three lines of products: comfort (next-to-skin), warmth (insulation) and shelter (weather protection).	Outdoor, mountaineering, yachting clothing, blankets and accessories, etc.[v]
Windstopper **WIND STOPPER**	W.L. Gore & Associates	Windstopper fabrics are engineered for peak performance and total comfort that provide windproofing and maximum breathability.	Outdoor, mountaineering, yachting clothing and accessories, etc.[vi]

Notes:

i   www.cordura.com/en/fabric-technology/index.html (accessed 18 June 2012).
ii   www.gore-tex.co.uk/remote/Satellite/content/what-is-gore-tex (accessed 18 June 2012).
iii   www2.dupont.com/personal-protection/en-us/dpt/kevlar.html (accessed 24 June 2012).
iv   www.lycra.com/g_en/webpage.aspx?id=963 (accessed 25 June 2012).
v   www.polartec.com/ (accessed 25 June 2012).
vi   www.windstopper.com/remote/Satellite/toc/TechnologyOfComfortFrameset/index (accessed 25 June 2012).

TABLE 1.2 Constituent brands and sport brands using them

Types of constituent	Brands	Producers	Examples of brands using them
Fabrics	Breathe	UCB	Wilsa-Sport
	Cordura	Du Pont de Nemours	Fusalp, Cimalp, Descente, Fjällraven, Mammut, Mexx Sport, Shöffel, Reima
	Dri-Release	Optimer	Casall, Salomon, Swix
	Dynamic	Schoeller Textiles	Haglöfs, Mammut, Marmot, Mellos, Schöffel Vaude
	Kevlar	Du Pont de Nemours	Garmont, Millet, Völkl
	Lycra	Invista	Adidas, At. One, Chillaz, Fjällräven, Odlo, Swix
	Meryl Micro	Nystar (Rhône-Poulenc/Snia Fibre)	Eider
	Setila Tergal	Rhône-Poulenc	Adidas
Membranes	3XDRY	Schoeller Textiles	Alberto, Cloudveil, Columbia, Eider, Goldwin, Mammut, Marmot, PhenixSalomon, Schöffel, Spyder, Swix, Tatonka, The North Face, Vaude
	Alpex	Dickson PTL	Technica
	Coolmax	Du Pont de Nemours	Quechua (Oxylane Group)
	Dermizax	Torayentrant	Kjus, Oxbow, SOS, Spyder, Tenson
	eVent	Event Fabrics	Pearl Izumi, Reusch, Spyder
	Gore-Tex	W.L. Gore & Associés	Salomon, Nordica, Rossignol, Dolomite, Bestera, Meindl, Salomon, Technica, Aigle, Vuarnet, Fjällråven, Lafuma, Quiksilver, Sun Valley
Textiles	Airvantage	W.L. Gore & Associés	Burton, F2, Rossignol, Schöffel, Sun Valley
	Airdrive	Toyobo	Descente
	Colibri	W.L. Gore & Associés	Exclusively for Loeffler clothes
	Coolmax	Du Pont de Nemours	Castelli, Chillaz, Mizuno
	Diaplex	Diaplex	Mc Pearson, Phoenix, Spyder
	Gelanots	Tomen	Salomon, Sun Valley
	Husky	Eschler	Allsport, Mellos, Vaude

products or services; (2) informational services and (3) relational services, by allowing a brand community to gather, discuss and share their opinions about the brand. The transactional e-brands essentially serve functional and utilitarian purposes; it has to be easy, efficient, clear and comfortable for the consumer. On the contrary, informational and relational e-brands rather serve a hedonist and experiential dimension of consumption (Holbrook and Hirschman, 1982). These e-brands offer many services traditional brands find difficult, such as providing information without time constraints or providing individualised and customised products. Sport markets have witnessed increasing numbers of online transactions and products sold which undeniably demonstrate the consumer appetite for this type of distribution. This is illustrated for instance by a 2012 Mintel report dealing with the UK sport goods retailing market[1] which found that two-fifths of sport goods buyers were happy to buy from an Internet retailer. In parallel with these forms of retail, new e-commerce actors such as websites organising private, discount and destocking sales (secretsales.com and vente-privee.com) have also emerged and are showing great success. For instance, vente-privee.com, which boasts to be the global leader in online private sales relying on 14 million members and featuring more than 1,450 major international brands, is present in eight European countries and has just launched a joint venture with American Express in the USA.[2] Consequently, several sport-specific websites following the same models have been emerging such as leftlanesports.com, theclymb.com and privatesportshop.com and are now competing with the generalist private sales websites.

The progression of e-commerce has forced traditional brands to invest in this new sector. This is the case of retailers which have expanded their offer online such as Sports Direct with sportsdirect.com and Made In Sport with madein-sports.com. Among them, professional clubs and franchises benefiting from a strong reputation have developed their own websites not only to promote their brand but also to sell tickets and products to a wider audience. In this sense, websites allow sport organisations to reinforce their link with their fan bases and communities, beyond their traditional geographical areas of influence. Some clubs and franchises can even provide free content (for example, results, ranking tables, transfer information) and charge for premium content (for example videos, partners' contacts) which then transform the website into a true profit centre. E-brands are also present in virtual environments where they encounter millions of e-consumers. They have intensively invested in social networks but also video games and virtual worlds such as Second life. One of the main advantages of e-brands is their ability to create a unique identity and use it to reach new markets and segments. Moreover, when they adopt a new name for the e-brand and/or the website, different from the corporate brand, the failure risks and consequences for the parent brand are minimised (Lehu, 2001). However, if failure risks are minimised, any positive feedback from a successful e-brand is also limited for the parent brand.

A good example of sport e-brand is Fogdog Sports. Founded in 1998 in San José (California), this pure 'click and mortar' brand (Fogdog.com) has rapidly become the unavoidable sport goods point of sale for sport participants (Carpenter, 2000). This e-brand was created following an Internet start-up model with an initial capital investment of 25M$ raised in two years and brought by various investors (including Intel, Sprout Group, Vertex Management, Novus Venture Partners). Its growth has been dependent on a solid network of partners (international sport brands, retail store brands) and the quality of the services they provide. From a strategic point of view, Fogdog has set up a network of partners including about 4,500 companies and brands which represent a significant proportion of the American sporting goods industry.[3] From a marketing perspective, the brand has been using an efficient mix by promoting its brand and articles through publications with wide audience support (for example *Cosmopolitan*), in economic reviews (for example *Sporting Goods Intelligence*), in technological reviews (for example *PC Week*) and in sport media (for example *Bowling Digest, Horse & Rider,* and *Snowboarder*). The brand also developed TV commercials (*ESPN, Golf Channel, Outdoor Life Network*) around the slogan 'Your anywhere, anytime sports store'. Finally, the brand has been sponsoring many sporting events (including beach volley, triathlon, cross-country skiing, local sport leagues). Among the services provided, Fogdog offers the possibility for (potential) consumers to email experts who will help to find the most appropriate products for them. Fogdog also created a newsletter, customisable per sport activity, which is widely circulated in the USA.

If we consider that the Internet allows sport brands to develop new lines of products unfeasible otherwise, Nike Id is certainly a good example. Surfing the wave of the consumer need for personalised objects and the customisation trend, Nike Id (www.nikeid.nike.com) offers sneaker addicts the opportunity to customise footwear, clothing and sports equipment (for example watch and backpack), changing colours, or writing names and words on a few basic models. This one-to-one service named co-parenting (Stanbouli, 2003) seems to be more and more popular and represents a growing industry even if product prices are higher. In some cases, clothing e-brands even ask consumers to propose some logos and designs that are used for products targeting wider audiences.

Sport-specific brands

The second main sport brand category corresponds to the specific brands of the sector which are not found in other industries, at least not in the same configurations. This is for example the case of professional club and franchise brands as well as brands belonging to sport governing bodies, leagues and federal organisations and which we gather under the term sport organisation. However, three other types seem to be also industry-specific: celebrity brands, event brands and media brands. These can also be found outside the sport sector but we will later demonstrate how they differ and are unique within the sport sector, showing distinct identities, characteristics and purposes which strongly structure the sport field.

Organisation and club brands

The strength of a brand is often related to its capacity to make consumers escape from reality and connect with imaginary and symbolic contents and this is something sport clubs and organisations do very well. In many cases, athletes have become heroes, their performances and achievements have been elevated to myths, and many sport clubs and organisations are aware of this element and have exploited it. In order to capitalise on the emotional bonds sport fans and spectators can have with them, sport clubs and organisations have developed more and more branding strategies which rely on their history and values, their strong identity, and their capability to develop their merchandising and diversify their financial revenue streams.

The development of a reputation does not only rely on the excellence of a product, such as a luxury brand item for instance, but on the excellence and the reputation of the club's players and on a strong history that values successes and trophies. This is for instance illustrated by the study of Chanavat & Bodet (2009) which found that many brand associations of the best English Premier League football clubs were related to former and current players, coaches and chairmen. A place can also be associated with a reputation such as for instance Old Trafford, the Manchester United stadium nicknamed the 'theatre of dreams', or Madison Square Garden for the New York Knicks. We are close here to what Lewi (2003) called mythical brands. Sporting facilities and stadiums are powerful vectors of communication which strongly contribute to the brand equity as well as the brand's sponsors and partners. All over the world, the trend seems to be for the (re)development of major sport facilities comprising a significant commercial dimension (shops, restaurants) and a recreational one as well (museum, fitness centres, swimming-pool); a concept coined as creating 'cathedrals of consumption' (Ritzer, 2010). In this regard, the new Yankee Stadium is a perfect example. Beside the commercial dimension, these stadiums are often designed by famous architects in order to make them unique and reinforce the prestige of the sport organisations using them. As an example we can cite Dan Meis, a very well-known American architect, who has specialised in sports and entertainment arenas and has designed the famous Staples Center in Los Angeles, the Saitama Super Arena in Japan and the Paul Brown Stadium in Cincinnati. Half-way between a club brand and an event brand, the Millennium Stadium in Cardiff (Wales) is another example of the development of stadium brands. It has mainly become famous worldwide due to its retractable roof and thanks to the 1999 Rugby World Cup final. This stadium now hosts many sporting (rugby, motorsport, football, boxing) and cultural (concerts and exhibitions) events.

The strategies implemented and the amounts of money invested make professional clubs look like non-sport brands with strong equity and growth allowing them to develop their line of products and extend their brand. Merchandised products are at the heart of professional clubs' brand strategy. As we are reminded by Kapferer (2006), what makes the wealth of a football club such as Manchester

United is the worldwide community of more than four million fans who buy its kits and products and want to watch the games. Professional clubs and franchise brands actively and increasingly target foreign fans and consumers and they fully exploit the benefits of merchandising and licensing. However, the brand's success is often related to the club's sporting success and to the profile of the celebrity brands of the people who compose their squads. In this regard, some club brands can even be shadowed by celebrity brands (Bodet and Chanavat, 2010), and this can be seen as a form of cannibalisation.

Like professional clubs and franchises, many sport organisations such as sporting federations and sporting event organisers adopt the same models of management focusing on the importance of the brand. The branding approach is noticeable both at a strategic level in terms of goals and objectives and at a commercial level through the exploitation of the positive attributes, symbols and associations of these sport organisations. This represents a revolution for the voluntary sport organisations, such as traditional European sport federations, and their not-for-profit culture. They seem however to have progressively realised the potential their brands hold, which could help them increase their financial revenues, which in turn would help them better achieve their long-term objectives.

In North America, the professional sport leagues represent the majority of institutional sport brands with universities and colleges. These professional leagues such as the National Football League (NFL), the National Basketball Association (NBA), the Major League Baseball (MLB) and the National Hockey League (NHL) have been almost naturally, by their profit orientation, focused on branding strategies which make them highly profitable. For instance the 2012 NFL league revenue is estimated at US$9.5 billion with an average NFL team value of US$1.04 billion.[4] Regarding another sport organisation, the Professional Golfers' Association (PGA), founded in 1901, has been developed as a global brand. With about 7,000 members across the world, this association manages the interests of professional golfers and their sponsorship contracts for instance, and many national and international tournaments. It has developed an efficient marketing strategy, 'exploring new opportunities for sponsors including partnerships, product endorsement, merchandising, direct marketing to golfers as well as corporate promotional activity, sponsorship, training and education platforms' (Barrand, Britcher and Curtis, 2004, p. 67).

In the second half of the twentieth century, the Olympic Games has also been the subject of an increased commercialisation. The main revenues were first generated through the sales of media rights then, during the eighties, the commercial exploitation of the Olympic rings and logo of each Olympic Games began. It has been increasing to make the Olympic brand probably the most powerful sport brand in the world today. Concerned by the diversification of revenue streams, J.A. Samaranch, a former IOC president, overtly put in place a commercialisation system, modifying the Olympic Charter and the not-for-profit nature of the event (Chappelet, 2006). For many, the 1984 Los Angeles Games was the turning point that embraced the global level of the Olympic brand. The branding dimension of the Olympics has been constantly prominent since and Ferrand (2007) comments that to be victorious in the Olympic Games bidding process, cities have to create and develop a strong relationship with the Olympic brand and its stakeholders who have to take into account its economic, environment and social dimensions.

Celebrity brands

Athletes and sport champions have now clearly understood the commercial dimension that their name holds. By looking at the table of the richest athletes worldwide, it is easy to appreciate that their fortune has been widely built by managing their name an international brand. Several well-known contemporary examples such as Kobe Bryant (basketball), Roger Federer (tennis), Cristiano Ronaldo (football), Lionel Messi (football), LeBron James (basketball), Tiger Woods (golf), Phil Mickelson (golf), David Beckham (football), Michael Schumacher (Formula 1) and Lewis Hamilton (Formula 1) can be cited. Because sport celebrities are perceived to carry positive values (for example effort, achievement, dedication, excellence), they become great levers to enhance brands' positive images. The main difference between traditional brands and celebrity brands comes from the way celebrity brand equity is constructed. In this sense, sporting performance is crucial for celebrity brands however the strength of the brand is not always proportional with the number of trophies and victories achieved. In this regard, Anna Kournikova, the tennis player, was a good example because she developed a strong brand equity although she never won a WTA title in singles.

Michael Jordan was probably the first case of an athlete who developed, with the pivotal role of Nike, his name as a brand and reached an international level (Andrews, 1998). Celebrities have the power to influence and orientate sport markets, promote a sport and then encourage its growth as a business. Through his endorsement with Nike, Tiger Woods helped the brand to become one of the leading golf apparel companies in the world. In the boardsports sector, Robby Naish is also a good example. Being a popular and great windsurfing champion, he strongly contributed to increase the awareness of his sport and enhance its image. Nowadays, his brand has become a popular corporate brand of sailboards, sails, boards and paddles, and kite surfing equipment all over the world. Celebrity brands use the media coverage of athletes and champions, generally still competing, in order to get economic and financial benefits. This is, however, an exceptional situation, because few sport people can reach this celebrity brand status. However, when they have reached such a level they can even exploit it even after their sporting career and try to surf on the brand equity previously created. This is what happened with Zinedine Zidane, the French football player, who became, after retiring from his sporting career in 2006, the successful ambassador for the Qatar bid for the 2022 FIFA World Cup in 2010. As illustrated with some of the above examples, some of them can even transfer to another status and become event brands (for example Naish Paddle Championship), service brands (for example David Beckham Academy) and corporate brands (for example Li Ning, Sergio Tacchini).

Event brands and media brands

Even if they share similarities with service brands from a legal and marketing point of view, event brands represent the only category whose awareness and reputation are jointly enhanced with the event. If from a theoretical point of view each sporting event is a brand because it distinguishes itself from other competitors, the brand level is achieved only when sporting events are successful enough, which takes time: nearly 100 years for the *Tour de France* for instance. However, it seems that sporting events have now been widely considered and managed as brands which make them reach their status quickly, or at least quicker than before. Although very few sporting events have been initially created solely for profit generation purposes, they are now seen as great opportunities to generate extra revenues for the rightsholders. Therefore, the sporting event is not only branded to guarantee its sporting success but also to maximise extra financial revenues. These issues are tightly correlated and the most popular sporting events are often those which are the most profitable. The logical sequence seems then quite simple: popular events attract media brands which provide extra income and increase the audience which in turn attract sponsors and consumers. The potential benefits are then massive and justify the valorisation of an event's brand equity.

Event brand management is strongly related to the communication and the promotion strategy of the sporting event itself. Furthermore, if the economic profitability is an important element, it is not the first mission of federal sporting organisations when managing the brand. The main objective is the success of the sporting competition and tournament for athletes, fans, spectators and the general public. Through the exploitation of its notorious brand, the Fédération Internationale de Football Association (FIFA) is fully involved in managing this balance with its main event the FIFA World Cup. As an organiser, FIFA has worked with Whitestone International, an agency specialised in brand building, marketing and communication to develop the logo of the event and We do Communication GmbH, a famous German communication agency, created the official poster. Like any brand, the 2006 FIFA World Cup™ has been launched following rigorous strategic, financial and marketing planning to guarantee a commercial success.

The Tour de France, which is the third sporting event worldwide in terms of audience, follows a slightly different logic as it does not have ticketing revenues and belongs to a private sport company Amaury Sport Organisation (ASO). Historically created by a French sport journal to increase its sales, the Tour de France is a trademark brand managed by the Société du Tour de France (a component of ASO) and which is profit oriented. The revenues come from four main sources: TV rights which represent about 45 per cent of the income, sponsors and partners (about US$5 million to be a key partner and between US$2 million and US$3 million to be an official partner or supplier), merchandising and hosting rights paid by cities to be the start or the arrival of a stage (about US$170 000 per city). In 2005, the profit made by ASO was estimated at US$21 million.

With regard to the importance of images and information in contemporary societies, it is not surprising to consider media brands as true brands or at least as companies that extensively use branding logics and approaches. Three main sectors can be identified within this category: specialised media, TV broadcasters and sport and information websites and electronic resources (which can sometimes also be covered by the other two). In the sport specialised press sector, the case of *l'Equipe* perfectly illustrates the brand management and particularly the development of brand portfolios in the media. Historically the only daily French sport newspaper, the group Édition Philippe Amaury (EPA) which owns the newspaper extended the line of products and created brand extensions while keeping the newspaper at the heart of the network. The group first developed a weekly magazine which can only be purchased with the newspaper on Saturdays and which looks at sports and sport information though a different, less specialised and sometimes more gossipy lens. EPA then created a collection of books in relation to sport and sold historical sport photos, used by the newspaper. This media brand has also developed a website which provides some of the information found in the newspaper, but also videos, podcasts and a shop. The group also developed a TV channel which is a sport information channel. Reinforced by these successes, the group extended its portfolio of media brands and acquired several magazines specialised in football, tennis and cycling.

In the sport broadcasting sector, thematic media brands suffer from competition with the more generalist media brands which often have more financial power to buy event broadcasting rights which should theoretically represent their main asset. For this reason, many of the major sporting events are broadcast by generalist media brands and sport specialised media brands often have to focus on certain segments made of highly passionate fans. For instance Eurosport TV channel focuses on lower profile events and sports such as the women's FIFA World Cup, winter sports, motor sports (except Formula 1), tennis (except major tournaments), snooker and triathlon (Abdourazakou, 2003). From this perspective, the media brands which can afford to buy exclusive broadcasting rights for major events such as the Olympic Games, men's FIFA World Cup or the football Champions League are similar to up-market or luxury brands with a mass audience because they hold a rare product and because their awareness and reputation increase thanks to this privilege. However, the recent arrival of a new entrant Al Jazeera Sports with almost unlimited resources may change the power balance on the market.

The development of sport media brands is also the result of the professional clubs' will (club brands) to have their own TV channel. Most of the best European football clubs such as Real Madrid FC or Manchester United have one. This allows them to create a closer relationship and proximity with their fans and to communicate with them on a more regular basis, particularly with satellite fans, to use the term of Kerr and Gladden (2008), which in turn enhances their loyalty to the brand which is an important dimension of the perceived brand equity as defined by Aaker (1991). This is also another way to offer new services and opportunities either to current sponsors or to attract new ones. Nevertheless, the cost of having their own channel remains an important issue which can dissuade many clubs and organisation brands from creating a TV media brand. For this reason, some club brands which share the same values and identity are currently planning to create common media brands in order to share the costs and use alternative online media such as YouTube channels.

Certification and label brands

Label brands designate the labelling systems used by companies, associations of companies, organisations, foundations, charities, governments and public authorities, intended for consumers and society at large to show that some products, services and brands conform to certain standards which can be ethical, ecological, high quality or technological. The use of these label brands in the sport sector has been increasing because they are thought to reinforce the credibility of products and therefore consumers and various stakeholders' confidence and trust. According to Kapferer (2006), labels are a proof of quality given by a certificating organism and demonstrate that products meet certain specifications. They caution, they legitimise, and they give credit to products and services. These labels should also be considered as brands because they are often in competition with other labels. However, they do need to be associated with other brands. Three categories of label brands can be identified in relation to sport: ethical and environmental labels, labels that are provided by sport organisations and professional entities and technological labels.

Ethical and environmental labels

In line with the changes in consumer expectations and the development of labels in many sectors and industries (for example, green stickers, energy star, Max Havelaar), sport and recreation consumers also demand ethical, social or environmental guarantees from the brands they consume. For Kapferer (2003), contemporary consumers no longer accept brand practices they judge unethical, even or especially if they are conducted in far away countries, and they are increasingly ready to sanction the brands which are not perceived to behave properly. Therefore, if brands want to maintain their market share, their reputation or the relationship they have with their consumers, they have to increasingly show, by communicating or setting specific programmes, their concerns regarding their impact on individuals, society and the environment, as well as their willingness to be (and not only be seen as) good citizens and actors of the world.

As an example, the outdoor clothing brand Lafuma has created a label named the Pure Leaf Project which defines, in collaboration with the World Wide Fund for Nature (WWF), a list of strict eco-design criteria to reduce the environmental impacts the production of a backpack or a T-shirt generates. The Pure Leaf label, which can be found on the product tags, identifies their eco-design credentials. Similarly, and also in partnership with the WWF, Rip Curl launched the Rip Curl

Project which aims to support environmental projects linked to the preservation of surf spots but also projects promoting education and eco-design. The products labelled Rip Curl Planet are made with at least 55 per cent eco-friendly fabrics, such as organic cotton, recycled fibres, linen or hemp. Interestingly and perhaps surprisingly, Rip Curl Planet Foundation's main partner is the automobile brand Renault which does not necessarily fit with all the statements of the brand and its label.

More and more sport brands are engaged in ethical, environmental and societal causes and are encouraged to support non-governmental organisations and charities or even to create their own foundations. An example of the latter is Surfrider Foundation Europe which is an association gathering professional surfers and surfing brands and aiming to defend, save, improve and manage in a sustainable way oceans, coastlines, waves and the people who enjoy them. In the same vein and in the dynamic of environment preservation and protection, other associations have created their own labels, which are independent from companies, governmental organisations and lobbies, and which represent labels sport brands want to be associated with. Table 1.3 describes three examples of these labels.

Sport governing body and professional labels

In order to guarantee a certain level of service quality to sport and recreation participants and to help them make the most appropriate choice of structure, an increasing number of sport organisations have set up labels. Following branding principles, labels assure consumers that facilities, frontline staff and service delivered conform to rigorous norms of safety and quality. This is extremely helpful due to the heterogeneity of sport organisations which display massive differences in terms of services (Pigeassou, 1993). Sport organisations' quality labels represent a marketing tool for sport organisations and a strategic means to increase the number of sport participants which is generally their main long-term objective. In the sport federal system, the number of participants and members also represents a significant asset in dealing with local and central authorities as well as negotiating with sponsors. To illustrate, we can cite the German Olympic Sports Confederation (DOSB) and the German Gymnastics Federation which together developed activities and labels in order to offer high-quality programmes to help people to stay fit and healthy. Specifically, the DOSB created the 'Sport promotes Health' label and awarded it to about 14,000 programmes while the German Gymnastics Federation created the 'Health Benefit – German Gymnastics Federation' quality label and awarded more than 40,000 programmes (Petry and Schulze, 2011). Another example is the safety label developed by the International Mountaineering and Climbing Federation (UIAA) which certifies pieces of equipment for mountaineering and climbing that meet the requirements of the relevant UIAA safety standards determined in collaboration with safety label holders (the corporate brands).

For sport organisations, the labelling policies represent a positive asset because they allow all structures to market and distinguish themselves from their competitors for a limited cost. Moreover, most of them, particularly voluntary sport

TABLE 1.3 Ecologically and environmentally friendly firms' independent labels

Labels	Characteristics
1% for the Planet 	1% For The Planet is an alliance of companies which are engaged in giving one per cent of sales to environmental groups around the world. This alliance was initiated in 2001 by Yvon Chouinard and Craig Mathews, respectively the founder of Patagonia and the owner of Blue Ribbon Files. In 2009, the alliance reached the 1,000 member milestone and memberships grow continuously. As for sport companies and brands, *Firewire Surfboards, Jackson Kayak, Loose-Fit Surfboards, Mountaingirl Ltd, Champion Soccer School, Skim Seakayaks, Venture Snowboard* among others can be cited.[i]
Surfers Against Sewage 	Surfers Against Sewage is an environmental charity protecting the UKs oceans, waves and beaches through community action, campaigning, volunteering, conservation, education and scientific research. It was created in 1990 by surfers who were 'sick of getting sick' because of infections after going in the sea. Among the sponsors can be found *Rip Curl Foundation, Speedo, Quiksilver foundation, Patagonia,* and *King of watersports.*[ii]
Summit Foundation Ecological Solutions 	The Summit Foundation Ecological Solutions is a Swiss foundation created in 2001. Its missions are to increase awareness of environmental issues and to provide applicable everyday solutions to promote responsible and environmentally friendly behaviours. It conducts education, prevention and consulting programmes. The foundation is partnered with 65 Swiss and French skiing resorts as well as sport and cultural events such as the *Rip Curl Freeski.*[iii]

Notes:
i   www.onepercentfortheplanet.org/en/aboutus/ (accessed 25 June 2012).
ii www.sas.org.uk/ (accessed 25 June 2012).
iii www.summit-foundation.org/index.php (accessed 25 June 2012)

organisations, cannot necessarily afford expensive promotion and marketing campaigns. Labelling also helps higher sport organisations in the federal pyramid to control the quality of services offered by the organisations below them. For the smaller ones or the ones at the bottom of the pyramid, being controlled is the price they have to accept to benefit from such a marketing tool. In theory, label brands should attract more participants and members in comparison with those who do not have them. Moreover, labelled organisations often receive extra support either from a material, financial, marketing or human point of view. The certification by a label also represents a symbolic and institutional reward for volunteers' and paid-staff's efforts and engagement which is a significant factor of motivation and satisfaction. Indeed, for labelled structures, the federal label is a means to limit the influence of self-organised practices, which represent an increasing and competing form of participation. Finally, this can represent a unique opportunity for sport organisations which are not allowed or restricted by law to implement marketing communication and promotion. From a consumer perspective, they present numerous advantages but mainly express a competence and the promise of certain levels of quality. In this sense, labels have the same roles as franchised brands. Like them, being labelled allow brands to be part of a network and to enjoy the associated benefits. By increasing the level of perceived quality, it enhances the equity of the brand. It can also have an influence on the three other dimensions defining perceived brand equity which are: brand awareness (the brand becomes better known because of the label), brand image (more positive associations such as safety and excellence are carried by the brand) and brand loyalty (switching to a non-labelled brand represents a risk) (Aaker, 1991; Keller, 1993).

Finally, sport organisations are not the only ones to develop label brands and companies and associations of companies do it as well in the sport sector, focusing essentially on the quality issue. The final targets of these labels are consumers but also companies (the B to B approach). For the latter, a good professional label is the most recognised one. For example in France, the Qualisport label is a certification for construction companies building sport and recreation equipment and facilities. In this field, this label provides a strong competitive advantage particularly when projects are funded by local authorities.

Technological labels

Technological labels are used by corporate and store brands to reassure the customer when a new technology is used in the production of sport goods, clothes and shoes (see Table 1.4 for specific examples). Generally speaking these labels are exclusive because they are only claimed by the brands that use them. Oxylane Group (i.e. formerly Decathlon Group) has for instance created a series of labels such as Novadry (www.novadry.com), which 'guarantee a finished product's water-proofing and/or breathability in conditions of strong rain', and Equarea (www.equarea.com), which characterises textiles that 'actively wick away perspiration', for its clothing brands Tribord and Quechua.

In order to add the specific label on the products' tag, brands follow specifications that they sometimes set up themselves. Because of this, their claims are difficult to dispute and do not seem extremely reliable. However, the brands play on the fact that consumers are not necessarily aware that it is a self-made label and just seeing a label associated with the product and the brand may increase the product's perceived quality.

For the rest, sport brands' technological labels fulfill the same objectives or purposes as industrial and constituent brands. They are created to give confidence to consumers and enhance perceived quality, and sometimes authenticity. The only difference is that constituent brands such as Gore-Tex concern all types of sport clothing brands whereas technological labels belonging to a brand only concern the products of that brand. When looking at the brand's discourse, particularly in

TABLE 1.4 Sport brands technological labels

Labels	Characteristics
Novadry (Oxylane/Tribord)[i]	Novadry is a waterproof and breathable garment which allows clothes to be lightweight, solid. This label guarantees that clothes are waterproof, breathable, water repellent and windproof.
Regulator Insulation (Patagonia)[ii]	Regulator Insulation fibre keeps body heat while keeping skin and body dry. Fibres are lightweight and highly compressible for packing. They complement climbing, skiing, and snowboarding shells and performance baselayer pieces.
Breath Thermo (Mizuno)[iii]	Breath Thermo technology creates a fabric that is knitted in all Breath Thermo products. The fibre is lightweight and resilient, and converts moisture to heat to keep the body warm.

Notes:
i   www.onepercentfortheplanet.org/en/aboutus/ (accessed 25 June 2012).
ii   www.sas.org.uk/ (accessed 25 June 2012).
iii www.summit-foundation.org/index.php (accessed 25 June 2012).

the case of Oxylane/Decathlon, we can see however that it tries to make consumers believe that its label brand is in reality a constituent brand without having to pay for it. It can then be seen as a strategy which aims to give more credit to the brand for a limited cost, but it can also be seen as a response to not being invited into the selected club of brands which have the right to be associated with famous constituent brands such as Gore-Tex. However, this could produce the opposite of the desired effect. De Pelsmacker *et al.* (2005) found that the issuer of the label brand was a very important factor for consumers of ethically labelled products.

2

THE TANGIBLE INFLUENCE OF SPORT BRANDS

The decreasing role of traditional landmarks such as states, unions, churches and families in postmodern societies seems to have created a space that brands have been increasingly investigating to become significant societal landmarks and powerful entities. In this general context, sport brands are playing a significant part as they possess this ability, as luxury and prestige brands, to make people dream. Some of these brands represent and feature the history and contemporary myths of their creators (for example it is said that Bill Bowerman, one of Nike's founders, used his wife's waffle iron to design the sole of what became the waffle trainer), products, athletes and even events which are associated with them. Therefore, it appears necessary to better understand the different dimensions and approaches which structure the tangible relationships between sport brands and their consumers, particularly in a context of market economies' globalisation.

The weight and impact of sport brands

For many consumers and young ones in particular, the value and the power of sport brands rely on past moments of glory, stories, symbols and imaginary contents they have been associated with which make them unique. Therefore, few brands can claim the same power and level of identification attraction. Consequently, sport brands represent profitable and enviable businesses. The sports and leisure markets show continuous and regular growth and some sectors have even become gold mines for intergenerational products such as shoes and sneakers. Retail stores have also become aware of the benefits of investing in this market and some have created their own brands and products to compete with the traditional international sport brands. Industrial holdings are also becoming interested in this worldwide market of an estimated value of US$230 billion with an annual growth of between 4 per cent and 6 per cent depending on country (Andreff and Szymanski, 2006). The interest of the financial group Pinault Printemps La Redoute (PPR) for Puma is a relevant illustration of this phenomenon. This sport brand represented a very good investment because its profit margin is close to the group's luxury brands. Moreover, Puma's worldwide reputation is also ten times higher than the one of PPR; although its turnover is eight times lower. Financial motivations then push American funds such as VF Corporation, which owns The North Face, Vans, Nautica, Napapijri and Reef, and European funds such as Airesis, which owns Le Coq Sportif, Fanatic and Mistral, to become interested in investing in sport brands. Nowadays, not many companies can show such high profit rates. The revenues generated by the major international sport brands now reach massive figures which make these brands highly profitable and attractive as illustrated by the estimated values of the brands presented in Table 2.1.

TABLE 2.1 The top four most valuable sport brands per category

	Club brands	Event brands	Corporate brands	Celebrity brands	Media brands
1	New York Yankees US$340,000,000	Super Bowl US$425,000,000	Nike US$15,000,000,000	Tiger Woods US$55,000,000	ESPN US$11,500,000,000
2	Manchester United US$269,000,000	Summer Olympics US$230,000,000	Adidas US$5,000,000,000	Roger Federer US$26,000,000	Sky Sports US$3,000,000,000
3	Real Madrid US$264,000,000	FIFA World Cup US$147,000,000	Gatorade US$2,500,000,000	Phil Mickelson US$24,000,000	YES Network US$600,000,000
4	Dallas Cowboys US$193,000,000	MLB World Series US$140,000,000	Reebok US$1,500,000,000	David Beckham US$20,000,000	MSG US$500,000,000

Source: Adapted from The Forbes Fab 40: The world's most valuable brands, 2011 edition, www.forbes.com/sites/mikeozanian/2011/10/03/the-forbes-fab-40-the-worlds-most-valuable-sports-brands-3/ (accessed 29 June 2012).

Major, international, national and regional brands

Among practitioners, it is common to differentiate markets with or without brands, and sport markets are undeniably brand markets. They are dynamic and characterised by intense rivalries between competitors. They also present various particularities which strongly influence the sport brands' strategic orientations such as the existence of strong barriers for entry, technological specificities, and strong cultural and marketing differences (for example between sports, between public, voluntary and commercial organisations and categories of products). In the sole sport shoes market, about 20 different segments can be identified (running, trail, street, skate, etc.). The sport goods industry is made up of major brands with international levels of awareness and reputation and medium and small specialised brands which compete in national and/or regional markets but can also have an international reputation on specialised niche markets.

The major sport brands adopt managerial and economic models which are focused on capitalistic growth (the biggest ones are present on the main stock exchange markets), on internal specialisation and diversification (including increasing the number of offers on small marketing and technological niches and diversifying with new products through merging and acquiring other firms and brands) but also on external diversification by providing complementary products displaying technical or commercial similarities outside sports markets. Some brands specialising in mountain sports equipment and accessories (for example Millet, Lafuma, Petzl, Beal, Scott) have diversified their offers to provide equipment for soldiers, firemen or high-height workers. Similarly, many sport brands have tried to leverage their reputation and brand equity to enter non-sport markets such as beauty products and toiletries, glasses, or luggage, including Adidas, Lacoste, Head and Slazenger.

These major international brands mainly search for economies of lines and scales, productivity gains and costs rationalisation. They also follow a strong exportation strategy as many of their historical and traditional markets are now mature, which see them making important turnover shares in foreign, and potentially highly profitable, markets. At the same time, financial and economic pressures force them to subcontract their work in countries with low production costs despite the criticism regarding ethical and social issues. In these globalised markets, the economic motivation is often a priority over other motivations, even if many concerns are raised in the companies' home countries. For instance as a consequence of the integration of Rossignol in the Quiksilver group, 160 jobs were axed and the production of skis was relocated to Romania whilst the production of snowboards was relocated to China. However, due to negative public perceptions and sometimes governmental pressures or incentives, a trend to relocate some foreign-based chains of production or create new units in home countries is noticeable. For instance, in 2011, Rossignol set up in France a unit of production for its high-end ski products and in 2010 Le Coq Sportif opened a small unit in one of its former buildings in Romilly-Sur-Seine (France), the city which saw the creation of the brand, 22 years after seeing the brand leave. However, these relocations remain marginal and never concern major chains of production. As analysed by Duménil and Levy (2011), the direct foreign investment of non-financial American companies represented 27 per cent of their physical investments (construction and material) in the seventies whereas it represented 81 per cent for the 1998–2007 period. The current trend is still for outsourcing and relocation and not yet for insourcing and de-relocation (coming back).

Up against these major international sport brands, numerous small and medium sport brands compete and seem to be more reactive to the changes in consumers' needs and expectations because they tend to be closer to them than the biggest ones. Often free from the constraints of intensive production, they can be profitable with smaller numbers of sales. They tend to favour strategies focusing on certain know-hows, a service quality, and proximity with their consumers and a human dimension. These micro brands, from a worldwide perspective, can usually be found on two types of strategic market: either on traditional and specialised markets such as orienteering and fell running shoes for which the annual volume of sales rarely goes beyond a few thousand, or on emerging but non stabilised niche markets whose products are potentially highly profitable because of competitors' scarcity but have extremely diverse product lifecycles. In order to remain competitive in these specific markets, these small brands often avoid mainstream channels of distribution such as the main retail stores and franchises because they want to maintain their margins. Nowadays, thanks to the Internet, it is easier to be in touch with demand and at a lower cost. As for communication, they tend to use different and alternative channels of communication and viral marketing is a well-used technique.

From a strategic point of view, the business model of national and regional sport brands significantly differs from the major brands. For the former, offers are often shaped to national and local specificities. Each product or range of products is adjusted for the market of the country of origin. Certain ski and snowboard brands try for instance to adapt their product to consumers' tastes by offering different colours and serigraphs according to different countries. The challenge is different for major brands as they heavily rely on standardisation to offer almost identical products to different geographical markets. For national and regional brands, the challenge is to integrate cultural, social and legal differences. It is more profitable for major brands such as Adidas and Nike to commercialise low-differentiated products because of the gains they can make in terms of economies of scale. The only way to make consumer demand uniform without or with few product adaptations is to implement globalised and standardised communication strategies and blueprints. For major brands, the worldwide market seems to maintain a relative stability and market saturation or a crisis in a single country represent an epiphenomenon. This stability is one of the reasons why major distribution groups such as Foot Locker and Oxylane Group have kept on investing in new foreign markets and countries.

Since the eighties and nineties, the strong concentration of the sector has created a new configuration of producers. First, international sport corporate brands and major sport-specific retail brands, representing no more than about forty actors worldwide, share most of the worldwide turnover (the first fifteen brands represent about 80 per cent of the sector's turnover) and dominate the market thanks to their positioning and targeting of the most profitable segments such as sport shoes and outdoor clothing. Second, there is a myriad of small and very small businesses which stimulate the market by targeting the numerous gaps and niche segments left by the dominant sport brands because the profit margins are not seen to be attractive enough for them and because they are not reactive enough to cope with the sudden changes in demand. Finally, due to the markets' globalisation which pushes for concentrations and alliances, we can observe the development of hybrid sport brands which are the outcome of close partnerships and collaborations between global and international sport brands with generalist or specialised retail brands such as Nike and Walmart and Nike and Foot Locker respectively. This recent phenomenon, known by economists as vertical extension or integration (see Chapter 6), seems to strongly and sustainably modify the market landscape because it produces more and more powerful brands which can control the whole chain of production from research and development to distribution. This represents an advantage for manufacturer brands because they can better control the selling price by reducing the role of retail brands. They can also reduce the production costs by mutualising them for several brands from the same group (for example using the same production sites for several brands) and can limit as well the numbers of new competitors by creating bigger entry barriers (Porter, 1982). Finally, this vertical extension allows a better cover of a geographical area and a diversification of their brands and products' portfolio. This trend can be observed with the integration of local and foreign brands by global brands in order to adjust to the local demand characteristics.

Globalisation and sport brands' concentration

Until the nineties, technical sport goods with a strong added value (for example skis, boats, windsurfing boards) were mainly exported by western European and North American countries although low-technicality goods such as sneakers and clothes were mainly imported to these countries. In the first case, goods were mainly exported towards developed countries although in the second case, they were mainly imported from emerging or developing countries from South-East Asia. The massive importation of these types of goods, clothes and shoes from emerging countries was explained by their cheap labour costs as well as the incapacity to master sophisticated and highly technological production processes. The situation changed when the low-quality goods' exporting countries such as China, Taiwan and South Korea acquired the know-how and the technological knowledge to conceive sport products with high added value corresponding to the norms and requirements of western countries and consumers. For instance, 90 per cent of globally commercialised windsurfing boards are produced by Cobra, a single manufacturer brand based in Thailand.

This new positioning of countries with a cheap labour reputation but also the capacity for producing high-quality products transform the production and value chains in the sports industries worldwide. For instance, South-East Asian countries have become more interesting because they can offer many different industrial products, from basic and simple small pieces to complex, engineered products relying on advanced research knowledge. For these reasons international sport brands increasingly locate their production and look for suppliers and partners in those countries. If countries from the Asia-Pacific region have become the biggest exporters of sport products in terms of numbers and varieties, as well as subcontracting activities, the G7 countries (Canada, France, Germany, Italy, Japan, United Kingdom and United States) have become the biggest importers and consumers.

This shift is also accompanied by the progressive migration of parts or whole production lines to exporting countries, leaving mainly R&D and marketing departments and registered offices in western countries. As mentioned in the previous section, a few cases of de-relocation of production units in western countries with the examples of Le Coq Sportif and Rossignol can be observed and are likely to serve marketing purposes rather than production ones. Because major parts of the production of international brands are subcontracted, it can even be thought that they have become more commercial companies than manufacturers as illustrated by the case of Nike which does not have factories in its name and which has all its production subcontracted outside the USA (Gratton and Taylor, 2000). This is certainly not an exception in the sport goods industry and these major brands are more and more assemblers and less and less manufacturers (Klein, 2001). Even if they have strong standards and requirements, they do not fully control the production process and only conception, communication, sales and marketing attract their full attention. If the role of assembler or adaptor of sport goods is not opposed to the role of producer and manufacturer, it highlights the fact that a growing strategy does not solely rely on an industrial model any more but also and mainly on the production of symbols, meanings and values. This strategic orientation seems increasingly profitable, especially on the fastest growing markets such as those dealing with surfwear, running and outdoor clothing. With fewer responsibilities in relation to the production, and especially human resources management and its cost, adaptors or assemblers can then focus all their resources on the innovation, communications and marketing aspects.

The market of sport goods brands finally seems bipolar with on one hand the main global and dominant sport brand groups which focus on sportswear, sport shoes, skis/snowboards and outdoor sectors such as Nike, Adidas, Reebok, Amer Sport (for example Salomon, Wilson and Atomic) and Quiksilver. Associated with these major brands can be found major retail brands such as Intersport, Oxylane Group and Sports Direct International, dominating the sport specific retail sector in Europe. On the other hand, we can observe a profusion of small brands characterised by a strong specialisation competing in many different market segments which are not seen as profitable enough by the major sport brands. However, it does not mean that because major sport brands do not compete for these market segments that they are not profitable for smaller organisations. The major sport brands' strategy could be seen as 'wait and see', where they let the small brands take the risks inherent to new markets and see if they are successful enough to invest in them when they are stabilised and profitable enough. This strategy was conducted in the eighties by Skis Rossignol within the emerging snowboard market by using the Canadian subsidiary company of its brand Dynastar to launch its first snowboards.

The concept of economies of scale explains a significant proportion of the market structures as well as the strategies operated. However, it also explains sport brands' internal dynamics which almost have an obligation to diversify in order to gain new market shares and remain sustainable. Many examples can be identified.

For instance, Adidas extended its initial production of traditional sport shoes to football boots and balls, then to sportswear because of the high-margin potential of these growing markets. The German brand has also tried to differentiate itself from its main competitors in emerging markets such as India where the brand aims to sell sport shoes for US$1. Another example of diversification comes from Rossignol, originally a skiing equipment specialist, which produced tennis racquets for a while and now plans to offer hiking boots and clothing. In another sector, the famous scooter and motorbike brand Yamaha has become a skiing equipment and tennis racquet brand. The brand Browning diversified from golf clubs to tennis racquets. Salomon diversified its production from shoes and ski bindings to skis, snowboards, golf clubs, bike accessories and outdoor clothing. And Babolat, the world leader for tennis racquet strings, now provides tennis and badminton footwear, grips, luggage and clothing. Babolat also diversified its offer through a partnership with the tyre brand Michelin to create tennis shoes. Finally, another example is given by the Italian brand Fila which established a partnership with Ferrari to launch a limited edition collection of sport shoes.

Nowadays, the diversification of sport brands appears as a strong component of their strategy. Many of them abandon their single-product or service strategy to adopt multi-products and services strategies and portfolios which sometimes go through co-branding strategies and alliances with brands from the same corporation or other brands. For instance, Rossignol created the Dynastar Ferrari skis, and Quiksilver snowboards and mountain bikes. Under the ownership of Quiksilver, the diversification is also accompanied by the share of industrial processes. The times when one production unit supplied one brand are now gone. The brands from the Quiksilver group now share all the factories and production platforms which allow the brand to consider other extensions in each brand category thanks to the know-how and knowledge transfer from the other brands. This concentration of knowledge and technological processes has become a significant driver for international brands to develop global portfolios to better cover different markets.

For sport brands, an external growth or diversification is generally made in a sector where the distance from the original products remains short. Brands do not have an interest to extend their products too far from their core activities in order to continue benefiting from a significant image transfer. A too big gap between the parent brand and the extension could create a confusion which would at least make the extension inefficient or at worst would create negative reactions from consumers of the parent brand. However, although theoretically important, a proximal distance between brands and their core market segments does not seem to block certain external acquisitions. This was for instance the case for Benetton, the clothing group, which successively bought Nordica (the world leader in ski shoes), Asolo (hiking boots) and Rollerblade. After a few years, the Italian group sold all three brands and made significant profit margins. The clockmaker company Ebel which acquired Authiers skis and the Agnelli Group which acquired the German cycle brand Heideman followed the same strategy.

This situation is not limited to international sport good brands and can also be observed among international, national and even regional club brands. Major sport clubs look to diversify their activities and their revenues by the creation of branches and brand extensions in different market sectors (for example hospitality, financial services), by managing brand portfolios and by investing in company shares. For instance Manchester United Football Club, one of the biggest club brands, has developed many different services and products. Their stadium Old Trafford is also a venue for conferences and meetings, exhibitions, as well as dinners and weddings. The club possesses its own TV channel (MUTV) which made the brand become a media brand and also provides financial products through its branch Manchester United Finance. However, it rarely considers investment in shares in other companies and brands and is rather limited at a brand level (brand extensions) compared to its group level (portfolio of brands).

Lafuma, an outdoor clothing, accessories and now furniture brand, is a good example of a brand which adopted a consistent and homogenous diversification strategy although staying in its original market territory, and keeping minimum distance between the original brand and products and the new ones. In a fifteen year period, the Lafuma group acquired seven companies and nine brands among which some have been abandoned due to strategic and competitive reasons such as Mac, a clothing brand, Rivory Joanny, a ropes and cords brand, Charles Dubourg, a sportswear brand and L'Esquimau, a hunting and country brand. After each acquisition, Lafuma obtained additional expertise and know-how, for example with the rock climbing shoes sector when it acquired the brand One Sport. Lafuma group's brand portfolio now comprises five main brands organised around four main divisions: Lafuma which represents the great outdoor division; Millet and Eider which represent the mountain division; Le Chameau which represents the country division; and Oxbow which represents the boardsports division.

Sport brands' dimensions and their valorisation

It now appears difficult to limit the consumption of sport brands to the simple aggregation of production, usage and image values. Besides the brands' functional aspects such as signal recognition, choice practicality, quality guarantee and choice optimisation as identified by Kapferer (2008), three other dimensions can be identified: sensorial, semantic and somatic dimensions.

The sensorial dimension

The sensorial dimension of sport brands refers to the tangible characteristics of sport products and services, those features which can be experienced via all consumers' senses (vision, hearing, smell, taste and touch). According to many authors (for example, Pine and Gilmore, 1999; Schmitt, 1999), brands are not simple markers and identifiers anymore, they are also experience producers. This is particularly the case for the sport context. Holbrook and Hirschman (1982) identified that the experiential dimension was fundamental with leisure, entertainment, and arts products; domains which sports belong to. Sports experiences strongly influence all human senses: the smell of a pitch grass, the vision in spectator sports, the taste of salty water in swimming, the sound of the skis on fresh snow, the feel of the grip of a tennis racquet or the comfort of running shoes. The focus on another function of brands, the symbolic function, limited the interest in brands' sensorial aspects although they create different emotions and enchantment that can be individual as well as shared with others.

The semantic dimension

The semantic dimension refers to the symbolic function of services, products and brands and their ability to carry meaning and values. This dimension relies on the semiotic paradigm which considers that each object has an explicit dimension (the object itself) and an implicit dimension which relates to the mental associations and signs related to it. Sport brands provide of lot of signs which can be interpreted in different ways by different individuals. Therefore their consumption sends implicit messages which help consumers to enhance their self-concept and/or social image. This corresponds to the badge function identified by Kapferer (2008). This semantic or symbolic function is something which is actively developed and promoted by sport brands' marketers but it should also be noted that sports themselves carry these kinds of signs and associations that may accentuate the impact of such a dimension for sport brands by using sports' signs within brands' signs.

The somatic dimension

The somatic dimension refers to body and corporal practices expressed and manifested through buying and consumption behaviours and rituals. Each culture, each country or region does not have the same codes of practice and uses regarding objects and brands. Generally speaking, consumption phenomena involve a scenic treatment, a script which requires sometimes ritualised, cultural routines. Sport behaviours rely on a specific syntax or score which favour the appropriation and the incorporation of an object and the related brand. For instance many brands play on the reproduction of these bodily actions and expressions in their commercial and promotional campaigns. This function was illustrated by Holt (1995) who analysed how sport spectators consume and identified the specific roles of both objects and actions in experiencing games as well as their use in shaping spectators' identity and self-concept.

Therefore, sports brands should be considered as transmission mechanisms of values, gestures and rituals because these dimensions can explain the fact that some of them are appealing or not, appealing to all or only to some individuals, purchased, hated and worshipped. However, although the sign dimension is important, sports brands cannot be reduced only to social meanings. They also have strong individual and personal values which are expressed though an appropriation or integration, to use the consumption metaphor used by Holt (1995). As stated by Eco (1985), objects – and then brands – are highly emotional signs because they also invite an incorporation/embodiment from individuals. The Adidas slogans 'Forever sport' or 'The victory is within us' are good examples of such incorporation as they encourage consumers to integrate with a certain sporting culture or ethic. In order to differentiate themselves from their competitors, big or small signs and logos, stores and brands have become powerful triggers of narratives whose main function is to dramatise and re-enchant products and services to make them desirable. Simultaneously, sports brands also promote certain ideologies and therefore contribute to the reproduction, the development and the marginalisation of social beliefs and practices. For instance, through its slogan 'Just do it', Nike enjoined us to do and act, to overcome barriers and limits, norms and rules, without excuses. Lacoste made the same kind of incitation with its slogan 'Become what you are'.

In the long-lasting debate about creation or satisfaction of existing needs, it seems that sport brands actively contribute to format tastes in offering new modes of consumption (for example using sport shoes for fashion purposes) or in creating new products which change life, sport and leisure habits and practices (such as mountain bikes, snowboards, scooters). However, the appropriation of sport brands' products goes through different phases which structure in time the consumer–brand relationship. Sometimes, products can even be diverted from their original uses and functions by consumers. Therefore, sport brands' uses can help to classify consumers and their behaviours, allowing the creation and the development of specific group identifiers, being either social groups, territorial groups or emotion-based groups such as the postmodern tribes and communities (Cova and Cova, 2002).

The valorisation of sport products should then go beyond the traditional dichotomy opposing usage and transaction value for consumption objects. From a consumer perspective, value is not necessarily an inherent attribute of consumption objects and brands: it depends on the way they are valorised because they are given different values in different contexts. As illustrated by Landowski (2004) with a beer example, the value attributed to the beer is not the same if you are thirsty under a very hot climate, if you are drinking it in a cosy atmosphere with beer specialists or if you are drinking it during a sporting event or at home watching a sport game with friends. This example demonstrates that sport brands' value should also be understood from an interactional and relational perspective. As consumers look for different experiences and functions, as Holbrook (1999) defined value as a relative preference characterising an individual's experience with a particular object, sport brands' value should not be considered as unique and universal. Their value is linked to all the brands' functions and meanings and then presents a multidimensional character.

The sport brands' influence on consumerism

Understanding the sport brands' influence on individual and group behaviours is made more challenging, but probably more exciting as well, in a world where exchanges between countries and cultures take a significant part in the activities of companies, whatever their size, their categories of products and services and the way these offers meet the consumers' needs. In this context, two commercial approaches could be identified: one is qualified as multicultural and the other one as standardising. On one hand, cultural, ethnic and religious differences between regions and countries would be manifested through diverse and heterogeneous consumption modes, in particular in developed and in-development countries. On the other hand can be found what some observers call the 'world village' in which similarities more than differences are emphasised and represent a strong component of marketing and promotional tactics.

The changes in nature of the relationships between consumers and their brands force commercial actors to try new strategies to provide new consumption and life landmarks such as humanising and providing meanings to brands, creating a partic-ular identity. In this sense, sport brands contribute to the creation of new consumption universes and the transformation of sport markets by initiating and accompanying a tangible change in cultures and habits. Understanding what we call the consumerist influence of sport brands consists in appreciating the effects of the creation and the diffusion of a 'tangible culture' linked to brands in terms of fashion, innovation, and intercultural transfers on consumers, even if it is sometimes difficult to separate it from the 'intangible culture' of consumption in terms of origin and impacts on consumer behaviours. In this context, we will see that sport brands exercise an influence on norms, symbols and rules of actions directly impacting on behaviours, values and practices.

Creation and diffusion of sport brands' cultures

The challenge for sport brands is to understand how the cultures we live in gener-ate sense and meanings for everyday products and services and how they are spread within societies to reach consumers. Advertising and fashion contribute to the spread of these meanings in associating functional products with symbolic features such as being sexy or sophisticated. In turn, consumption objects and brands provide consumers with these significations which help them construct and affirm their individual identities. For these reasons it is therefore important to understand how sport brands infiltrate cultures and societies. The world offers a profusion of styles and consumption modes and consumers are sometimes overwhelmed by all these possibilities and choices. However, despite this apparent abundance, the options really are not that many and seem to be progressively filtered in a process of cultural selection (McCracken, 1986). These options constantly evolve, which explains how some brands, such as Fred Perry for instance, can become obsolete one day and become trendy and fashionable on another.

Culture and fashion display structuring features which explain this perpetual change in the clothing sector and styles often reflect deeper societal trends as well. They can emerge from minority groups representing edgy or marginal attitudes and behaviours before becoming more popular and taken up by various layers of society. Styles are often the outcome of the interaction between innovations from brand creators and designers and spontaneous consumer actions adjusting them to their needs. They can travel far and go across country borders thanks to media. However, most of them have a finite lifetime and their adoption progressively disappears with the consumer's desire to be different and search for new identity attributes. To a certain extent, sport fashion (for example sportswear, vintage, surfwear, streetwear) seems to correspond to the aspirations of many consumers in their identity quest. However, we should wonder if this trend will last even if all growing sport brands hope and try to actively maintain this situation.

Not one single designer, brand or communication agency is solely responsible for the diffusion of a tangible culture. However, in a context of strong concentration, sport good industries tend to produce more similar goods, such as in the sector of water sports. Specifically Speedo and Arena dominate the worldwide swimwear and accessories markets leaving the other competitors far behind them. In all the the countries considered, either Speedo or Arena holds the leader position. On the contrary, multiple actors provide a higher diversity of products such as in the case of ski, surf and bike industries. Also, numerous socioeconomic actors actively or passively contribute to the production of tangible cultures making the prediction of consumers' tastes extremely difficult, even if all brands and marketing and communication agencies aspire to do so in the long term. Nevertheless, they seem to all rely on three main components to create a strong cultural impact on consumers. These are:

1. a creative sub-system able to generate new symbols and products;
2. a management system whose purpose is to select, mass produce and distribute these new symbols and products;
3. a communication sub-system which aims to make sense of the new product as well as defining a set of attributes which will serve as communication supports (Solomon, 1988).

In the case of major sports brands such as Nike, Adidas, Reebok or Asics, these three components or sub-systems can be found integrated within the company. However, numerous agents play a filter role which limits or increases the success of certain products and brands. Parts of the symbols are all types of criticisms coming from the main competitors, consumer associations, newspapers or columnists and acting as cultural intermediaries (Solomon, 1986). In the sport markets, specialised retail stores, champions and consumers themselves seem to play this role which regulates the influence of brands.

Sport brands and consumers' everyday life

The engineering of everyday life corresponds to the appropriation by marketers of popular cultural elements which are transformed in promotional media (Solomon and Englis, 1994). It becomes then more and more difficult to identify what is authentic from what is (re)produced to appear authentic. The 'new vintage' mode is a good example of that because it qualifies new products sometimes using old or vintage designs and it is then difficult to identify what is really vintage – an old product found in an attic or a car boot sale – from what is new but made to appear vintage.

In the sport shoes industry, major brands have restarted the production of old models which made them successful in the past. For instance Reebok re-launched 15 years later the Pump system; Adidas re-commercialised the Tokyo trainers, a replica from the sixties' model, after doing the same with the Stan Smith and Gazelle models; and Nike redesigned the famous Air Max model from the nineties. In doing so, these brands aim to offer products which resonate in consumers' memories and souvenirs and are appealing because of a certain period in their life. However, as these products also appeal to younger generations it seems that these trends are just part of a continuous cycle. This vintage trend has been then accentuated by imitation from other brands such as Le Coq Sportif (see Figure 2.1) and Puma, which wanted to surf that wave.

FIGURE 2.1   Le Coq Sportif's Eclat vintage model

Vintage fashion clearly plays on nostalgic feelings about almost mythical 'good times', turning points in life and champions. For sport brands, this strategy is low-risk and very cost effective. It is through the frame of authenticity that Adidas tries to interconnect its own history of the brand with consumers' own history in talking about its own roots. Adidas named its line Originals and targeted consumers with a non-sporting and fashion use of the products. In the same vein, to celebrate in 2007 its 100 year anniversary, Rossignol re-produced, in a limited edition, the legendary Olympic 41 (the first ski in laminated wood structure) and Strato (the first ski combining fibreglass on a wooden core) models as well as related vintage clothes and accessories.

Many physical and experiential elements are also used by marketers to have an impact on consumers' everyday lives. For instance they place their products and brands in movies, they manipulate atmosphere features (for example using sounds and smells) in retail stores, and invest public spaces with many different supports, events and promotional tactics and material. The goal seems to be to continuously try to surprise and entertain consumers to attract their attention in an over-crowded environment of signals and messages. It is now common to see giant billboards amplifying the physical presence of sport brands in public spaces such as streets and buildings.

Street and guerrilla marketing tactics are also used a lot to generate this element of surprise as well as an element of exclusivity due to the absence of direct competitors in these time-bound events and happenings. Brands can use wild posting, street murals, mobile showcases, pop up events, and mobile and walking billboards. All these promotional activities have a tangible influence on consumers' everyday life and environment. As sport brands examples we can cite the case of Converse's ambient marketing in England, featuring 'In case of Emergency' boxes containing several pairs of shoes which can be taken by lucky finders. Another example comes from the 'seatless benches' from Nike's run campaign which fit perfectly with their environment except that they are slightly unconventional.

The growing influence of sport brands on consumers' everyday lives appears unstoppable as marketers and creatives search to extend the scope of diffusion places for their message. For instance, in the USA, a professional female bowling player sold empty zones of her kit (parts of her shirt – front, back, sleeves) to potential sponsors on *eBay* (Solomon, 2003). This influence of brands and sport brands in particular on people's life is not restricted to commercial environments and public places such as streets and public transport. More controversially, brands are also investing in schools, and not only with clothes, school bags, lunch boxes but also, in the USA, through sponsored educational material such as booklets, posters, book covers and CD-ROM computer programs featuring brands such as Coca-Cola and BIC (Frith and Mueller, 2010). Obviously sport brands such as Nike, Reebok and Foot Locker, for whom children constitute one of their main targets, are also heavily engaged in such programmes. American Colleges and University campuses have also been targeted and brands have been hiring students called 'brand ambassadors' or 'campus evangelists' to represent them on campuses. It seems that we are closer and closer to the story of a 2009 movie entitled *The Joneses* which narrates the life of a fake 'normal family' made of actors paid by brands to promote their products and services in suburban neighbourhoods.

Fashion styles are more diverse than ever before and for many analysts, this diversity seems linked to the existence of sub-cultures or identity groups rather than only social and economic factors. There are indeed many different ways of wearing certain clothes and shoes, to associate and combine different clothing items which highlight an important customisation and personalisation of styles to integrate with or to be in opposition to specific groups. From a sociological perspective, being trendy means that a reference group positively evaluates a mix or a combination of clothing items in a consistent way which defines a style. The significations associated to brands therefore reflect underlying cultural categories which correspond to simplified ways of seeing the world (McCracken, 1986). For this reason, the clothing styles and brands of celebrities, champions and politics influence brands' awareness and success such as the yellow Asics shoes worn by Uma Thurman in the movie *Kill Bill*.

Fashion trends, similar to products lifecycles, are generally characterised by a slow and progressive acceptance, a climax point, maturation and then decline. However, as illustrated with vintage or new vintage trends they can re-become popular and start a new cycle. Although the cycle seems to be the same, its duration seems much longer for sport brands. A difference can, however, potentially be made between sport brands with a strong technological component in comparison with sport clothing brands for instance. For the technological ones, their strength is strongly associated with the duration and success of the product which could either be a craze or become a classic. Many sport crazes have been known, such as the 'mono-ski' (a single ski with the feet side-by-side) and the 'skwall' (a single ski with a foot in front of the other), scooters and double strung tennis racquets. Because of the introduction of new innovations or rules, the craze for these products did not last. The fate of the brands was then dependent on the brand's single or multiple-product strategy and its capacity for adaptation. On the contrary, classic brands such as Lacoste, Ferrari and Converse seem to rely on longer cycles which make them always fashionable even if their success does not follow a regular progression. These brands are often popular across various generations and geographical regions, but remain rare. This limited number can be explained by the quality management of the decline period which should be anticipated either via investing in a larger brand portfolio or in redeveloping and repositioning the brand and its products. This is what Lafuma tried to do in signing a partnership in 2007 with Thierry Mugler, a famous French fashion designer, to create a high-end skiing clothes line.

Opinion leaders and interpersonal diffusion

In terms of consumption, opinion leaders are people who are able to influence purchases and uses of certain branded products and services. They present particular attributes which give them a lot of importance to brands as well as a strong reputation and recognition in their field of expertise. These opinion leaders can be considered 'super consumers' and are believed to be objective to recognise an appropriate level of quality, price or innovation about a specific brand, product or range of products. They are generally strongly connected with the media, either because they often use them to find specific, relevant and unique information or because they are frequently featuring in them due to their expertise. They are very well informed which make them attract more information as they become the targets of many commercial and promotional messages but they also aim to share this information with others. Because opinion leaders are listened to and observed they can therefore influence others. Marketers actively search to identify them, to inform them, to provide them samples of new products and invite them to consume new services, to equip them and to invite them to feature in special promotional events.

Nevertheless, within sports markets, some categories of products are not always pushed by trends and it is common to see sport celebrities voluntarily or non-voluntarily initiating new product lines and clothing styles. An Italian sportswear manufacturer for instance used the famous/infamous head butt given by Zinedine Zidane to Marco Materazzi in the final of the 2006 FIFA World Cup to create a brand named Perché, meaning phonetically 'why' in Italian, and whose logo featured the action. Right after the 2006 FIFA World Cup, the general manager of a sports publicity company based in Beijing, Zhao Xiaokai, tried to exploit the 'Zidane effect' in registering a trademark. The trademark was registered for clothing, shoes, hats and beers under the name Tietougong meaning 'Iron Head Kung Fu'.[1] Following this event, several trademarks and brands have been registered in various countries such as Headbutt (clothing and shoes), The head of god (clothing, shoes, stationery) and Zheadbutt (clothing, shoes, sodas) which is a portmanteau for Zidane and head-butt. For the latter, the venture started with the launch of an energy drink and was rapidly followed by USB keys and a MP4 player named Zheadbutt Blade. However, in most cases these brands do not last as they mainly surf on the wave of the event and then disappear in line with the vanishing memory of the event. If these examples are in fact quite rare it is, however, frequent to see athletes and sport celebrities being recognised and used as opinion leaders by corporate brands: featuring in their advertising campaigns and being endorsed by them. At the same time, many athletes and champions exploit their reputation and image to create their own brands as for RF for Roger Federer (tennis), Rafa for Rafael Nadal (tennis), 15 for Serge Blanco (rugby) or 39Pro for Nicolas Anelka (football) playing on the interpersonal influence they can have.

The influence of sports products

Can branded products and services be qualified as consumption objects? Yes, they can, if we adopt a restrictive definition of consumption objects as elements of an external reality which are manufactured and can be handled (Moles, 1969). However, it seems that sport brands are more than consumption objects as they participate in social life as elements of desire, regulation and interaction with others. Their desirability not only depends on their utilitarian dimension but also depends on the way they contribute to social and cultural systems. Sport brands are not solely consumption objects because they are influenced by and because they influence social practices, which can be seen as a tangible effect. They act as social regulators because they enrol or exclude individuals from social and cultural groups, according to the groups' explicit rules and prescriptions. Sport brands definitely contribute to this classifying role as their products are often subject to technological and semantic processes which transform natural elements into cultural objects, comparable to understandable categories to specific groups. Whether it concerns the transformation of chemical constituents into Gore-Tex or Teflon, or the recycling of plastic into Patagonia clothes, the process looks like a transformation mechanism of nature into culture. With its Trash Talk shoe model, Nike and the former Phoenix Suns player Steve Nash transformed manufacturing waste into a basketball sneaker that sold for US$100 a pair.[2]

The consumption of sport brands responds to a cultural, and often subcultural, logic which imposes implicit rules and obligations regarding their purchase or avoidance, and use. Sport brands represent cultural objects because they follow three rules allowing, according to Lévi-Strauss (1968), the structuring of a culture:

1.   interdiction rules;
2.   permission rules;
3.   prescription rules.

Many sport brands play on the transgression dimension of their products with the use of celebrities in their advertising campaigns. Nike played this card in featuring Pete Sampras and André Agassi playing an ever-lasting game in the heart of a city (demonstrating sport place transgression), and used this technique again by transforming an airport in a playground for the Brazilian football team.

Sport brands' products as 'special' goods

From one perspective, it is possible to consider that sport brand products and services possess their own social life in acquiring or losing value, in changing their meanings, in becoming cult or in becoming simple utilitarian goods. Kopytoff (1986) demonstrated that consumption objects construct social identities because they carry interpersonal influences and because their significations are transformed. This is the case for sport shoes which have become highly significant consumption objects in our contemporary societies. They represent a singular category within what Belk (2003) described as self-transforming objects. Given the fact that brands spend about US$200 million each year on marketing and advertising, it can be thought that sport consumers firmly believe that their performances will be affected by their purchase decision (Bloch, Black and Lichtenstein, 1989). Athletes also seem to acknowledge that they influence others' performance (Albert, 1984;

Nash, 1977). However, it would be a mistake to consider that athletes represent the majority of sport shoe consumers as it is estimated that more than 80 per cent of them are bought for fashion motives rather than sporting ones (Pereira, 1988). For the ones which are bought to be used in a sport setting, the criterion of comfort seems as important as the performance criterion.

As previously mentioned, sport brands' products do not only hold exchange and usage values but also symbolic and social values. They play an active role in the valorisation of the self-concept and can provide a framework which gives a sense to consumers' existence in achieving personal, social, cultural and environmental goals. Sport brands represent significant integration and classification objects. Although their instrumental possession provides pleasure and joy, which represent their hedonistic and experiential values, their symbolic possession is valorised because it provides a feeling of continuity and extension of personal life. Moreover, when sport brands are related to certain goods and sport participation services, they enhance consumers' feeling of self-control in contrast to sport spectacle services which are more passive – even if many spectators have the sensation of being actors in the sporting events. For this reason, teenagers often seem, with regard to action objects like sport shoes, to choose justifications related to the pleasure provided by their manipulation and handling rather than their contemplation. On the contrary, for older people, objects seem to essentially play a memorial function in reminding of them past events, interpersonal and fundamental social links. Ultimately, sport brands' products represent consumption objects able to hold numerous roles depending on the people, places and past and present events they are associated with in people's minds (Csikszentmihalyi and Rochberg-Halton, 1981).

The various meanings of sport brands' products

A particular meaning associated with the possession of sport brands' products refers to the sacralisation process. It explains how consumption can become a permanent activity, allowing consumers to express their values. Sacred products refer to acquisition or usage experiences which are deemed important for consumers. They are seen as extraordinary, sometimes mysterious and can provoke strong reactions of attraction or repulsion as well as very high levels of attention and attachment from the possessor; they are opposed to ordinary objects; they can contaminate objects and individuals; they require commitment and sometimes sacrifice (Belk, Wallendorf and Sherry, 1989). They are often part of caring, customisation or exposition rituals. Specifically, these possessions are rarely given or sold by their possessors to people who are believed not deserving of them. These objects are either part of a collection or kept in a special and sometimes secret place.

Moreover, this sacralisation can also correspond to some fetishism which refers to the objects' raw material or shape. This phenomenon tends to transform brands' products into idols or icons and sometimes to personify them by attributing them a soul such as for major professional football clubs. This sacralisation and fetishism are demonstrated by the fact that many English football fans ask to have their ashes scattered on their favourite team's home ground. In 2008, in Germany, the Hamburg HSV football club opened a club's official cemetery section to fans, located just yards from the pitch and featuring a football atmosphere (it had an entrance like a football goal, graves arranged like football stands).[3] The first football club to do this was the Argentinian Boca Junior, opening a cemetery dedicated to Boca fans and former players 18 miles from Buenos Aires, where grass has been transplanted from the club's stadium La Bombonera. The cemetery has a capacity of 3,000 plots and each of them costs about £500 up to £2,000.[4]

This almost animist phenomenon allows consumers to reinforce their self-image as well as their social image. It is very close to what Sahlins (1976) described as totemism. Precisely, totemism refers, for a specific group of individuals, to processes of associations to plants, animals and objects and is a feature of tribal societies. For Lévi-Strauss (1968), in totemism, objects are both natural and cultural in the sense that their meanings express social hierarchies for the group of individuals which worship them. Sahlins (1976) extended this thinking to contemporary societies by hypothesising that these plants, animal and natural objects have now been replaced by manufactured goods. Therefore, sport brands and products can be seen as totems in contemporary western societies. For instance, sport clothes function like symbolic codes representing belonging to a specific community. They work as classifying totems which allow the communication of distinctive social identities. This can be extended to clothing styles which significantly rely on sport brands and products by which consumers are classified in tribes or communities (for example skaters, or surfers).

Consumers' perceptions of brand innovations

In order to facilitate the success of an innovation several factors have to be considered (Rogers, 1995). Applied to sport brands, they are:

- level of fit with consumer lifestyles;
- easiness to try and to learn how to use;
- simplicity of adoption;
- potential for widespread adoption;
- competitive advantage in comparison with existing products and services.

These factors will determine the consumers' level of acceptance or resistance. Levels of resistance are closely linked to perceived risks which can either be physical, psychological, economic, social, or performance. When the perceived risk is low, acceptance and adoption of innovations are generally quick. Conversely, when it is high, so resistance will be high. Consumers who are risk averse will tend to be more loyal to the brands they consume and then will be less likely to adopt innovations, especially from other brands. However, when consumers look for hedonistic experiences, they are more likely to be open to innovations if they are thought to provide new sources of pleasure and excitement.

The specific brand's approach towards innovation is an interesting issue as it depends on the way consumers are guided by their perceptions and their experiences. The notion of novelty is relative and subjective because it is linked to the adoption or resistance factors which are different among regions, countries and cultures. However, it seems that the attractive power of sport brands' premium products remains strong, particularly for the youngest consumers, indicating that despite the importance of social influences, individual attitudes should still be considered important. Sport experts will more likely want the latest innovations in order to optimise their performances and then become opinion leaders and influence the diffusion of these innovations within the sport. Innovations are not accepted according to a progressive linear curve but rather by waves. For Rogers (1983), five successive waves of adoption can be identified:

1. innovators who represent about 2.5 per cent of the potential market;
2. early buyers who represent about 13.5 per cent;
3. the first majority which represents 34 per cent;
4. the second majority which also represents 34 per cent; and
5. the late buyers who represent about 16 per cent.

For sport brands, the different categories of adopters are influenced by different factors and individual traits more or less important according to the market sectors considered. Among them, the relative innovation superiority, its fit with consumer values and expectations, the complexity and its social visibility seem to be significant factors influencing the innovation diffusion (see Chapter 5, pages 111–16). The relative innovation superiority refers to the consumer's perception that the new product is superior to the ones already available on the market. Many sporting innovations have failed not because of the products' technological dimension but because they did not match the social expectations of the consumer targets such as mono-skiing for instance in comparison with snowboarding, which provided more than just a different feet orientation. Innovation complexity includes the easiness of use, especially during a time when consumers want to do something by themselves without passing through a long-lasting learning stage (Bodet, 2009). This factor can surely explain the success of snowblades. Finally social visibility is an important factor illustrating the tangible impact of sport brands. It refers to the easiness with which new products and their benefits can be seen, noticed, imagined, described and communicated to potential adopters. For instance, it is easier to notice a new folding scooter than the Adidas 'Intelligence Level 1.1' shoe model whose sole integrates a computer and a motor to adjust each stride.

3

THE INTANGIBLE INFLUENCE OF SPORT BRANDS

In any given consumption society, intangible culture expresses its personality through its companies and brands. It includes abstract ideas such as values, morals and ideologies which are embedded within the goods and services produced and consumed in it. A culture is an accumulation of meanings, norms, traditions and rituals among members of a stable community directly influencing consumers' decisions, behaviours and relations to objects. However, the observation of these influences is often complex as they are often overlapping and interconnected. Therefore, sport brands do not only exist for their functions or utilities but also because they take part in the social interactions, meanings and rituals which define the culture. This chapter aims to better understand why and how purchasing and consumption behaviours are influenced by sport brands' intangible features.

The social and cultural influence of sport brands

Sport brands' social and cultural influences are expressed in norms of behaviour in relation to one or several more or less formalised groups, and which directly impact on individuals' values, attitudes and practices. The following sections deal with sport brands' symbolic functions, relations with social classes and cultural norms and values.

The symbolic roles of sport brands

Because culture appears as the sense people give to the world surrounding them, each consumer purchase or consumption behaviour can be interpreted as a sign or symbol (Levy, 1980; Solomon, 1983). People who share the same culture share as well verbal and non-verbal signs and symbols which facilitate their communication. Therefore, different cultures and societies will share different signs and symbols and certain objects, practices, visuals and colours will not have the same symbolic meanings accordingly. In relation to sport, cultural influence explains why football is mainly a boys' sport in Europe although it is mainly a girls' sport in the USA. A thorough understanding of the cultural elements and differences should allow brands to optimise the distribution and the communication of their products and services. Embedded within people's interaction and communication between each other, sport brands' symbolic dimension plays a crucial role. A symbol is a social construction, a stimulus associated to a learnt meaning and a socially-shared value. It can be more or less complex. When symbols are simple and direct, they do not require much information processing. Complex symbols require a much more complex interpretation. It is therefore logical that marketers try to include simple symbols when communicating about their brands to facilitate consumers' cognitive treatment and in turn positive attitudes. Nike has seemed to almost always use simple symbols and concepts associated with its endorsed athletes such as the Air Jordan shoes. In this case the name of the brand does not even appear, leaving the recalling function to the logo. Beyond the fact that symbols and signs are socially constructed stimuli, they also influence people's self-concept and are part of people's everyday life (embedded in family, workplace, and leisure activities). In terms of sport brands, they are used to manage people's image and identity as sport participants, to affirm people's belonging to a specific sport community, and to affirm a positive or distinctive role or position. However, not all symbols and signs have the same meanings and roles as they depend on both cultural groups and individuals.

Each society and community develops its own network of shared symbols. Through the socialisation process, consumption goods acquire a meaning with an allusive value more or less consensual (Solomon, 1983). In the basketball world, the brand And1 has been for instance associated to playground and hip-hop symbols in opposition to the more institutionalised brands such as Nike and Champion USA associated with the NBA. It seems now evident that some sport brands are regularly purchased for their strong symbolic meanings by groups and communities who use them as totems or emblems. For instance, a skater or a surfer style implies the purchase and consumption of brands such as Ethnies, Vans, Reef, Rip Curl, Quiksilver or Billabong. The origins of brands' symbols and signs come from both commercial actors (for example marketers, advertisers, designers) and interpersonal and informal influences (for example opinion leaders, heroes and myths, word-of-mouth). Although these sport symbols often come from a specific sociocultural universe (for example outdoor, boardsports, teamsports, watersports), they are almost always re-appropriated and diverted from their original meaning by consumers and practices and are not any more in the sole control of marketers.

These symbols acquired by consumers via their branded purchases help them reinforce their self-esteem as well as setting a scene for the expression of their self-concept in affirming a belonging, in supporting social roles, in facilitating the acquisition of new social status and in participating in the interpretation of people's environment. They are used on a daily basis by consumers. Via its symbolic features, a brand generally organises three stages of self-image communication (Levy, 1980). During the first stage, consumers adopt one or several elements of a brand which best represent their self and which convey a vision and a presentation more or less idealised. In a second stage, consumers hope that the members of their social environment will perceive the brand and its symbolic features and third, they will hope that these features will be transferred to their self in people's mind. Therefore, as each purchase and consumption can be perceived and interpreted as a symbol, consumers can then strategically manipulate them to the benefit of their self-image (Levy, 1980; Solomon, 1983). Conversely, if consumers use these brands strategically, brands can also manipulate these elements to appear favourably and attract these consumers. For instance, surf boards, long boards and snowboards are extensively used in advertising and as part of stores' decorum even in situations where their presence can appear unnecessary as illustrated with Figure 3.1 featuring a tattoo shop using surf boards for its front decoration.

FIGURE 3.1 A tattoo shop using surf boards for its decoration

The aim is to reach young consumers in making implicit references to the surf culture which conveys associations such as fun and cool. This is for instance what Belair Direct, a Canadian insurance company, did within one of its 2005–2006 promotion campaigns which aimed to attract potential new employees and which featured a business woman on a skateboard. Some symbols are, however, difficult to associate with individuals who do not belong to specific groups when they are attached to technical and highly-specialised material and equipment. In these circumstances, casual participants hardly try to be associated with these symbols either because the goods are not accessible to them, because they are too expansive, because of their lack of knowledge, or because the gap between the symbols they want to be associated with and their level of expertise is too big to be real. For this reason, clothing styles are so important and clothing and brands are so popular, in particular among young people: their symbols are easy to acquire and less likely to be challenged.

Nevertheless, for a product or a brand to become a symbol, its possession and/or implicit use have to involve a differentiation in order to project a distinctive image between consumers and non-consumers. In this sense sport brands play an important differentiating role, particularly with the use of their logo. Logos have become real identity indicators just as tattoos and piercings signify belonging to a specific social group or postmodern tribe. For these reasons, logos have sometimes become objects of true worship. One traditional argument to explain the worship of brands and their goods and services relies on the decreasing importance of traditional institutions in people's life such as family, the state, religions, clubs and associations which do not provide enough sense and do not make people dream enough any more. One explanation among others is that brand worship seems corroborated by the fact that shopping malls and stores have become social, recreation and leisure places called by Ritzer (2010), 'cathedrals of consumption' underlying their sacred dimension which will be later analysed in this chapter.

The impact of income and social class factors

The influence of symbols and signs on people's purchase behaviour and product use should not hide the importance of classical factors such as income and social classes, particularly during difficult economic times. Undeniably, brands and their products and services are often purchased and displayed to refer to a real or wanted social status. In this sense, brands allow people to define their individual location in the social space (Bourdieu, 1984). However, it is necessary to take into consideration the fact that demand also depends on people's financial capacity to buy these products and services and their capacity to access them. Nevertheless, each individual has his own relationship to money which will depend on his own associated meanings (for example freedom, success, integration), his own behaviours in terms of acquisition and spending, his own fears and social antecedents such as familial education (Borneman, 1978). Despite all these individual factors, the relationships are still dependent on disposable income and belonging to a social class. Despite the development of individualism in developed and in some in-development countries, social factors, whether they define certain classes or not, have a strong influence on consumption behaviours. In the analysis of the relationship between consumers and their brands and sport brands, social factors and class allow the segmentation of social groups more or less homogenous in terms of consumption practices. Each of these social groups, whether they are formal (working class, lower middle class, upper middle class, upper class) or not (yuppie, bobo) is characterised by its own symbols and associated meanings which can be used by individuals to affirm their belonging, their desire to belong to this group, and by mirror effect their non-belonging from other social groups. It is important to consider these groups not to be set in stone and that they are constantly reconfigured. For instance, the late nineties saw the apparition of the term bobo, a portmanteau of the words bourgeois and bohemian, to designate upper-middle and upper class individuals with politically liberal views and environmental and ecological concerns. These bobos are believed to be the descendants of the yuppies (young urban professionals) from the eighties and nineties and are associated with particular brands and consumption habits. The social group is spread over different North American, European and Asian countries with slight local variations, indicating that it crosses cultural, economic and political boundaries (d'Astous et al., 2002). In the United Kingdom for instance, 'chav' is a derogatory term which designates a working class youth subculture group whose members are associated with branded sportswear and certain sport brands. Despite similarities observed in different countries such as in the case of the bobos, the social stratification and the number of groups and classes are highly dependent on the cultural and economic context. Therefore, when analysing consumption patterns, the choice of social indicators to segment similar individuals will be affected. However, three main characteristics can be identified in relation to the influence of social groups and classes. First, the influence of social classes is more significant for products with high symbolic value and which are not very expensive such as clothing items. Second, income is the most significant factor for expensive products without strong symbolic elements such as sports equipment. Third, social class and income are both important for expensive and high symbolic value products such as cars, tourism, cultural and leisure activities.

Various studies have established a link between social classes and the adoption of specific values and lifestyles which are expressed through particular consumption behaviours and where brands play a significant role. For instance the lower-working class often includes people with precarious financial situations and unstable working status. Companies and marketing departments have increasingly tried to target low-income consumers while avoiding discrimination. This business model has been called B-2-4B and stands for business to four billion, which is the size of this socio-economic group worldwide. For instance, some low-cost fitness chain brands, such as Pure Gym in the United Kingdom, aim to attract this group of people who have never been members of gyms before, by offering low prices, no monthly contract and 24-hour opening. This strategy has been successful for Pure Gym which has opened 22 gyms since late 2009 and is expected to have up to 65 gyms by 2013.[1] The trend is being followed by other brands such as Gym Group and EasyGym, a brand extension of the flight low-cost company EasyJet, as it seems to be the fastest-growing fitness sector.

For an increasing number of consumers, luxury brands seem to be considered as a response to both quality and social status concerns and purchasing these kinds of item does not represent an economic and social risk. However, in difficult economic times, this attitude seems to be replaced by the search for good deals and opportunities with lower profile brands. One explanation can be linked to the increasing numbers of reduced-price designer items and counterfeited products which negatively influence luxury brands' image and reputation. This phenomenon is also amplified for sport brands by the fact that many of them have followed downward line extension strategies to have their products distributed by mass-market retail stores. Therefore, for many consumers, brands' logos and emblems have lost their power of attraction. It seems particularly the case for older and upper-class consumers as loyalty seems to decrease with age, which is a big issue for brands as these segments have high disposable incomes. It seems that when the competition for symbols and signs is too intense or when they are not meaningful enough, these consumers are more likely to switch for other brands (d'Astous et al., 2002; Solomon, 1983). In this context, price remains a strong barrier as illustrated in the case of Chanel which created a luxury rugby ball for an expensive price of €130.

Rules, norms and language

The evolution of dominant values in societies is often a concern for market research institutes and brands' marketing departments because they are highly influential with regard to consumption patterns. Intangible culture is at the origins of these systems of values and norms which in turn create rules about what is correct, good or acceptable to purchase, use and wear. These rules of being together, which concern any kind of society (Lévi-Strauss, 1976), deal with what is recommended (prescription rules), allowed (permission rules) and forbidden (interdiction rules). All these rules can influence the design of sport brands' products and services as well as their purchase and consumption. These norms are embedded within a specific culture and are expressed through interactions between members of the same community. They participate in a social play defining what is mainstream and dominant and what is marginal and dissenting. Therefore, to construct their identity, individuals manipulate and play with these rules and norms. Sport brands like playing with these rules and sometimes transgress them, most often symbolically, because they allow them to target different segments such as teenagers, rebels and minority groups. In this case, brands can contribute to the development of a counter-culture and the edification of new norms and rules. Several examples of brands using anti-heroes or rebels can be identified such as the young André Agassi (tennis), Allen Iverson (basketball) or Eric Cantona (football) with Nike. However, it is important that these norms are not always conscious or verbalised. Explicit norms are named enacted norms whereas implicit norms are named crescive norms.

From a cultural perspective, language is an important dimension in the establishment of a system of values as it materialises and communicates shared meanings. In the sport context, all the members of a community use the same language to both enhance the sense of belonging and to differentiate themselves from the other sport and non-sport communities (for example in team sports, skateboarding, freeriding, surfing and snowboarding, gymnastics). Only experts and community members are meant to understand all the terms. On this basis, sport brands have to adapt their language and vocabulary in order to be able to properly communicate their messages to these specific groups and to be able to appear favourably to them. As these words are directly connected to specific group meanings and values, their understanding represents a key asset for brands' marketers. Moreover, as sport brands increasingly target globalised groups and communities the language issue is particularly important, especially when consumers are global citizens who speak many different languages. For global consumers, the question concerns which language brands should use to try to connect with them. Outside the sport area, a study conducted with Chinese residents in Montreal (Canada) showed that publicity in English had more impact than publicity in Chinese in terms of positive attitudes towards the brand concerned (Toffoli and Laroche, 1998). This surprising finding can be explained by the fact that expatriated communities are less trustful of messages communicated in their home language when they do not come from brands from their own country; the source's credibility is seen as suspicious.

Language as a culture and subculture component mainly intervenes at a cognitive and affective level. Brand names, when they are pronounced in another language can mean nothing, and therefore do not convey any symbols and explicit meanings, or on the contrary mean a lot and can create positive or negative consumers' reactions either because they explicitly refer to an inappropriate or crude term or because it conveys culturally undesirable meanings and symbols. When meanings are explicit this represents an unforgivable mistake from marketers because it is easily avoidable, although implicit meanings are more difficult to appreciate especially because they can only concern specific sub-groups. This was for example the case of Nike in France: when pronounced in a French way it corresponds to the English 'F word'. For the brand, it was therefore crucial to impose the English pronunciation of the brand in this country. Another example is the Crusaders rugby union franchise based in Christchurch (New Zealand) which seems to be considered as a neutral term in Australasia although the name would probably not be given to a European club or franchise as it could be considered as offensive for Muslims in Europe, referring to the religious wars between Christians and Muslims between the eleventh and thirteenth centuries. To avoid these kinds of problems, sport brands increasingly look for basic and neutral names which do not try to have any implicit meanings as it is difficult to manage them on an international and global scale. One strategy to get round this obstacle is to emphasise on the logo and the brands' visual identity such Adidas, Nike, Reebok or Puma have tried to do, even if it does not fully exclude any symbolic meanings and then misperception cases.

Cultural differences and sport brands consumption

After having identified the different mechanisms related to the notions of culture, social classes and groups, symbolism and self-concept, it is now possible to identify the main elements which drive cultural differences as well as their influence on brand purchase and consumption behaviours. It is, however, necessary to first identify the different elements which shape countries' national cultures and the different elements which shape consumers' sensitivity to certain products, prices, distribution channels and communication campaigns because they represent crucial information for brands' strategies. According to Hofstede (2001), each nation possesses cultural differences which can be articulated around five main dimensions:

1. **power distance:** the relationships between two levels of power and the propensity of less powerful individuals to accept the unequal distribution of this power;
2. **uncertainty avoidance:** the degree to which individuals feel threatened or not by unknown things and situations;
3. **masculinity:** the degree of dominance of male sex role patterns;
4. **individualism:** the strengths of ties between individuals;
5. **long-term orientation:** individuals' anticipation of the future.

According to this author, these main dimensions explain why the launch of new products and brands and promotional messages are not perceived in the same way in different countries. According to numerous experts such as Aaker and Maheswaran (1997), the individualism/collectivism dimension dominates all the other dimensions as it directly affects individuals' self-construction, the role of others, values and lifestyles, motivational factors and consumption patterns. Therefore, it is better understood why Adidas centred its marketing campaign during the 2008 Beijing Olympics on the collectivism dimension where star athletes were magnified by others and literally supported by them in numerous posters.

In mainly individualist cultures such as in many Western European and North American countries, consumers seem to favour a central cognitive treatment of communication campaigns where they scrutinise all different relevant elements of a message to understand it, whereas for more collectivist cultures such as in many Asian countries, a peripheral treatment relying for instance on the identification of peripheral cues such as the source's attraction to understand the message, seems to be favoured in the formation of attitudes (Aaker and Maheswaren, 1997). Consequently, sport brands' publicity campaigns targeting consumers who predominantly belong to an individualist culture have to provide rich informational content, a strong argument which focuses on the most relevant and salient attributes, whereas the credibility of the source or the association with athletes and celebrities might be more relevant for more collectivist cultures. Consumers from more individualist cultures seem also more sensitive to messages which emphasise individual benefits and values whereas consumers from more collectivist cultures seem more sensitive to collective factors such as family, interpersonal relationships, and community interests.

For sport brands these cultural differences linked to political and economic systems demonstrate the necessity to integrate these issues in the definition of brands' marketing strategy and mix. These differences also shape other cultural determinants which are particularly relevant and used by sport brands such myths, legends and rituals. Correlated to these cultural differences are also differences in relation to religion and cultural stereotypes.

Myths and legends

Each culture develops its own stories and practices which help individuals to make sense of the environment which surrounds them. People seem also particularly fascinated by extraordinary stories, facts and mythical heroes which are part of each culture. Sport brands extensively use this rhetoric and often qualify athletes and sport participants as modern heroes or modern adventurers who risk their life to dominate natural elements. This is for instance what many outdoor sport brands emphasise and, even for less experienced participants, this mythical head-to-head with nature via sport practices is thought to create a real fascination to them and in some cases change their lives.

A myth is a story in which the symbolic elements represent emotions and ideals that are shared by a common culture or subculture. It is a mean to symbolically resolve unthinkable non-assumable contradictions and conflict situations by including them in a narrative. Consequently, myths reduce stress and anxiety levels because they provide behavioural patterns which can be adopted by anyone. For this reason, they are often used in sport brands' marketing and communication campaigns. As an example, Solomon (2003) referred to one Spanish sport TV channel's publicity which featured a basketball player going to a dunk as if he was elevating himself to the sky in the manner of a thirteenth-century painting depicting a scene from Greek or Roman mythology. Myths often refer to supernatural and sacred dimensions and usually feature gods and heroes. In the sport world, it is common to use the expression stadium's gods to characterise athletes and this was also the name of the calendar of the Stade Francais Paris' rugby club. Star athletes are often attributed power and skills which are so spectacular that they can be seen as supernatural and divine. This was for instance the sense of one publicity campaign from the swimwear brand Arena attributing magnetic powers to attract precious metal (medals) to the featuring athletes. It is important for sport brands to understand the cultural myths of the countries to which they want to sell their products and services, either to mimic them, to mock them or to transgress them.

Brands themselves often have a history made of foundational myths, based on real events or rumours, and which pass through employees and loyal and passionate consumers. Nike has for instance understood their importance and designates experienced employees to be tellers and to transmit this heritage to new employees. They are told about the history of the founder, an athletics coach who used his wife's waffle iron to design its first shoe model, about the commitment and dedication of coaches and athletes to the company, and new employees even visit the tracks where the founder operated to seize the full meanings of Nike's myths and its identity (Ransdell, 2000). And it is not surprising if brand names often refer to mythical sporting athletes, events or places to operate a direct transfer and provide to the brand a mythical status. For instance the French rugby brand Eden Park is a direct reference to the Eden Park stadium in Auckland, New Zealand, which is seen as the 'Olympia' (this is also a sock brand's name!) of rugby players and particularly French ones because of the rare and so famous victories the French team had against the All Blacks.

Very similar to myths are legends which are representations of events and characters, often real but distorted and amplified by collective fantasies and popular literature and poetry. Originally, legends often referred to ancient Greek, Roman or medieval epic tales such as Odysseus, Sinbad the Sailor or King Arthur but contemporary legends refer to celebrities such as actors, singers, athletes and even fictional characters. Legends can even refer to particular products but constitute a marketing denomination rather than a real popular perception and definition such as in the case of the Dynastar Legend Pro Rider ski series. As do myths, legends also refer to special places for sport participants such as Mount Everest, Hawaii or Cape Horn and which are often exploited by sport brands such as Patagonia, Eider, Annapurna, K2, Himalaya Mountain and McKinley. The distinction between myths and legends is relatively thin because it is easy to consider that self beliefs are based on real and historical facts, which create legends, rather than fantasy, which creates myths. Another very similar cultural support is represented by fairy and folk tales which are increasingly used by brands because of the collective power and meaning they have. This is for instance what Reebok did in 2004 when creating its own version of Cinderella by replacing the glass slipper with the 'Fairytale Classic' model.

Each brand aspires to become mythical: it is synonymous with pride and glory but more than anything, immortality. For Lewi (2003), mythical brands rely on longevity and their origins have often been forgotten. It seems that a minimum of three generations is required. To reach this status brands have to lose their origins to be able to be appropriated by society at large. They also have to fulfil a social integration function, to identify all the elements composing their reputation on which they could have an influence, to be part of people's everyday life, and to use archetypical heroes. Within the sport industries, it is difficult to determine whether or not many brands have reached this status as few of them have passed two generations. Numerous major event (Olympics, FIFA World Cup, Wimbledon tennis tournament, the Stanley Cup) and club (Real Madrid, FC Barcelona, Manchester United) brands can be considered as mythical brands, particularly for many sport clubs which were founded at the end of the nineteenth century. However, regarding sport corporate brands, their number is smaller mainly because of their young age, and only a few such as Nike and Adidas could eventually be considered as mythical. Other brands can be considered as mythical such as Zodiac the world leader brand for inflatable boats, but without reaching all the previous enounced criteria due to a less broad public profile.

To become mythical, three stages broadly corresponding to lifecycle stages are needed (Lewi and Rogliano, 2006): heroism, wisdom and myth. During the hero-ism stage, brands differentiate themselves from the main competitors because of unique values stemming from innovations and/or different ways of thinking which in turn create for them a unique, real and symbolic territory. The strong differen-tiation will normally create a public fascination which will be expressed by forming a strong and rich relationship with the brand. During the wisdom stage, brands try to consolidate the relationships they have established with the public and their consumers and try to enrich them. When brands' identity and positioning are well established they can grow via internationalisation, brand, target, and line extensions. It relies on the search for new frontiers and universes to expand the consumer base and attract new and different consumers. This is what Salomon did by developing new bindings, new ski boots and skis, embracing golf clubs through the acquisition of TaylorMade, adopting bike wheels through the acquisition of Mavic, developing shoes (for example their Adventure line) and in line roller skates. During this stage, brands always take the risk of going after new markets, segments and consumer expectations which are increasingly difficult to satisfy and eager for novelty. The final stage is the myth one and means that brands have reached a universal and global status, and that consumers have the impression that brands have always been part of their life, been part of their own personal history.

Consumption rituals: sacred versus profane

One of the most frequent classifications about cultural symbols relies on the oppo-sition between sacred and profane. For each individual and culture, certain persons, events, experiences, places, objects and by extension brands can be considered as sacred, and therefore worshipped, or on the contrary totally ordinary. In some cultures, living places are seen as sacred and people will try to valorise, enrich and personalise them. In the same vein, sport places have become sacred for many sport participants and fans for whom a visit can be seen as a pilgrimage. Numerous examples can be cited: Roland-Garros (tennis, Paris), Indianapolis Motor Speedway (motor racing, USA), Maracanã stadium (football, Brazil), Everest (Climbing, China–Nepal), Hawaii (surfing, USA), Eden Park stadium (rugby union, New Zealand), The Madison Square Garden (boxing, ice-hockey and basketball, New York City). Therefore, these places represent either strong brands or symbols brands want to be associated with.

Persons can also become sacred and are then designated as icons or idols. Celebrity brands can exist and be successful because they are seen as sacred in the eyes of their fans and for whom they can develop a real fan base in the league of rock or pop stars. Their power lies in the fact that the ordinary sport and non-sport objects they use or touch become special and sacred (such as the contamination characteristic of sacred objects). A random baseball ball can become a sacred object if caught during a special game and batted by a star athlete. From then, its place is not any more in a baseball field but in a museum, a special place such as a personal collection or mausoleum. It seems that over the past fifty years, numerous events which were considered in the past as sacred have become ordinary or profane whereas ordinary and casual events have been sacralised (Belk *et al.*, 1989). Under the pressure of an increasing commodification process, it seems that almost everything can become sacred. Many companies now make a living out of the commercialisation of such objects (for example old shirts, shoes, balls, photos or autographs), and auction houses have even been specialising themselves for such objects. Many athletes have become idols or 'living gods' because of their sport prowess, their charisma, their political and social engagement, their appearance, or just for who they are. David Beckham (football), Muhammad Ali (Boxing), Babe Ruth (baseball), Michael Jordan (basketball), Wayne Gretsky (ice-hockey), Tony Hawk (skateboarding), Nadia Comăneci (gymnastic), Pelé (football), Carl Lewis (track and field), Dick Fosbury (athletics), Martina Navratilova (tennis) have certainly reached this dimension. For this reason, many brands want to be associated with these great champions and human beings, hoping for some positive elements to be transferred to them. However, when these athletes are too sacred, brands take the risk of being overshadowed by these celebrity brands. Moreover, these sacred statuses are not eternal, and the cases of O.J. Simpson, Mike Tyson and more recently Zinedine Zidane and Tiger Woods are there to prove it.

From an anthropological perspective, rituals are the substance of sacred and profane sociocultural relationships (McCracken, 1986). Their primary function is to provide a structure of meanings in relation to events, exchanges and behaviours happening within a group or a community. Rites and rituals are then repeated behaviours differentiating habits according to their level of personal identification and involvement, and the symbolic and affective load they carry (McCracken, 1986). They can be private, public, individual or collective, religious or secular, etc. When talking about rites and rituals, we often think first about large-scale public collective religious celebrations and events (for example baptisms, weddings, funerals), but many of them concern micro-individual private events. The reason why they are important to understand for sport brands is that some rituals are sport related and because many sport objects underpin rituals and constitute personal and identity landmarks. Professional sport universes are full of rituals (for example changing-room rituals, cheering and singing rituals, victory celebration rituals) and marketers and advertisers extensively use them in their campaigns. Rituals are not immutable. They evolve and sometimes disappear while new ones are created and institutionalised. Being part of a ritual is a guarantee of use and consumption and for this reason sport brands either try to be inserted in existing ones or to create new ones around their brands.

McCracken (1986) identified four main categories of rituals: exchange, possession, divestment and grooming rituals. 'Exchange rituals' contribute to interpersonal communication, to the creation, the enhancement and the reinforcement of the links between persons. These rituals have both strong symbolic and functional dimensions. 'Possession rituals' underline the ownership of objects and are linked to activities such as cleaning, discussing, comparing, reflecting, showing-off and photographing. They refer to the personal history of the owners and the way they define themselves in regard to others. They are fundamental in the construction and affirmation of self and social identity. This explains for instance why people keep game tickets, scarfs, shirts, match-day programmes, autographs and all kinds of memorabilia. Conversely, sport club brands and leagues can increase their financial profits by selling these objects while increasing their social and emotional bonds with their fans. 'Divestment rituals' characterise the separation and abandon process as well as the erase of the meaning associated with the previous owner. Mirroring the acquisition rituals, these processes aim to break and annihilate the bonds and ties consumers have created with their objects via reselling them, offering them or destroying them. As these objects are not fully emptied of their meanings and symbolic value, some brands have set up recycling programmes which produce new objects. Sport brands such as Patagonia with the recycling of clothing items, Nike with sneakers, and Millet with old climbing ropes are examples of this. These programmes have probably been primarily set up because of environmental considerations but they are also likely to recycle symbols, meanings and attachment. The last category of rituals concern 'grooming rituals' which are meant to reactivate the link individuals have with these objects. These rituals can also concern the body and sport brands (for example Lacoste, Adidas, Stade Français Rugby club) have realised this and increasingly extend their brands in this direction and now offer toiletries and moisturisers, which are more or less linked to sport and physical activities.

Celebration rituals do not necessarily represent a distinct category, but are worth noting. On these occasions sport brands try to be present and often try to be part of them, via communication and promotional campaigns, the launch of new products or the re-launch of old models. It is very common to see professional sport clubs and leagues organising special events or offering special prices for games scheduled on Valentine's Day or Father's Day. They can also initiate these celebrations. This is what Converse did to celebrate its 100-year anniversary with its campaign named Connectivity and which gathered sport, arts and music icons. Finally, we can also mention rites of passage which are culturally important and signify the transformation of individuals and/or the achievement of another status. These are often related to celebrations and ceremonies. They can concern the passage from childhood to adulthood, becoming independent financially, becoming a parent, etc. In the sport context these rites are very important and common, particularly when they are associated with sporting expertise levels, achievements and records. They are often enacted during initiations, and sport objects and brands are very often part of them (for example the presentation of the first baseball glove, the first snowboard, the first golf putter).

Religions, nations and regions

In many countries, religion is a key characteristic of the culture which therefore influences collective and individual modes of consumption and many other areas (language, family, education, work). From a consumption perspective, religion intervenes in the setting of norms, values, rituals and celebrations influencing the purchase of specific products, services and brands. However, religious influences are not homogeneous and practices differ among countries, societies and groups, even for the same religion. Moreover, the influence does not necessarily concern a whole country and can concern only religious communities and groups. These religion and cultural elements should be understood by sport brands if they want to avoid making mistakes and creating negative reactions. For instance many brands such as Marithé + François Girbaud (clothing), Paddy Power (sports betting, online poker, online casino and bingo) and Volkswagen (cars) have parodied the Jesus Christ's last supper scene from Leonardo Da Vinci's painting in their commercial campaigns, provoking many protests among Catholic communities which ended with a ban for some of them. Many controversial advertising campaigns have also featured either Jesus Christ or the Christian cross. Even if in many European countries the influence of religious traditions and values has been decreasing in people's everyday lives and sometimes replaced by postmodern values such as individualism and consumerist hedonism, this is certainly not the case for all communities in Europe and most countries worldwide. On the contrary, it seems that these issues are becoming increasingly important as more countries become wealthier and consumption levels increase. Religions also keep an important role in rituals and celebrations which are often associated with the consumption of products and brands.

Generally speaking for sport brands, respecting religious traditions concerns the use of appropriate symbols and icons, specific words and vocabulary, nudity and prohibited products in marketing campaigns. Nike's adverts featuring the football player Wayne Rooney and the boxer Manny Pacquiao forming a cross with their arms and then mimicking the position of the Christ on the cross were perceived as offensive to Christian sensibilities. More recently, Real Madrid has removed the Christian cross, which is on the top of the crown from its official logo, in order to 'strengthen its fan base among Muslims in Europe and the Middle East' (Kern, 2012). This removal was required by the ruler of Ras al-Khaimah emirate where Real Madrid is building a resort island which raised some criticisms about the influence of religion, and in particularly Islam, on European cultures and traditions (Kern, 2012). However, Real Madrid was not the sole European football club concerned: FC Barcelona also removed the San Jorge cross from its shirts sold in the Middle East; Inter Milan was sued by a Turkish lawyer because the shirt designed for the one hundredth anniversary of the club featured a 'Crusader-style' red cross; FC Shalke 04 (Germany) was asked to change some lines of its anthem perceived as insulting to the prophet Mohammed. Sport brands are also concerned with sponsorship-related issues. Particularly, they are mindful of Muslim populations and countries for which gambling and alcohol are prohibited although many sponsors come from these industries. For instance in 2011, the Istanbul-based Efes Pilsen professional basketball club had to change its name to Anadolu Efes S.K. because of a bylaw issued by the Turkish Tobacco and Alcohol Market Regulatory Authority banning alcohol-related contents in sports activities and sponsorship and because Efes Pilsen is the name of the flagship product of the Efes Beer Group. Even if these kinds of bans are not necessarily issued because of religious motives – France, a secular country, passed the same type of legislation – the fact that the Turkish government at the origins of this decision is rooted in Islam indicates the religious dimension alongside other factors such as public health and well-being has to be acknowledged. In the same vein Qatar's Sheikh Abdullah who is the owner of the Spanish first division football team of Málaga CF intends not to renew the shirt sponsorship contract the club had made with the online betting and gambling brand William Hill because of his religious belief.

Another category of cultural influencers concerns the national and regional characteristics of consumers on one hand, and brands on the other hand. As evoked in the introduction of this section with the reference to the work of Hofstede (2001), country and national dimensions of culture are important elements in the consumption of brands and the comparison of consumer behaviours in different countries highlights significant differences in terms of cognitive, affective and behavioural reactions. It was for instance found that French and Chinese fans of English Premier League clubs did not perceive the business dimension of their favourite club in the same way (that is positive for Chinese fans but negative for French fans) (Bodet and Chanavat, 2010; Chanavat and Bodet, 2009). Nevertheless, these differences should not only be attributed to cultural differences as they can also come from structural differences linked to purchase contexts, commercial environment and distribution networks. Another aspect of this issue concerns the importance of sport brands' national and regional characteristics which are embedded within the concept of cultural stereotypes. Cultural stereotypes, which can be defined as simplified conceptions and beliefs about other cultural groups, also exert an important influence on sport brands consumption. There are many different types of stereotypes but the ones concerned here are linked to nations and regions – other stereotypes which are associated with specific subculture groups and communities are studied later in the book (see Chapter 4). National, regional and sometimes local stereotypes have appeared in terms of strategic positioning and valorisation of know-how and expertise due to the globalisation phenomenon. More and more regions, in a wide sense, develop a more or less specific reputation in relation to services, goods and brands which can become a significant asset in terms of quality and authenticity. These are the famous 'made in'. For example, the retail brand Holland Bikes, which is the official and exclusive retailer of Dutch bike brands such as Batavus, Gazelle, and Koga in France, strongly capitalise on the Dutch cycling tradition and expertise. For some category of products, referring to specific countries or regions perceived as legitimate and expert represents a strong commercial asset. However, it has to be noted that these perceptions vary strongly according to consumers and their cultural and geographical belonging alongside their sensitivity to the exotic and patriotic values brands may hold. These perceptions can be used to target foreign consumer segments as well as targeting local consumers. The Chinese dimension seems for instance to be a significant dimension of Li Ning's communication.

It is indeed common to see sport brands building their strategy or reinforcing their identity by playing on a local and regional anchorage allowing them to differentiate themselves easily from their competitors. Almost every professional sport club brand plays this card. The difference is the size of the local community which can be very small without a strong identity or on the contrary very large with a strong sense of belonging, pride and sometimes independence. For the latter, this is for instance the case for FC Barcelona in football which is strongly associated with the Cataluña region and identity; Athletic Bilbao football club with the Basque region; and the Montreal Canadiens ice-hockey franchise with the Canadian French-speaking community in the city. However, this strategy can sometimes have its downsides because emphasising on a regional or community link can alienate and exclude fans and consumers who do not strongly perceive themselves as belonging to these communities. During the nineties, this is for instance what happened with various Australian soccer clubs (for example Marconi Fairfield, Sydney and Melbourne Croatia) that were perceived as associated too closely with specific ethnic groups and so were not perceived as inclusive, which created tensions at times (Skinner, Zakus and Edwards, 2008). For corporate sport brands, this regional identification is emerging, and increasingly employed. Sport brands such as Airness and M.Dia have for instance emphasised during the early stage of their development on the brand and founder's anchorage and identity within the Parisian region and its suburbs. In the same vein, the boxing and clothing brand Lonsdale also highlights its origins by having London on their logo. The fact that New Balance has maintained a strong manufacturing presence in the USA can also make it seen as a brand which is strongly associated to America and American culture. Just because of its name Champion USA is another example. Some studies have demonstrated that consumers seem to better memorise brands and products which are made in their own countries in comparison with imported brands (d'Astous and Ahmed, 1999). Patriotism explains these kinds of results and for instance Canadian people are extremely proud of Canadian sport brands such as Garneau (cycling, triathlon, running cross-country and alpine clothing, accessories), Easton (hockey, baseball and softball), and Bauer (ice-hockey) and CCM (ice-hockey), even if the later ones have been respectively acquired by Nike and Adidas. It is, however, difficult to generalise this trend for all countries and it can be thought that consumers from developing countries might be more attracted to brands from developed countries. The exception to this could be local brands which are well-known and quite successful in developed countries and for which local consumers would feel a patriotic attachment. For instance, it could be said that the fact that Li Ning has been sponsoring the successful Spanish basketball national team, has been an official partner of the NBA and has also been sponsoring several NBA players positively affect Chinese consumers who could identify themselves to these successes. Furthermore, in a globalised economy brands' origins and products are more and more difficult to trace and a brand clearly identified by its country origins could have all its production based in other geographical areas. This is the case for Nike which has 99 per cent of its shoes made in Asian countries. In these conditions it is more and more difficult to associate a specific country of origin to the brand. Finally, these perceptions and stereotypes are important but become less significant after consumption of the brands. Consequently they seem to be more important for first-time buyers than for consumers who are already familiar with the brands.

Sport brands' identity and perceptions

The relationship between culture and consumer behaviours is always a two-way process. If services, products and brands are influenced by cultural dimensions, they also influence cultures and subcultures. In consumption societies like ours, cultures constantly evolve and sport brands play a significant role in these changes. Therefore, if it is acknowledged that brands and sport brands provide meanings to consumer behaviours, it should be recognised that they correspond to shared representations for specific communities at a specific moment in time. Based on these principles, brand image, identity and personality represent three important dimensions which are revealing factors of sport brands' intangible influence.

Sport brands' identity

Brand identity appears to be a complex and sometimes blurred concept even if its importance remains undeniable. To be able to talk about brand identity, four conditions are necessary and concern the existence of four elements (Sicard, 2001):

1. a name;
2. a product or service;
3. a logo;
4. intangible characteristics.

According to this author, two mistakes have to be avoided when defining brand identity. Brand identity cannot be reduced to visual elements and cannot be reduced to the brand's DNA, which is often used by practitioners and academics, as this would mean that brand identity is set for ever, as for a genetic code. Therefore, brand identity has to be defined by both its tangible and intangible elements, and should also be defined by permanent elements but also changed and past elements which are part of the brand history, traditions and culture. Brand identity aims to provide a direction and a project for organisations and their employees (Aaker, 1996), and therefore define the way the company or organisation wants to present itself to the markets as an issuer of intangible signals. For this reason, identity appears a crucial factor in the success of brands and the development of their equity (Aaker, 1996). Brands' successes necessarily rely on the construction of a strong identity which should be tightly linked to the company or organisation's strategy. This identity therefore defines the mission, the promise and the originality of brands. For Quiksilver, this is the service of people who like sliding practices and sports; for Adidas, this is the victory which hides inside everyone; for Lafuma, this is freely enjoying natural landscapes; for Salomon, this is instinct and technology based practices; for Aigle, this is the spirit of nature and freedom; for the Olympic Games, this is the struggle and not the triumph; for Manchester City FC, this is pride in battle, etc.

For sport clubs and leagues, identity is often linked with history, traditions and trophies and the older and more successful they are, the stronger the identity will be. For corporate sport brands, identity is strongly associated with the success of their products and innovations. The identity of Petzl was shaped by its headlamps; Spalding by its basketball; Vuarnet by its famous sunglasses model Skilynx; Helly Hansen by its long sleeve baselayer; New Balance by its running shoes.

Each brand identity, which can be summarised in few words as shown with the previous examples, comes from a certain vision of the world, a philosophy or a personal history which should transpire from both visual and intangible elements. What is said and signified by brands is important because they want consumers to fully project themselves through their products. For some brands such as Patagonia, this identity is intensified through an ideological and philosophical positioning. However, contrary to appearances (visuals, logos, mottos) which give the impression that it is clear, simple and explicit, the mechanisms which produced this identity are quite complex. They indeed rely on underlying values, dynamism, skills and expertise, visions, beliefs, commitments, and personal history of the founders and individuals who compose companies and organisations. As for Patagonia, the identity has been very strongly shaped by the visions and intuitions towards ecological and environmental issues of the founder Yvon Chouillard. Overall, brand identity relies on a sum of structuring factors characterising and defining the real face of the parent organisation, the reasons for its commitment, as well as the main ideological and strategic orientations.

For Kapferer (2008), brand identity presents six facets which are gathered in what he called the identity prism: 1. physique, 2. personality, 3. culture, 4. self-image, 5. reflection and 6. relationship. The first facet represents the physical dimension and mainly concerns the symbols, logos, colours, shape, ingredients and intrinsic quality of the brands' products and services. This is for instance the three stripes for Adidas; the Olympic rings for the Olympic Games; 'Phillie Phanatic', the mascot of Philadelphia Phillies Major League Baseball team. The second facet represents the personality dimension and corresponds to the characteristics of a person the brand would be. In the sport context, it is often related to the characteristics of the brand's founder, to endorsed athletes, to famous players, coaches and chairmen. This facet is further analysed in the section 'Sport brands' personality', page 73. The third facet is cultural and corresponds to the brand's system of values, its norms, its rules, its beliefs feeding the brand's inspiration (Kapferer, 2008). For instance Shimano's cycling accessories and equipment incarnate Japanese rigour and advanced technology; Fila and Kappa symbolise the Italian know-how in terms of textile; Champion USA incarnates the American sporting roots and values. The fourth facet is relational and corresponds to the types of relationships brands want to establish with their consumers or want their consumers to establish between each other and with other people. For many surfing brands, it is about proximity, coolness and friendliness; for others it is about transgression; for others it is about establishing a strong relationship with their true selves; for others it is about being the best and beating others. The fifth facet reflects the main stereotypical profile of the brand's consumers. Conceptually speaking, reflection is distinct from the brand target but a match between both would mean that the brand is successful because it attracts the kind of consumers it targets. For instance, Quiksilver consumers may be seen as cool and fun; Liverpool FC fans may be seen as working class people whereas Chelsea FC fans may be seen as posh; Lacoste consumers may be seen as classy; No Fear consumers may be seen as extreme and daredevil. The more generalist and inclusive the brand is, the less this dimension will be marked. The sixth facet deals with consumer self-image and corresponds to consumers' personal identity rather than social identity, which is conveyed by the reflection function. It corresponds to how consumers want to picture themselves for themselves. For instance some brands can indicate that sport participants are beginners or on the contrary experts of the discipline. It also corresponds to sport fans that support successful teams and clubs in order to make them feel successful. This was for instance expressed by a Chinese fan of Manchester United who expressed that supporting this team met 'his ambition to become successful' (Bodet and Chanavat, 2010, p.61). These symbolic values and meanings should be held and exploited by sport brands.

For a single brand, the Lacoste identity prism analysed and presented by Kapferer (2008, p. 183) constitutes a good example for understanding the different facets of brand identity. For this author, Lacoste's physique elements are 'shirt 12x12', 'soft', 'airy', 'crocodile' and 'colours'; personality elements are 'well balanced', 'authentic' and 'serene'; culture elements are 'aristocratic ideals', 'sophistication', 'simplicity', 'sport and classicism', 'individualism'; relationship elements are 'valorisation' and 'accessible'; reflection elements are 'non-conspicuous men and women' and 'real class'; self-image elements are 'discretely elegant' and 'always correct although casual'.

Sport brands' image

Brand image can be defined as the sum of all mental representations that a person or a specific group hold about a brand. Image is a reception concept which corresponds to a decoding process, an extraction of meaning and an interpretation of signs operated by consumers. As Kapferer (1991) indicated, brand identity and image are different concepts in the sense that brand identity is part of the marketing strategy and corresponds to the way the company wants the brand to be portrayed (for example the wanted image) whereas brand image corresponds to the way this identity is received and perceived by consumers. The aim of companies and brands is to reduce the gap between brand identity and image but they do not fully control the process as many external factors can increase or maintain it. For this reason, brand image can be either positive or negative and can strongly vary according to consumers and segments. In 2004, the Oxylane Group's brand Quechua tried to reduce its image deficit in the mountain sport sector and in particularly toward young consumers, compared to well-established brands such as The North Face, Salomon and Eider. To fill the gap, Quechua developed its products' colours line, created limited editions, launched several innovations and launched Chullanka, its consumer magazine. With this example, it can be seen that many elements and characteristics are used by consumers to evaluate a brand and compare it with others, and that its products and services play a significant role. From an image perspective, the link between products and services and brands is also a two-way process. The relationship helps to construct brand image but conversely, brand image helps consumers to infer characteristics, symbols and meanings to products and services when they are not experienced. Brand image also serves as a short-cut which avoids consumers having to become aware of and memorise all a brand's products and service characteristics. Brand images are influenced by various elements and dimensions but it does not mean that they all have the same weight in particular when considering the different consumer segments. In this sense, some brand images can be dominated by certain dimensions which are more or less manageable and controllable by brand managers. Figure 3.2 illustrates the complexity of brand image and identifies its different components.

The major sport retailers' image is influenced by communication and promotional campaigns but also by the experiences consumers live in their stores. In a research studying various sport retailers located in France (including Courir, Decathlon, GO Sport and Intersport), Bouchet (2005) found that there was a strong correspondence between retailers' brand image and consumers' memories of their visits. These results tend to advise retailers to improve their image in enhancing in-store experiences offered to consumers and adopt experiential marketing strategies. The development of flagship- and concept-stores, as Nike did in London and Li Ning in Portland (Oregon), also represents a strategy to improve consumer experiences which would in turn improve retail brand image.

Brand image has been recognised as an important component of brand equity and defined as the added value a brand provides to a product or service in comparison to an identical unbranded product or service (Aaker, 1991). For Keller (1993), brand image is composed of the different types of associations consumers hold in mind and can be classified into attributes, benefits and attitudes. Attributes represent the descriptive features of the product or service and can be product/service related or not (for example price, packaging and appearance, user imagery and usage imagery). Benefits represent the 'personal value consumers attach to the product or service attributes' and can be functional (for example the utilitarian aspect), experiential (sensory pleasure, variety, cognitive stimulation) and symbolic

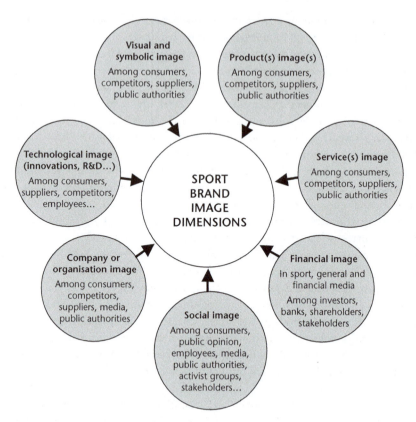

FIGURE 3.2 The different sport brand image dimensions

(for example a badging function) (Keller, 1993). Last, attitudes represent the consumers' overall assessment of the brand and can be positive, neutral or negative. Keller (1993) further classified brand associations in terms of favourability, strength and uniqueness. Basically, the more favourable the associations are, the more sustainable they are and the more unique they are and the more the brand image will be positive and solid. All combinations are possible, and some brands can hold positive but common associations whereas some can have strong negative associations. For instance Bodet and Chanavat (2010) compared the brand images of four clubs of the English Premier League of football and found that Chinese fans associated the terms sexy and beautiful to Arsenal FC, successful and dominant to Manchester United, firm will and perseverance to Liverpool FC and no-history and money to Chelsea FC. The authors also identified four types of benefits associated with these four brands: 1. emotional ('enjoyable', 'feel excited', 'nervous', 'relaxed', 'happy'), 2. cognitive (learn and appreciate), 3. social (meeting friends and sharing common experiences') and 4. psychological (matching victory and power ambitions) (Bodet and Chanavat, 2010).

The communication mix (advertising, public relations, sponsorship, corporate social responsibility, etc.) is probably the most important lever to improve brand image. However, it is important to keep in mind that many external factors such as media, the company and organisation's social, environment and economic impact, and word-of-mouth, particularly with the role of social media, represent crucial influencers which are not easily controllable by brand managers. In many cases perceptions and associations can be false or exaggerated by public rumours and it is imperative for brands to take that into consideration. Even if they consider these perceptions to be wrong, they need to be proactive to reduce the gap between brand image and brand identity. They have to accept that there is no one single reality – brand identity, but several realities for consumers and consumer groups creating several brand images. For instance, many consumers still associate Nike with child labour or sweatshops' poor working conditions even though these related scandals happened about twenty years ago and the company is now engaged in many social and responsible programmes. Finally, it has to be noted that brand image is related to brand awareness in the sense that consumers need first to be aware and familiar with the brand before elaborating a mental image.

Sport brands' personality

Brand personality is a topic of growing interest and can be seen as a variation of brand image analysis. This approach consists of considering that brands' characteristics can be compared to and assimilated to individuals' characteristics. The importance of brand personality can be then compared to the role of brand image. However, this approach also estimates that consumers engage in relationships with brands as they would do with individuals. In this sense, the relationship is more personalised and personally meaningful. Nowadays, marketing studies are more interested in the personality attributed to brands (the brand image) than the brand's intrinsic personality (its brand identity), and many experts estimate that consumers naturally attribute personality traits and characteristics to brands. This projection, or humanisation process, seems to rely on the observation of brands' tactics, strategies, operations, discourses and behaviours. Consequently, a brand using an exclusive distribution channel may be perceived as bourgeois and sophisticated whereas a brand which uses recycled constituents for its products may be perceived as concerned, generous and sensitive; see Table 3.1 for further sport brand related examples. Brands have indeed realised this process and often implement personification strategies using their logos, mascots, and characters (for example Green Giant, the Bibendum Michelin man, Ronald McDonald) or their founders, executive and employees such as Gert Boyle for Columbia.

Specifically, the brand personality approach aims to evaluate brands based on a set of personality traits which are comparable to those used to characterise human individuals (Koebel and Ladwein, 1999). As previously mentioned, the underlying principle relies on the fact that consumers will develop more or less positive attitudes to brands according to these personality characteristics. Contrary to

TABLE 3.1 Brands' actions, associated personality traits and sport brands

Brands' actions	Associated personality traits	Sport brands
The brand was re-positioned several times or has regularly changed its slogan	Unstable, versatile schizophrenic	Reebok – Rbk, Salomon
The brand always use the same character in its advertising	Familiar, reassuring, consistent	Columbia, Foot Locker, Philadelphia Phillies
The brand is expensive and uses an exclusive distribution channel	Posh, sophisticated	Nautica, Lacoste
The brand is often sold with reduced price	Common, random, fake	Starter, Koodza (Oxylane Group)
The brand offers many line extensions	General, multi-tasker, skilful	Nike, Adidas, Manchester United
The brand uses recycled material	Responsible, empathic	Patagonia, K2
The brand uses practical packaging or talks simply to consumers	Warm, accessible	Kanuk, Lafuma
The brand is often bought during special sale periods	Organised, opportunistic	15 from Serge Blanco, Helly Hansen
The brand proposes long-term guarantees and consumer services	Reliable, serious	Mavic, Shimano, Gore-Tex

Source: Adapted from Fournier (1994)

product/service related attributes whose functions are primarily utilitarian, brand personality holds a strong symbolic function allowing consumers to express their self-concept (Keller, 1993). Aaker (1996) identified five main dimensions which are: 1. sincerity, 2. excitement, 3. competence, 4. sophistication and 5. ruggedness. These dimensions can help brand managers and experts to position a brand in comparison with its main competitors in a given market and for specific segments. Ferrandi et al. (2003) for instance did it for Nike and Adidas and found that these two brands have more similarities between them in terms of sincerity, conviviality, feminity and ruggedness than with other non-sport brands. This kind of study is very interesting because it compares the gap between brand identity and brand image, considering the brand perceived positioning with the main competitors, and analysing the different realities of each consumer segment. However, it should be noted that the use of pre-existing scales, measuring a set number of characteristics almost mechanically, blurs the differences between brands as it does not allow for subtle and unexpected differentiations in the personalities. Precisely, is it possible to seize the full complexity and diversity of brand personalities by using a limited number of personality traits? Our response tends to be negative.

For various marketing experts, the notions of brand humanisation and person-ification echo new forms of animism in consumption helping to better understand the relationships individuals establish with their brands. In consumption societies, brands and products are truly worshipped and are supposed to bring desirable characteristics to their owners, making them highly important in their lives. If diamonds are a girl's best friend, brands can certainly be considered as many consumers' best friends. Two forms of animism seem to concern brands (Fournier, 1998). With the first form, people believe that the object owned is possessed by someone's soul which helps people to get close to that person. This is one lever used by sport brands to sell memorabilia and to extensively use athlete endorsement to give the impression that a part of the loved athlete is embedded within the object. With the second form, objects and brands are humanised and described as if they were real persons. This is particularly the case with sport brands which have a long history. Although some brand personality characteristics can be seen as universally positive and appealing (for example sincere, trustworthy, generous), this is not the case for all of them. Some personal characteristics will be praised by some consumers whereas they will be avoided by others (for example aggressive, ambitious, solitary). Therefore, the brand strategy consists, if possible, of identifying the main characteristics their different consumer targets will seek, and matching them and offering them. Some consumer profiles have been therefore drawn by several marketing experts and researchers. For instance, Horney (1945) distinguished consumers based on their personal orientation and identified three types:

1. accommodating people who are willing to encounter others;
2. aggressive people who act against others;
3. detached people who avoid interpersonal contact.

However, even if the simplicity of this kind of classification is quite appealing for brand managers, it seems quite caricatured to truly describe human nature and behaviours. Other approaches have then focused on certain personality traits which are deemed to be stable enough to be reliable. They are, for instance, need for personal accomplishment, need for affiliation, aggressiveness, conservatism, dogmatism, emotional stability, search for variety, excitement, spontaneity and sociability. However, this knowledge is relevant only for brands which are mainly consumed for their symbolic value and not primarily for their utilitarian value. Moreover, this matching tactic relies on the principle that consumers display consistent behaviours independently of the purchase and usage contexts, which is difficult to assume. Consequently, it can appear too risky to base a brand strategy mainly on the supposed consumers' personal existing or sought characteristics as they may change quite often. Moreover, as for brand image, it is likely that different consumers perceive different personalities for the same brand. Finally, this approach should not also make managers forget the importance of other socioeconomic and cultural factors which may strongly influence the perceptions of personality traits and their appraisal.

4

SUBCULTURES, COMMUNITIES AND SPORT BRANDS

Subcultures seem to be present within many different countries and also internationally as they take the same values, attitudes and behaviour to any new country. For instance some studies have shown that big cities' residents have more similarities with big cities' residents in other countries than residents from rural areas from the same country (Catoera and Graham, 1999). This is illustrated by the launches of worldwide marketing campaigns for books, video games and movies. This example would tend to demonstrate the existence of similar consumer behaviours and reactions among different groups of individuals, creating subcultures which are understood by marketers. However, two types of subcultures have to be identified. On one hand, there are consumption subcultures whose members are gathered around common consumption practices, products, services and brands (Schouten and McAlexander, 1995; Kozinets, 1997). On the other hand, there are social subcultures whose members share specific behaviours according to ethnic (Marshall *et al.*, 1994), religious (Hirschman, 1981) or sexual criteria (Kates, 2002). In the first category, consumption practices are similar although individual characteristics may be different. For the second category, it is one or several common individual characteristics which determine more or less similar consumption practices. The subcultures' influence on consumer behaviours is real and significant but highly complex. Therefore, the identification of the sole subcultures is not enough to understand the relationships between individuals and their sport brands and in some cases a focus on smaller groups within these subcultures is needed. These reference and belonging groups play an important role in choice of sport brands due to the tight links between their members and their social identity management strategies. This chapter focuses on the analysis of the influence of these specific social and cultural interactions on consumer behaviour and sport brands preferences and uses. Specifically, these influences take the forms of norms, symbols and behavioural rules directly shaping consumer tastes, practices and choices and they will be studied in this chapter through the lens of the subcultures and communities perspectives

The influence of social subcultures

A social subculture can be defined as a society component which is self-identified but also identified as such by other people outside of it. Within this subgroup individuals display specific cultural characteristics (sharing norms, values, symbols) which are different from the dominant cultural patterns. Therefore, the belonging to a subculture directly influences lifestyle and most consumption related practices for its members and creates certain beliefs towards the dominant culture. However, these subcultures are not mutually exclusive and individuals can belong to several of them, either at different moments of their lives or at the same time. This belonging plays a significant role in the definition of individuals' self-concept and consequently influences brand preferences, choices, purchases and uses. For brands operating on culturally heterogeneous markets, clustering and segmentation become necessities requiring a strong understanding of each subculture and its implications in terms of brand consumption to identify the most relevant and profitable ones. This challenge can appear extremely difficult as subcultures can display many different characteristics. Some subcultures are defined by ethnicity, nationality and religion whereas others are defined by age, sexual orientation, income, appetite for technology or regional location. As for sport brands, it seems that generational, minority and economic subcultures are the most significant and are therefore further developed within this chapter.

Generational' subcultures and sport brands

From an identity perspective, age seems to play a very strong role in consumer behaviours and this role can even be exacerbated when one generation's objectives and practices are in contradiction with those of another generation. The age variable has been widely used in marketing and on some occasions brands have focused more on age categories than on product and services ranges. This is for instance the case of Sony Electronics where products have been segmented into 'Generation Y' (under 25 year olds), 'DINKs' for double income no kids (25–34 year olds), 'Families' (35–54 year olds) and 'Zoomers' (55 year olds and over) (Solomon, 2005). From a sociological perspective, an age category consists of individuals who have lived similar experiences. They have many common souvenirs, they have experiences of the same historical events, and they know the same celebrities (politicians, athletes, movie stars, singers, etc.). These souvenirs and experiences are thought to be crucial factors in shaping lifestyles, values, preferences and behaviours. Even if there is no universal way to segment individuals according to their age as it is highly contextual, each of us has a pretty good idea of where she/he belongs when a reference is made to her/his generation. Brands cleverly play on this perceived belonging and their related landmarks. Beyond the trends towards vintage and return to authenticity, it is common to see commercial messages using nostalgic tones and elements (for example context, music, celebrities) which are powerful levers for commercial attraction. Consequently marketing research still focuses on generational patterns and recently has been particularly interested in very young and senior segments. In between these two extremes of the continuum, researchers have focused on a particular segment named 'kidults' or 'adultescents'. Each of them is further discussed in the following sections in relation to their sport brand preferences and consumption.

The youth segment

For many years, people less than 12 years old were considered relatively passive consumers by marketers as they estimated that most of the decision-making in terms of consumption was assumed by their parents. However, the current commercial campaigns tend to demonstrate that this is not the case any more. On the contrary, publicities are now directly targeting these young consumers, particularly during youth television programmes, as they are often seen as captive and not highly critical towards the profusion of messages. This trend led Quart (2004) to say that young kids were hostages of brands and media because the media are highly influential and the children permeable to the marketing actions targeting them. Within sport markets, professional leagues and clubs extensively target these consumers and they often represent the main targets for their merchandised products such as replica shirts, caps, shorts and scarfs. The almost systematic association of corporate brands with league and club brands for the commercialisation of their merchandised and cobranded products represents another example of this active seduction enterprise. It is not surprising then that sport brands appear to be among the top-ranked brands for kids. In 2003, Adidas, Nike, Reebok, Decathlon, Quiksilver, Fila, Champion USA and Lacoste were among the ten most preferred clothing brands among French boys whereas Nike, Adidas, Decathlon and Reebok were among the top ten for French girls (Garnier and Guingois, 2003). More recently, babies now represent a new targeted segment even if it is obvious that the first targets are parents as they are the decision-makers. As an example we can cite 'The Little Gym' which is the world leader in terms of physical activity and motor development for young kids from four months to 12 years old; the baby gym shoes from Domyos developed for kids aged from one to four years old; and the No-Spill Sports Sipper offered by Nûby.

Youth is a period stretched from birth to the passage to adulthood and in which adolescence represents an identity transition. Marketers consider children and teenagers as in-formation consumers as brand loyalty starts to be built during this period. They believe that the earlier they start buying a specific brand the more likely they will continue to do so during their life and the stronger their relationship with the brand will be. Obviously, if this loyalty is beneficial for one brand it represents a threat for those which have not been chosen during these crucial years as it seems more difficult to break a bond between consumers and their brands than create one. Consequently, brands are increasingly focused on these segments. They consider that the 'Generation Y', which represents teenagers and young adults between 12 and 25 years old, represents the best target as their identity is still in construction and because brands will play a strong part in it. During this pre-adulthood period, teenagers search for the right style and the right look and copy the behaviours of those who are perceived to be displaying the wanted identity. The choices of activities, friends and clothing styles are fundamental for being accepted and integrated within a specific social subculture (for example 'emo', 'surfer', and 'gothic'). The results from the 2000 European socioeconomic barometer entitled *Teen Generation* showed how brands have impregnated teen cultures. Among the preferred brands, only three brands were already cited in 1995: Coca-Cola, Nike and Adidas. In 2000, six more sportswear brands appeared in the results: Reebok, Lacoste, Fila, Quiksilver, Ellesse, and Sergio Tacchini. For about 30 million European teenagers, these brands were the beneficiaries of a third of their budget dedicated to clothing and fashion accessories.

In regard to contemporary societies, teenagers seem to face four different types of conflict (Kim, 1993): autonomy versus belonging, rebellion versus conformity, idealism versus pragmatism, and narcissism versus privacy. Fashion clearly illustrates the contradictions teenagers are facing as they are pulled in two different directions in terms of clothing style. On one hand they are inclined to accept norms and conform to them to avoid being excluded and marginalised but on the other hand they are inclined to reject them and be original to affirm their uniqueness and their difference (Marion, 2003). This issue seems particularly salient among teenagers who participate in certain sports. Whether expert or beginner, each member of a sport acquires a sentiment of belonging by adopting the brands promoted and valorised by the group. Clothes represent teenagers' favourite channel of expression to claim their belonging and association to certain groups by following specific clothing styles which often require particular brands. As an example, Solomon (2005) identified several subcultures or tribes in the USA with their own clothing style and for which a set of acceptable or required brands is defined (see Table 4.1). However, it seems that due to media and globalisation these styles do not appear so unique to the USA and many of them can be found in European and Asia-Pacific countries. Obviously, some differences exist, particularly due to the existence of local brands, but this analysis shows the transnational dimension of clothing styles and in turn brands and sport brands consumption.

In order to comprehend the complexities of these youth subcultures and properly identify their members' expectations, sport brands have used innovative market and research methods because traditional techniques no longer seem to be accurate. As an example, brands use consumer diaries which can be print, audio or video in which teenagers tell what they do during a typical day. Another method is to identify trend spotters in order to discover new trends and fashions. This strategy has been used for instance by the American brand Airwalk. Some companies send observers into places that are home to subcultures in order to analyse consumption habits, as anthropologists would identify practices' structuring

TABLE 4.1 Tribes' clothing styles and their brands

Tribes	Clothing style	Brands used
Rap	Hoody, baggy trousers, unlaced sneakers.	Nike, Fila, Helly Hansen, Ellesse
Grunge	Second hand and shabby clothes, cut jeans or trousers, t-shirts without logo.	Converse, Doc Martens, Levi's
Skater	Tight trousers, worn on hips showing underpants and covering shoes, caps or bob hats.	Van's, Nike, Volkom, Four Star, ES
Classy	Classical clothes, Shetland sweater, pleat front trousers. Suit and court shoes for women.	Hermès, Todds, Paraboots, Weston
Rave	Fans of techno music, flashy tight t-shirt, fatigues, big sole shoes, psychedelic hair.	Xuly Bet, E-Mail, Adidas, Cop Copine
Neutral	Instinct purchase, jeans trousers, sport shoes, trendy scarf; casual and discrete people but the biggest tribe.	Levi's, Nike, Kangol, Eastpack, Caterpillar

Source: Adapted from Solomon (2005)

elements. Last, sport brands use social media and forums of discussion to connect with their consumers and identify emerging trends. The brands can also use these forums for pilot testing new ideas and designs. This is a cheap and effective method as it provides almost immediate feedback.

'The 'kidults'

Now in their thirties or forties, these consumers have been named 'Generation X' based on Coupland's (1991) book. Slightly different in terms of start and end and meanings associated according to countries, individuals from Generation X seem generally speaking to be born between 1965 and 1980. They are therefore associated with major stressful events such as the 1973 oil and 1979 energy crises and the Chernobyl disaster, unemployment growth, and overall a loss of landmarks in rapidly changing times. Its members grew up in an era of leisure, are often urban, educated and single (or in a couple without kids). They seem, however, more diverse than the previous generations and are less inclined to follow leaders and rules. They are thought to be constant switchers and zappers who want to do by themselves. They also appear nostalgic and do not hesitate to buy products and brands which characterised their childhood. They are addicted to the diversion of objects, are passionate about customisation and are sensitive to innovation and design. They have been named kidults or adultescents, two portmanteau terms made respectively of kid and adult and adult and adolescent. This generation is stigmatised by its consumption patterns which for Maillet (2005) can be defined by the idea of 'a child's soul within us'. Half kids and half adults, they display unusual and sometimes unpredictable behaviours. They love brands but are rarely loyal to them, at least not in a modern and exclusive way. In their highly consumerist universe, sport brands play a significant identity function. For this reason, some brands have developed specific strategies emphasising kidults' childhood or rebellious attitudes towards dominant norms. In terms of sport brands, some of them have created specific products to fit within their universe of reference. For instance the brand KanaBeach, which is a direct reference to cannabis even if kana means 'chant of travel' in old Briton dialect, is a surfwear brand which claims that one of its ingredients of success is its rebellious spirit. In the same vein, the motto of the brand Volcom is 'youth against establishment'.

Other means are used by brands to reach these kidults such as sponsoring and communication strategies which are defined as community or tribal (Cova and Roncaglio, 1999). For instance the sweets brand Haribo managed via its sponsorship activities to reach different age groups: kids, teenagers and kidults, through its partnership with the Tour de France and the Classic Haribo cycling race. Besides sponsorship and co-branding strategies, sport brands also try to create anniversary celebrations to reactivate the link they have with their consumers through old products. This is why for instance Adidas organised an exhibition in London to celebrate the thirty-fifth anniversary of its model 'Superstar'. Reebok did the same to celebrate the twentieth anniversary of the 'Pump' model and asked fashion designers to personalise them. In 2004, this is also what Nike did in a Parisian metro station when the brand organised a free exhibition dedicated to the Air Jordan models, with stalls presenting the 'Nike Terminator' and a customising workshop for the 'Air Force 1' model. Sport brands try to increasingly capitalise on their history which is meaningful for kidults who look for links with and remembrance of their past. In this context, old logos, slogans and visuals are often used. In the previously cited exhibition, Nike celebrated the 30 year relationship between Nike and basketball with posters featuring its famous models ('Blazer', 'Vandal', 'Air Force 1') with old-fashioned graphic styles and symbols giving the impression that the models just came out of a teenager's workbook from the seventies and eighties. In this example, the goal was to create an affective link between old and recent models and give credibility to the new ones. Along the same idea, in 2003, Converse tried to bolster its legitimacy with the advertising campaign named 'Invisible Game' aiming to highlight the historical link between the brand and basketball and to show that the brand had remained faithful to its authentic sporting heritage.

From baby-boomers to seniors

Baby-boomers were born between 1946 and 1965 and form a segment of individuals whose parents formed their family after the Second World War. They grew up in the sixties and seventies and most of them are part of the Generation 68 which is at the origin of cultural and political revolutions strongly modifying social and consumer practices. This generation is for instance associated to the hippy movement in the sixties, 'yuppies' in the eighties and the 'bobos' after 2000. Now that they are getting older, these forty to sixty year-olds are more active and sporty than the previous generations and are wealthier as well. Sport brands have tried to keep this aging segment loyal and the resurgence of old models from the sixties offered by Converse, Le Coq Sportif and Champion USA demonstrate that they are motivated both by a vintage fashion trend and an attempt to attract baby-boomers by plying a nostalgic tone. Moreover, some sports and physical activities such as tennis, cycling, sailing and golf are increasingly associated with these consumers because of their income and because these practices are quite distinctive. Alongside baby-boomers, seniors seem to strongly influence brand strategy. Seniors represent a population of young and old retired people who want to enjoy life after a long period of stressful and hard labour and who also look for a better experience of aging. Life quality improvements, progress in science, medical treatments and care have made this segment more and more important from a demographic point of view. This represents a big segment with relatively comfortable disposable incomes looking to spend on leisure and recreation activities, which represents a good recipe for attracting sport brands. However, it has to be recognised that seniors do not represent a homogenous group because it gathers individuals from 50 years old to more than 80 years old. Therefore, this segment is often divided in three subgroups which are 50–59, 60–74 and 75 years old and more, as they are significantly different in terms of professional, social and physical activities. In terms of communication and marketing, senior people's image is nowadays far from the stereotype which featured them as old, disconnected, bedridden and declining. Within the sport markets, few products are currently specifically made to target this population, and only a few sectors such as golf, aquagym, hiking and tennis have realised their potential. The brands involved have tried to prioritise the criteria of comfort, technicality, welcome and service. The craze for cycling, thalassotherapy, snow rackets (Bouchet, 2002), and more surprisingly for the Wii Fit and Wii Sport in homes and retirement homes seem also to demonstrate that senior people want to remain active. The latter are especially popular because they are encouraged by numerous doctors and medical experts.

In order to help brands to define specific marketing strategies, market researchers and consultants have identified several values and needs which are specific to senior persons: a need for autonomy (remaining active for as long as they can), a need for social interactions (loneliness is common among older persons), and a need for altruism (helping people and giving back). They also display specific characteristics in terms of consumption behaviours. Two thirds of them consider that consumption is a necessity and only 27 per cent consider it as a source of pleasure, against 41 per cent for the 18–29 year– olds (Lehuédé, 2003). They rarely purchase spontaneously and are not very receptive to new products. However, they are sensitive to brands' promises and images; more so than younger consumers. For instance, 63 per cent of them declare that they are inclined to buy a product when the brand seems trustworthy (Lehuédé, 2003). They seem less influenced by prices and promotions, except obviously for the poorest of them. The marketing approaches towards these groups also try to distinguish chronological and perceived ages which can be quite different. For this reason many brands feature old persons being active, participating in 'young' and diversified sport and leisure activities such as aerobics or motorcycling. According to Leroux-Sostenes and Rouvrais-Charron (2008), the motivations of senior people to participate in physical activities can be summarised down to four: fitness, health, relaxation and communion with nature, all contributing to an improvement in general well-being, which constitutes a relevant marketing axis for sport services. A recent example of this is the development of adult playgrounds which particularly target older people and aim to provide health, wealth and happiness, and which are created by companies and brands such as The Great Outdoor Gym Company or Lappset with its senior sport products.

'Minority' subcultures and sport brands

Part of a classical social identity construction process, the majority–minority dynamic has never been so utilised by brands. Particularly, sport brands recognise and increasingly target minority subcultures helping them to reinforce their specific identity and image as well as occupy a distinctive positioning. However, this strategy is not without any risks because subcultures do not all convey the same values and symbols and being too much embedded within one minority subculture can alienate the members of the dominant culture as well as other subcultures. Subcultures are numerous and can concern large or very small groups, which make it impossible to set an exhaustive list. In the following section, several subcultures will be looked at according to the strong or weak links and associations they have with sport brands.

Ethnic identity is a significant component of values and consumption behaviours. From a theoretical point of view, an ethnic subculture is a group of individuals which is self-defined and self-sustained, cemented by cultural links and perceived by its members and others as a distinctive category. Ethnicity is very often related to other dimensions such as nationality, regionalism, language and religion. These ethnic minorities generally try to maintain their distinctive identity, and consumption (for example through food or clothing) is a good way to achieve it, either consciously or unconsciously. This therefore makes these groups relevant and attractive for brands and sport brands. However, ethnic consumption trends are not homogenous and do not correspond to single subculture categories and differences in terms of values and lifestyles are noticeable, particularly in relation to socio-demographic characteristics.

For sport brands targeting these subcultures, it becomes necessary to integrate certain elements in their offers and marketing. For instance, it is now shown that these minority groups seem to attribute more credibility to offers which are endorsed by members and leaders of their own group, creating in turn more favourable attitudes to the brands concerned (Deshpandé and Stayman, 1994). In the USA, the tennis player Arthur Ashe represents an icon for the black community thanks to his victory at Wimbledon in 1975. Among other brands, Le Coq Sportif has been able to leverage its link with this athlete and increase its popularity among young black people. Because of their role model dimension, champions represent powerful marketing figures for their related ethnic subcultures. The impact Tiger Woods had in golf, Serena and Venus Williams in tennis, Lewis Hamilton in Formula 1 and car racing, Zinedine Zidane and Park Ji-Sung in football, and Jeremy Lin in basketball have been real which have made them icons and consequently wanted by many sport brands to attract consumers from similar ethnic backgrounds. Athletes' ethnicity and nationality have now become so important that they have been fully integrated in some clubs' recruitment strategies of players alongside sporting considerations in order to attract new fans, media focus and sponsors. Some ethnic groups are involved, voluntarily or not, in adjustment processes within dominant cultures. This process named acculturation can be understood as a fitting and learning process which therefore defines different levels and intensities of relationships between individuals and their ethnic groups. Consequently, some consumers will prefer brands which underline their particularities in relation to their ethnicity and ethnic background whereas others, on the contrary, will prefer brands which make them part of the wider dominant culture. Therefore, it would be inaccurate to consider that ethnic subcultures are made exclusively of highly identified members who always try to manifest their distinct identity through their consumption. Regarding sport brands, the relationship between consumers and their ethnic subculture is special as there is strong link between sport activities and ethnic groups and nationalities. As an illustration, Pons *et al.* (1998) showed that French Canadians were more oriented towards hockey and consumed more hockey than Italian Canadians who, on the contrary, were more oriented toward soccer/football. These results have implications for sporting event club brands as well as for potential sponsor brands.

Besides ethnic subcultures, but not necessarily independent from, can be found new sorts of urban cultures such as neighbourhood subcultures. They have generally emerged from poor economic, peripheral and suburban geographical areas of major cities and been built in opposition to dominant cultures. They can be interpenetrated with other subcultures such as ethnic, religious or musical ones. Beyond the social appropriation of brands and sport brands such as Burberry, Louis Vuitton, Ralph Lauren, Nike, Adidas and Lacoste by these groups, which is not necessarily appreciated by these brands, more and more individuals from these areas have created their own brands. Sometimes just ephemeral collections, the most successful ones become popular brands due to the strong identification and pride of the consumer base who want to support a brand which comes from one of their own and uses innovative marketing approaches. In these cases, the 'made in the neighbourhood' constitutes a strong asset, at least to take off. That was for instance the case of Airness, created 1999 in the suburbs of Paris, and which is now a well-established brand supplying kits for several French premier league football and basketball teams and African national football teams.

Although important and well recognised by many brands and clothing brands in particular, the gay and lesbian subculture does not seem recognised or strongly associated with sport brands. This situation can probably be explained by the non-gay friendly sporting culture (for example during the recent 2012 UEFA Euro championship, the Italian footballer Antonio Cassano caused controversy when he said that he 'hoped' there was no homosexual player in the Italian squad) and the fact that very few athletes and former athletes have come out. Despite the existence of the Gay Games highlighting the link between the Lesbian, Gay, Bisexual and Transgender community and subculture and sport, sport brands do not seem to be explicitly targeting their members. In terms of club brands, we can cite the cases of the German football club FC St. Pauli because the club and its fans have adopted a strong anti-homophobia stance and the Stade Français Rugby club which targeted or at least tried to appear positively to the LGBT Parisian community when it launched its semi-naked players' calendar, its famous pink shirt, its moisturising product line and in using symbols and references from this community. In terms of sport corporate brands, if the Australian swimwear and sportswear brand AussieBum does not explicitly target the LGBT subculture, its advertising and promotional material can be said to refer to gay iconography.

The influence of sporting subcultures

According to Sitz and Amine (2004), consumption is able to make groups of individuals appear who will create their own cultural system; this is how they define the consumption subcultures. On the basis of the consumption of common activities, products, services and brands, subcultures gather heterogeneous individuals from social, generational, minority and economic perspectives. Their members share the same norms, values and representations coming from their culture of reference but are also producing their own. A subculture can be subdivided into sub-groups on the basis of particular consumption patterns. From a theoretical perspective, consumption subcultures are different from brand communities as several brands can be part of the consumption pattern of a given subculture.

Sporting subcultures are gatherings of individuals around the participation and the practice of similar sporting activities (for example skiing, basketball, running). These subcultures, which are sometimes called tribes or networks, are sometimes interpenetrated according to the observers' level of focus and analysis. For instance, the skaters' subculture is different from the surfers' subculture and the snowboarders' subculture, but skaters, surfers and snowboarders can be considered to belong to a macro boardsports or riders' subculture. As previously mentioned, subcultures are not entirely uniform and several groups can compose them according to their level of identification to the subculture, the intensity of consumption and practice, and a geographical or socio-demographic proximity. For instance in the cycling subculture, it is possible to differentiate the segments of cyclists who are members of a club, road cyclists, track cyclists, off-road cyclists, down-hill cyclists, casuals from competitors, solitary from group cyclists, weekend from holiday cyclists, etc.

Besides sporting subcultures, sport brand communities represent gatherings of consumers who are not bound by geographical locations, who share certain values, norms and representations, who recognise strong links of belonging with other members of the group and the whole group on the basis of a common attachment with a specific brand (Sitz and Amine, 2004). To illustrate this concept, the examples of Porsche, Harley Davidson, and Apple are often cited but many sport clubs (for example FC Barcelona, Manchester United), leagues and events (for example The World Series, The Super Bowl, The English Premiership of football), corporate (for example Quiksilver, Nike) and media (for example ESPN, L'Equipe, Corriere dello Sport) brands can be cited as well. Sometimes, a brand community can be associated with one or several subcultures which make it aggregate people with different values and characteristics. For instance, the Ferrari community gathers individuals who can belong to both the luxury and sport car subcultures. In each sport brand community, different sub-communities can also be identified. As for the Helly Hansen brand, some products have been adopted by rappers, generating two kinds of community: on one hand the community of outdoor sports' participants and on the other hand rappers and fans of rap music.

Within sport markets, the distinction between consumption subcultures and brand communities is sometimes difficult to make as brands and consumers' strategies tend to make them overlap. For instance, many sport brands sponsor and endorse teams, athletes, clubs, coaches and referees who promote and positively speak about the brands to the other members of their sporting subcultures. Besides, sport brands are extensively appropriated by consumers who do not participate in sport but use them as fashion items. Cova and Roncaglio (1999) characterised these segments as sympathisers alongside participants, casuals and sport institution members. These sub-segments can be more or less similar but the main common feature is that all individuals believe they belong to their sporting subculture. Consequently, Rollerblade did not hesitate to communicate about this diversity and promoted a general lifestyle called 'living and skating' which would include all community and subculture members.

The various forms of sporting subcultures

Various forms of sporting subcultures can be differentiated according to the initial sport or activity and the number of individuals who are a part of them. It can be said that each corporal activity created a sporting subculture whose members are often qualified by nicknames created by members of other subcultures. They are therefore quite easy to identify because of the visibility and access of the sport practice and then easy to target by brands. Due to their numbers, it is impossible to list and study all of them. Consequently, we will only focus in the second part of the following section on runners and joggers and on football and rugby fans subcultures. However, it is more difficult to identify sporting subcultures which are transversal to various sports and four of them will also be analysed. The first one to be studied is the female sporting subculture, followed by the lifestyle sporting subculture, the sporting countercultures and the e-sporting subculture.

The female sporting subculture

Within western cultures, if males are often associated with virile sports, females are rightly or wrongly often associated or expected to participate in aesthetic and graceful sporting activities. Part of this perception is certainly shaped by socialisation, parental education and ultimately, social reproduction which tend to see parents to consciously or unconsciously push their boys to do rugby or boxing and girls to do dance or gymnastics. Consequently, this social phenomenon tends to shape both male and female subcultures, and this distinction is largely encouraged, directly or indirectly, and favoured by sport brands which see straight landmarks and guidelines to follow to understand, attract and satisfy their respective targets. Sport brands love playing with stereotypes and particularly sexual ones as illustrated by Lange's promotional campaigns associating women – sexiness – with sport, and which correspond probably more to the ways men fantasise sporting women and not necessarily to the ways sporting women see themselves or want to see themselves. Reebok's commercial campaign for the 'Reetone' model is another example of how sport brands can emphasise stereotypes.

The growing female market presents interesting values, social originalities and new representations influencing the creation of promising subcultures from a brand perspective. Because of the development of this female sporting subculture, numerous sport brands have decided to invest into this segment, either in the sector of sport and physical activities or fashion. For instance, the fitness franchise Curves founded in 1995 targets only women who want to achieve their weight loss and tone up with machines specifically adapted to the morphology of women bodies. The 'Curves circuit' is a training workout which lasts 30 minutes and which claims to burn up to 500 calories. The brand boasts nearly 10,000 locations in over 85 countries.[1] In the sportswear sector, many corporate and club brands which were primarily targeting men are now designing specific products and lines for women. These adaptations also concern sporting event brands. For example, in 2006, in order to celebrate the arrival of the new title sponsor BNP Paribas for the Fed Cup (the international womens' tennis competition), the International Tennis Federation designed a new look and asked 260 players from 64 countries to vote for the new colour scheme[2]: fuchsia was the winning colour.

In France, Nike has for instance made 20 per cent of its turnover with its female products and the world leader brand aims to increase this number to about a third by 2015 (Garnier, 2002). After having mainly focused its strategy and efforts on the football sector until 2002, the brand has decided to give an important place to women with its core targets made of young girls aged between 12 and 18 years old who use the brand's items as part of their clothing style and women aged between 22 and 30 years old who mainly participate in individual sports. It seems that the brand's strategy primarily focuses on products and clothes design as for these consumers the notions of body shape, look and colours are very important. Other means to serve its strategy were to use female magazines for its marketing communication and offer a refreshed design to its retail stores which were perceived too masculine.

The lifestyle sporting subculture

Sport represents a privileged entry for many markets linked to generational and ethnic subcultures. By participating in a sporting activity, people exert, perform, play with others, and express their selves and their own personalities. Consequently, sport and clothing brands have targeted these sporting segments very early on either by extending their ranges and lines or by adjusting their offer to specific niche markets. Through the consumption and use of sport brands, people try to experience a tribal belonging which serves their social needs and/or sport passion. In this context, the transactional and utilitarian aspect of the offers has to fade in front of the sought values, symbols and meanings.

Various sport clothing subcultures are currently popular and increasingly so, such as the streetwear and surfwear ones. The related subcultures are interpenetrated with other social subcultures which are related to other consumption practices. Streetwear for instance echoes the rapping, hip-hop, street and graffiti subcultures. They embrace an urban spirit of rebellion and freedom expressed via the clothing style made of large hoodies and T-shirts, polo shirts, tracksuits, caps and flat-sole shoes from the main sport corporate brands such as Nike, Adidas, Fred Perry, Helly Hansen, and Lacoste. The surfwear subculture has been, however, influenced by the hippy and Californian spirits and manifests a relaxed and independent spirit associated with boardsports practices and being close to nature. For many members of the surfing subculture, surfing is an attitude which links people who do not necessarily surf but adhere to the same values and spirit of freedom, brotherhood, respect for others and nature, in opposition with the hectic modern and urban lifestyle focusing on professional careers and money. Many brands symbolise this spirit (for example Quiksilver, Hurley, and Volcom) but they do not appear exclusive as many of them can appear in other subcultures such as the snowboarding and skating ones.

In order to fit with the lifestyle trend, numerous sport brands are now developing two different product lines: one oriented towards sport participants and one oriented towards fashion and the lifestyle subculture. Following this logic, it is not surprising any more to see sport brands' advertising campaigns featuring non-athlete celebrities such as Snoop Dogg, Katy Perry or Noel Gallagher as for Adidas Originals. To target young urban and trendy consumers these brands sometimes collaborate with famous clothing designers and artists to produce limited series and collections which are often popular among fashion victims, sneaker addicts, collectors and fans. This is for instance what Puma recently did in 2012 when the brand asked Cedella Marley, the daughter of Bob Marley, to design a new line for Usain Bolt and the Jamaican team and whose core product is a new version of Bob Marley's military jacket named 'Iron Lion'. In a sense, sportswear brands have managed to capture the lifestyle subculture and redefine it as a lifestyle made in sport. It has forced non-sport brands to invest in sporting subcultures, for example Ralph Lauren supplyed clothes to the 2012 American Olympic team; Dolce & Gabbana clothed the 2012 Italian football team; EA7, the sporting line of Emporio Armani designed kit for the 2012 Italian Olympic team; Bogner and Sioux for the 2012 German Olympic team.

The sporting counterculture: an authentic subculture

As discussed by Loret (1995), sport can also be the place for the expression of a counterculture opposing the dominant one, and for instance Nike and Reebok have used transgressing cultural dimensions to make their success. Precisely, one of Reebok's slogans was 'Break the rules' which is an appeal for a rejection of dominant cultures. Similarly the use of athletes such as John McEnroe, André Agassi, or Eric Cantona in marketing and advertising campaigns tends to shake sporting conservative values as the rebellious behaviours of these athletes was a source of intense polemics. Besides their talent, these athletes have fascinated people because of their transgressing behaviours despite moral or ethical condemnations. Using the same idea, the American basketball player Charles Barkley claimed in a 1993 Nike commercial: 'I am not a role model. I am not paid to be a role model. I am paid to wreak havoc on the basketball court. Parents should be role models. Just because I dunk a basketball does not mean I should raise your kids'.[3] This statement which was written by the player himself followed and was followed by many iconoclastic statements and claims in comparison with the traditional perceived values of sports and athletes and the social role attributed to them. At that time, the narratives used by Nike with numerous athletes aimed to position itself in opposition to the traditional values conveyed by other brands and its main rival Adidas in particular which was seen as the representative of classical fair play, respect, honesty and exemplary values. Therefore, it probably should not be seen as something more than a tactical move relying on the identification of the main values and symbols of the sporting subculture to promote contradictory values to create another subculture, which would become a sporting counterculture, to differentiate the brand from its main competitors. Nevertheless, due to the intense brand associations and positioning on this segment – most of them want to appear as rebels to particularly attract in-rebellion teenagers, we can wonder if this sporting counterculture has not become at times the dominant sporting subculture, and indirectly pushed the classical 'clean' sporting subculture to become the real sporting counterculture. Moreover, it should be also mentioned that the frontier between sporting dominant and counter-subcultures is something moving and certainly not set in stone. What appeared in the past to be part of a sporting countercultural movement can be nowadays seen as part of the dominant sporting counterculture.

This sporting countercultural movement was particularly manifest during the birth of Californian and sliding sport practices and the appearance of associated brands. However, many observers, hard-core and pioneer participants are now regretting the loss of this spirit and the loss of a certain soul which means these practices are not transgressive any more. For instance Heino (2000) explained the success of snowboarding because it was developed in opposition to skiing and its dominant culture which was seen as orderly, disciplined, expansive, bourgeois, bureaucratised, rationalised with a must-win mentality whereas snowboarding was promoting personalisation, entertainment, spectacle and camaraderie. However, we can wonder if it is still the case now that snowboarding has been democratised and widespread and integrated into classical sporting governing bodies and competitions such as the Winter Olympics. To paraphrase Heino (2000), is snowboarding still so punk, and is it still a counterculture? As for surfing, hard-core participants criticise the fact that it has become a mass consumption product, although at its start it was deeply against consumer society. Similarly, the German football club FC St. Pauli is famous for its unique counterculture made of left-leaning politics, social activism, anti-racism, anti-fascism, party atmosphere and resistance towards commercialisation and marketisation of football but in 2011 a group of fans called the Social Romantics launched a petition asking for a stop and limitation of the club's commercial activities and criticised the installation of business seats and VIP boxes in the stadium. When marketing takes over counterculture, can it still remain countercultural?

The e-sporting culture

The e-sporting culture aggregates two sporting subculture categories: the first one deals with consumer-players who play against each other in virtual competitions and the second deals with video-game participation generating a physical activity in relation to virtual characters. In both cases, the e-sporting culture constitutes a very recent and contemporary social phenomenon where real and virtual worlds interpenetrate as much for sport consumption as for product and brand purchase. Video-games are increasingly popular and the physically passive player, except for few fingers, is increasingly being transformed into a physically active player. In the first case, the multi-player aspect is crucial in the success of games, such as for Fantasy Leagues and online football tournaments, and in the creation of a subculture. For instance in 1999, for the launch of its new car the 'Toyota Tundra', Toyota Motor Sales USA in collaboration with MSN Gaming Zone set a race tournament name Tundra Madness whose winner won one Tundra car. The tournament attracted more than 500,000 spectators and more than 1,000 registered players residing in the USA. Following the tournament, Toyota Tundra broke Toyota sales records and experienced the fastest sales start for a new product in Toyota's history.[4] In this specific example, a direct link could be seen between the e-sporting subculture and Toyota's brand community. Pro Evolution Soccer (PES), a game developed by Konami, has been organised and played in leagues since 2002 in various countries such as Germany, United Kingdom, France and Spain.

In France, the 2012 PES League covered a period of eleven months, with one event every weekend in different venues, gathering 18,000 players and ending with a national final. Purely virtual competitors are different from virtual competitors who may go to organised events to play virtual games such as in the example of the PES Leagues because physical interaction, shared enthusiasm and excitement, and atmosphere are elements which cannot be found in purely virtual games, despite the existence of forums of discussion. Purely virtual players can sometimes be a group of friends, or on the contrary not know each other, such as in the case of Fantasy Leagues. Nevertheless, they have their own codes, languages and practices (for example reading sport media websites regularly to see if certain players are injured) representing subcultures' constituting elements. The website Virtual Regatta[5] offers to participants the possibility to run famous races like Vendée Globe and Velux 5 Oceans with a virtual boat in choosing sail and capes based on the real weather conditions. During the 2008 Vendée Globe edition, 340,000 virtual sailors took part in the race and the website now claims 1,000,000 registered skippers.[6]

As exercise bikes, treadmills, fitness and abs exercises remain highly popular, new technologies have revolutionised home physical activities, even reaching retiring homes, which was not particularly expected. Thanks to 'Wii Fit' from Nintendo, 'Kinetic' from PlayStation and 'My personal trainer' from Nintendo DS, taking part in electronics-led physical activities is not only virtual anymore. In 2008, 'Wii Sport' became the bestseller video game with 40,520,000 copies sold since its launch. If Nintendo achieved such successes, it is because the brand has been able to target two types of consumers: teenagers and seniors. For the latter, the brand has become leader thanks to cognitive training games and physical and sport games graphically simple and very easy to play. The brand has even created the Wii Balance Board which is an accessory for the Nintendo Wii video games and which measures users' centre of pressure displacement and weight, and then allows the reproduction of the users' movements on screen. The craze for these games and virtual-real practices has been so important that a particular type of pain or numbness has appeared named the Wii-elbow, very similar to a tennis-elbow pain, due to the excessive use of a Wii remote control. For this particular e-sporting subculture, fun is more important than calories burnt, even though that remains important, and has to be shared with family and friends. It remains different from 'real' sporting cultures, because as far as we know, no sporting virtual champions have become sporting real-world champions. However, the contrary is certainly true. Fitness equipment brands have started to react and invest in this segment such as Mattel did with its Smart Cycle and WaterRower. Other video game brands such as Electronic Arts have followed the trend with EA Sports Active which acts like a virtual personal fitness trainer. Either tailored for young kids, teenagers, women or seniors, these video games have created new sporting subcultures which now represent real competitors for sport services, clubs and associations even if members of sporting and e-sporting subcultures seem different for the moment. Nevertheless, bridges can easily be established and it can be imagined that some participants may move from virtual to real sports and conversely as for as recovering participants or those who are prone to injuries. In this case, the different subcultures may interpenetrate each other. The mix of subcultures could be illustrated by the example of the Tour de France which created for one stage of the 2012 edition a website where spectators could put pictures taken from the side of the road. Online spectators could then follow the race live thanks to these pictures.

With the development of the e-commerce and online sales websites, which represent a significant component of the e-sporting subculture, consumers look for the best deals from a multi-channel context. However, few studies have looked at the specific behaviours of these e-consumers in comparison with their behaviours in traditional retail stores. The current mixed commercial situation made of physical and virtual realities considerably changes the relationships between sport brands and consumer groups and subcultures. This reflexion can be extended to online sport viewership and fandom in relation to sporting clubs, leagues and events. Through forums of discussions, chats, blogs, and social media, sport brands are increasingly under the threat of parasitism and critics. The massive expansion of electronic commerce has defined new rules, norms and relationships between brands and their consumers where the levels of control and power have progressively shifted from the former to the latter. They have defined specific online forms of consumption but it is very likely that they also influence physical forms of consumption. Sport brands are probably the first to be concerned as the majority of online transactions concern video games, sport clothes, shoes and accessories. Therefore the emergence of these specific e-sporting subcultures will have an impact on sport brands' strategies such as whether to remain 'brick and mortar' or move to 'click and mortar'.

Sport subcultures and segments

The sporting subcultures gather or differentiate various subgroups of individuals who, at a given moment, purchase and use similar services, products and brands. From this analysis, the concept of tribe has emerged from the literature referring to diverse segments that share a common consumption subculture. Tribes are mainly defined by affective and social criteria compared to segments which are mainly defined by cognitive and sociodemographic criteria. For many sporting subcultures, it seems that people's involvement in practices and sporting objects' attachment are the most accurate ways of identifying these tribes. For instance within the joggers, cyclists and hikers' subcultures, members can be clustered based on heterogeneous characteristics, practice patterns and levels of expertise. In front of this complexity, sport brands increasingly try to adjust and segment their offers within each targeted subculture. For outdoor related subcultures, the level of innovation seems to strongly modify the type of relationships consumers have with their activity independently from their form of practice. Thanks to its numerous technical innovations, Petzl has revolutionised potholing, climbing and mountaineering practices with its descenders, pulleys and its famous Jumar clamp. Petzl also initiated new bindings for Nordic skiing. In water sports, which represent subcultures which have been considerably changed by innovations, few brands have tried to contribute to the promotion of activities while broadening their offers. Precisely, the brand Mastercraft has specifically created boats for wakeboards for participants to have big enough waves to do acrobatics. Moreover, some companies have created water-ski lifts allowing participants to be pulled up and then not requiring boats anymore. Consequently, these innovations have considerably modified the types of practices (Hillairet, 2006), which have then modified the sporting subcultures and created new subgroups and tribes, because they attracted new participants. Sport brands increasingly try to target multiple segments which are more or less similar in terms of expectations and needs. When they are not so different, slight variations in offers are sufficient to satisfy the different subculture's segments. However, when they are too distinct, companies and brands sometimes have to acquire other brands or create new ones. This is for instance what motivated the Oxylane Group to continuously create new brands to reach the number of 19 (including Quechua, Tribord, Wed'ze, Kipsta, Kalenji, Inesis, Domyos, b'Twin). The group started with few brands and progressively recognised the existence of different sporting subcultures and segments within them which then pushed them to create more specific brands. In turn, the creation of these specific brands reinforces and officialises these subcultures and segments.

The skiing subculture is illustrative about this diversity of tribes. With the emergence of new sliding practices, the new segments of free-riders, free-stylers and racing skiers now represent about 20 per cent of the skiing subculture. Consequently, sport brands have developed ranges of products which fit with these consumers who are very visible on slopes. Free-riders are off-piste adepts, mainly men, aged between 25 and 40 years old and often come from mountain regions; for them, skiing is a way of life. They are easily recognisable because of their highly technical equipment and material which are often endorsed by famous sport brands. Free-stylers can be either skiers or snowboarders and are mainly oriented towards acrobatics. They are often gathered like a tribe or a pack around snowparks and half-pipes. As for the racing skiers' family, they are essentially competitors either in downhill or slalom disciplines. Among these three tribes of regular skiers, free-stylers appear as opinion leaders for other skiers in terms of clothing and appearance, material and equipment, and in terms of spirit which seems to symbolise freedom, fun and camaraderie.

The diversity of subcultures is high from a sport participation perspective but there are also various sporting subcultures from a sport spectacle and viewing perspective. As for sport participants, sport spectators are not homogenous and different segments and tribes can be identified based on demographic, gender, social, geographical, attitudinal and behavioural characteristics. From a subculture analysis perspective, Bromberger (1998) estimated that participation forms vary according to passion levels explaining the intensity and types of social affiliation and expression, the levels and forms of commitment and support from spectators and fans, either for live or mediated sporting events. Professional football clubs have for example become true brands, with their own market territory, their promises, merchandised products and their loyal consumers, even if they often do not see themselves as consumers and do not like being described that way. Hunt *et al.* (1999) identified five types of sport fans based on three theoretical orientations which were fans' propensity to bask in reflected glory, information processing and attachment as it relates to the self. Specifically, these authors identified:

1. temporary fans who are bound by time;
2. local fans who are bound by geographical distance;
3. devoted fans who are not limited by time or geographical boundaries but for whom being a fan is only peripheral to their identity;

4. fanatical fans for whom being a fan is a core dimension of their identity and who engage in fan-like behaviours;
5. dysfunctional fans for whom being a fan is the most important thing and which sometimes hinders them to fulfil normal social roles and make them adopt anti-social, disruptive and violent behaviours (Hun *et al.*, 1999).

The latter can be associated to hooligans and some 'Ultra' movements and are widespread among European football and focus attention and principally media attention. Historically, European football supporter culture emerged following two movements (Bernache-Assollant, 2006). The first movement developed in the sixties in England and was strongly related to teenagers and working-class subcultures such as teddy boys, punks and rockers; the model was further spread in Northern Europe (for example in Germany, Belgium, and Holland). The second movement was set up by Italian supporters ('tifosis') and spread through southern Europe. In both cases, these movements were strongly associated to other subcultures such as teenagers, students, and working-class people. However, it would be simplistic and incorrect to reduce all forms of spectatorship and fanship to this sole particular subculture segment as shown in Hunt *et al.*'s (1999) classification. Therefore, several authors have tried to look at the different tribes or segments composing spectatorship subcultures. Holt (1995) estimated that baseball fans mainly consumed for four reasons which he classified as consuming as experience, consuming as integration, consuming as classification and consuming as play. Although he emphasised the diversity of reasons why people would consume sporting events, he did not identify specific tribes and segments. His work was further extended by Bourgeon and Bouchet (2001) and Bouchet *et al.* (2011) who identified four spectator profiles based on dominant experiences sought, which were validated in rugby and tennis but aimed to be generalised for many sports. They are Aesthete, Interactive, Opportunist and Supporter profiles and are described in Table 4.2.

Even if these profiles identify specific subcultures within sport spectacle and event consumers, it should be noted that some variations should be considered based on the type of sport and the cultural contexts considered, which could create subcategories among these profiles. Last, regarding the spectators presenting a supporter profile, their level of loyalty towards certain league, club, team and event brands can be compared to another type of consumers' groupings which are structured around specific brands, sport brand communities.

The influence of sport brands' communities

When they are relatively successful, sport brands can become objects of a cult and worship which end up with the creation of a community of fans and passionate consumers. These communities of fans represent a guarantee of regular financial revenues as well as promoters and defenders of the brands. They can also provide interesting feedback which can help the brands to develop in their strategic

TABLE 4.2 Sport spectator profiles and consumption experience sought

Spectator profiles Consumption experiences sought

	Description	Verbatim
Opportunist	Behaviour expresses relative neutrality with any demonstrative support being forced by a collective movement, such as a Mexican wave. Participation is linked to the hope of receiving benefits from positive rewards.	'He's not necessarily a connoisseur.' 'He looks for personal contacts with political power.' 'He attends occasionally, according to the importance of the event.' 'He's attached to the team for different reasons.'
Aesthete	Behaviour is oriented towards quality, beauty, exceptional performance, fair play, and the drama and theatrical intensity of the show.	'Even if the team loses it's beautiful.' 'When we pay it's to watch a beautiful display.' 'The play needs to be artistic, spectacular.' 'He comes to observe the players, their technical abilities.'
Supporter	Behaviour is characterised by a degree of support for the players. Fans want to have the feeling of being co-producers by showing a physical and vocal presence or superiority.	'He's passionate, he's fanatic, a clubber, a die-hard fan.' 'He spends a lot of energy. He lives almost exclusively for that.' 'He supports his team all the time.' 'He's a little bit patriotic. He wants to win by all means.'
Interactive	Behaviour is oriented towards entertainment and shared emotion in reaction to objects or people's actions. They react and interact, and project themselves into the event, sometimes beyond the sport venues.	'Spectacle – this is sharing, exchanging, letting off steam.' 'We go there to escape, to have fun.' 'We go there for the pleasure. We love sport.' 'Vibrating differently.'

Source: Originally adapted from Bourgeon and Bouchet (2001). Bouchet *et al.* (2011).

orientations. However, when dissatisfied by some products and services or marketing practices, these communities can become tough opponents, not to say enemies
in the worst cases. These communities do not have geographical boundaries, due
to the globalisation of communication and goods. This is typically the case for
professional leagues and clubs who now have massive communities of satellite fans.
These fans are generally exclusive which means that they cannot purchase or
support the main competitor of their favourite brand as for Adidas versus Nike,
Quiksilver versus Oxbow, Salomon versus Rossignol, Aigle versus Lafuma,
Patagonia versus Columbia, Manchester United versus Manchester City, Real
Madrid versus FC Barcelona, Chicago Bulls versus New York Knicks. Finally, brand
community members are linked together through habits, rites, traditions, media

technical innovations for its shoe models in collaborating with elite athletes, either in basketball with the 'Chuck Taylor All Star' model, tennis and baseball with the 'Jack Purcell' model, or in badminton with its 'One Star' model. Nevertheless, the brand has also diversified its offers and ranges in launching clothing lines in limited edition and designed by famous creators such as John Varvatos. In terms of products, Converse regularly relooks its models, but the 'Chuck Taylor All Star' appears to be the most successful one, with a true community of fans supporting and purchasing it. It has become a cult object for many consumers throughout several generations. Some fans do not hesitate to draw on them or customise them by adding a variety of pins whereas others paint, tag or cut them. According to the model's managers, these shoes cannot be out-of-date because of the variety of models and the fact that consumers can customise and then truly appropriate them.

Adidas is one of the most famous and valued brands worldwide. After a period of leadership until the nineties, the brand lost its dominant position because of its sport specialist image and because it did not appeal enough to the youngest consumers and new consumption modes. The re-conquest of its consumers was achieved through a very strong investment in football which contributed to its popularity among the youth segments. Since, the brand has developed products targeted at athletes which are gathered under its line 'Sport Performance'. However, many of these products have been diverted from their initial function by some of the brand's fans who are not sport participants. Consequently, in 2001, a new range of products was created to target 20–25 year-old consumers. This line was named 'Adidas Originals' and its primary role was to rejuvenate old models to fit with these young segments. The 'Superstar', initially launched in 1969, 'Nastase' and 'Stan Smith' models have for instance re-appeared and all these re-launched models represent about 20 per cent of Adidas' turnover.[7] For the 32 year anniversary of the 'Superstar' model, the brand collaborated with artists, musicians, and famous retail stores. In 2005, 35 new models were offered in limited editions and progressively revealed to the public such as the versions with Andy Warhol, the Disney version with 'Goofy Sport', the manga version with 'Captain Tsubasa' or the version realised with the 'Upper Playground' store. All these specific models aimed to attract new consumers in many different and contemporary subcultures and boosted the sales of the 'Superstar' by more than 30 per cent.[8] Beyond the economic and financial success, this strategy and the new products allowed the brand to acquire another identity closer to pop and street cultures. Quite surprisingly, Adidas is now popular within the hip hop and rap subcultures and has worked with famous icons such as Run-DMC and Missy Elliot. In 2003, the brand launched a new line named 'Sportstyle' under the brand name Y-3 which was the fruit of a collaboration with the fashion designer Yohji Yamamoto targeting 30–40 year-old consumers keen on fashion and style. This represented another brand community initiated by Adidas via its new products and collaborations. The collaborations with Stella McCartney and Karl Lagerfeld are also illustrative of this trend. The launch in 2002 of Adidas Originals' flagship store represented the last tactic to materialise the brand community and cement it around a specific place of consumption and cult.

Quiksilver's community: a surfing culture

Created in 1970, *Quiksilver* started to commercialise surf suits and boots to over-come the lack of comfort of the existing ones. These products were light and comfortable, dried quickly and did not hinder surfers in their acrobatic move-ments. Alan Green and John Law, the two surfer-founders of the brand, were the first to wear the products. The members of the surfing community rapidly tried to acquire them and since, the brand has been synonymous with authenticity, origi-nality, functionality and innovation at the service of hard core surfers. A posteriori, it could be said that the marketing strategy adopted by the brand was targeting surfing communities and tribes from its start as the founders have always wanted to offer products created by surfers for surfers. However, because of the craze for beach and fashion subcultures and their demands in terms of style, Quiksilver had to hire creators and designers to offer products which would satisfy surfers' expec-tations as well as adopt aggressive marketing and commercial strategies to face the intense competition of other brands such as Rip Curl, Oxbow, Billabong and O'Neil.

Nowadays, Quiksilver is still targeting expert surfers as well as sympathisers who have never put a foot on a surf board, but who feel part of the surfing subculture and share its values and lifestyle. The product extensions regarding accessories such as sunglasses and watches are now launched via licensing to better attract this group of consumers. There is therefore nothing surprising in the fact that the brand holds a leader position within the surfwear and lifestyle segments due to its broad range of products and collections and its powerful universe of meanings and symbols. Furthermore, the brand manages to carry a cool image which features the ideas and values of the sporting counter-culture associated with boardsports. A clothing collection launched in 2005 and named 'Quiksilver Edition' particularly focused on the 20–45 year-old consumers of the brand, and aimed to valorise the emotional dimension of the brand which appeals to consumers across generations and segments. The brand is also actively involved in sponsorship, public relations and corporate social responsibility activities such as the 'Quiksilver Initiative' programme which aims to support projects to make people aware about environ-mental issues and protection. These projects aim to strengthen the links the brand has with its loyal consumers who are very often sensitive to these issues as part of the surfing subculture where nature has a fundamental place, as well as its employ-ees, creating a true brand community.

5

THE ECONOMIC AND SOCIAL VALUE OF SPORT BRANDS

A brand truly becomes a brand with time, when its offers finally meet consumers' needs and expectations. The brand is translated into awareness levels, perceived images and loyalty and thanks to its different value dimensions justify its role in a market. Numerous parameters which can be economical, marketing, strategic, managerial and sociological take part in the brand valorisation process. For instance, the necessary marketing and communication costs now encourage and even force firms and organisations to focus on brands with the best valorisation, penetration rates and brand equity. This is a direct consequence of sport markets' concentration. All firms also try to make economies of scale at production, human resources, research and development, design and facilities levels. The concentration trend is particularly important where innovations represent a strong component making Desbordes (2001) wonder if there was enough room for small firms on these markets.

Also, the globalisation phenomenon has strongly influenced sport brands' valorisation process. For instance, the standardisation of consumers' tastes beyond local and national markets justifies the creation of specific and local brands less and less. In many aspects, American consumers are similar to Australian, German, and Japanese consumers. Obviously differences remain, in particular from a cultural perspective, but they do not seem big enough to maintain different brands per market as products and services are very similar and often identical. Within the same continent or the same economic space, markets' segmentation, lifestyle and expectations seem more and more homogeneous and this is particularly the case for sport brands due to the increasing globalisation of sports and their universal appeal.

Brands as drivers for companies' profitability

Globalisation increases the number of competitors and therefore competition intensity, reinforcing the role and power of brands. For many experts, a switch is even being operated from market economies to brand economies and this seems to apply to sport brands. The sport brands market is evaluated at about US$230 billion with an annual growth of between four and six per cent.[1] Obviously this market is not uniform and comprises many different sub-markets with their own brands. As an example, the sport shoes market alone comprises about twenty different sectors and segments (for example running, trial, outdoor, athletics, indoor, tennis, football) with hundreds of specialised brands.

Financially speaking, sport brands show very attractive profitability rates making them safe investments for groups such as PPR (for example Gucci, Yves Saint Laurent, and Puma), Airesis (for example Fanatic, Ion and Le Coq Sportif) and Activa Capital (for example Pro Natura, Bruno Saint Hilaire and Sport 2000) in Europe; VF Corporation (for example Wrangler, Lee and The North Face) in the USA; Sumitomo Rubber Industry (for example Dunlop Japan, Srixon, and Roger Cleveland Golf) in Japan. Brands have become prosperity tools and are then managed as real assets. They undoubtedly represent competitive advantage levers for companies because they summarise within their reputation all the firms' and organisations' tangible and intangible differentiation efforts and strategies (Kapferer, 2006).

Sport brand portfolios

Nowadays, sport brands' internationalisation and globalisation are achieved with large scale alliances, mergers and acquisitions. The groups which own Quiksilver, Adidas, Nike or Lafuma cannot optimally grow without acquiring other sport brands, which is a process known as external growth. For this reason these groups own and manage bigger and bigger brand portfolios. However, they remain small or modest in comparison with food and consumer goods giant brands such as Nestlé, Danone, Procter & Gamble and Unilever; the latter owned for instance 1,600 brands in 2000 and 'only' 400 brands in 2011. Since the nineties, the groups from the sport sectors and industries have been clearly and progressively acquiring other sport brands to reinforce their portfolios and their dominant positions. Quiksilver Inc, Amer Sports, Jarden Corporation, Head Tyrolia Mares (HTM), Sports Authority, VF Corporation and Lafuma are the owners of more than a hundred sport brands among the most powerful and profitable (see Table 5.1). Besides these sport industry giants, there are smaller companies owning only two or three sport brands and whose scope and awareness are regional and national.

For a company, having such portfolios responds to a strategic necessity. When the Finnish group Amer Sports acquired Salomon, its main objective was clear: maintaining its leader position ahead of Quiksilver Inc. The strategy adopted by Adidas responded to the same needs and intentions when it acquired Reebok for about €3.1 billion to reduce the gap with its main competitor, Nike. In 2004, before the acquisition of Reebok, Adidas' turnover was about €6.48 billion and increased to €8.9 billion with the adjunction of Reebok. With this acquisition, the German brand increased its market share from nine per cent to 21 per cent in the

TABLE 5.1 The main corporations' sport brand portfolios

THE BRANDS OF QUIKSILVER, INC (USA)			
Quiksilver	Surfwear brand	Roxy	Women surfwear brand (created by Quiksilver)
DC Shoes	Skate, BMX and motocross (the urban brand of Quiksilver)	Raisins	Swimwear brand (USA)
Hawk	Skateboarding shoes, clothes and accessories (the name comes from the skateboarding legend Tony Hawk)	Andaska	Specialised outdoor apparel retailer (bought by Napali, the European subsidiary of Quiksilver)
Gotcha	Surfwear (licence for Europe)	Fidra	Golf apparels
Lib Technologies	Snowboards	Never Compromise	Golf putters
		Bent (Marvin)	Bindings
Radio Fiji	Swimwear	Island Soul	Swimwear
Bent Metal	Snowboards bindings	Gnu	Snowboards
Fidra by John Ashworth	Golf apparel line	Leilani	Swimwear

THE BRANDS OF OXYLANE GROUP (France)			
Nabaiji	Swimming accessories	Tribord	Water sports
Quechua	Mountain sports	Kalenji	Running and jogging
Kipsta	Team sports (e.g. football, rugby, basketball, volleyball, handball)	Domyos	Fitness, aerobic, gym-dance, martial arts, running
Oxelo	Skateboarding and ice sports	b'Twin	Bikes
Newfeel	Sport walking	Artengo	Racket sports (tennis, squash, badminton, table tennis)
Aptonia	Accessories	Géonaute	Nature equipment (walkie-talkie, watch, compass)
Inésis	Golf	Fouganza	Equestrian sports
Wed'ze	Snowboarding sports	Simond	Climbing and safety material and equipment
Caperlan	Fishing	Solognac	Hunting
Skimium.com	Franchise retailer		

TABLE 5.1 continued

THE BRANDS OF AMER SPORTS (Finland)			
Wilson	Team sports, racket sports, golf	Precor	Fitness equipment
Wilson Staff	Premium golf equipment	Volant	High-end skis
Suunto	Diving, training and outdoor precision instruments	Oxygen	Snowboards
Salomon	Snowboard sports and outdoor	Mavic	Bicycle and related components
Bonfire	Snowboarding clothes	Cliché	Skateboards
Arc'Teryx	Clothing outdoor gear	Dynamic	Skis
Atomic	Skiing and snowboarding equipment		

THE BRANDS OF ADIDAS (Germany)			
Adidas	Footwear, sportswear, sports equipment, toiletries	TaylorMade	Golf products
Reebok	Footwear, sportswear	RBK	Hip hop and dancing

THE BRANDS OF NIKE (USA)			
Nike	Footwear and apparel, sports equipment	Hurley International	Skateboarding and surfing clothes, equipment and accessories
Cole Haan	Casual footwear, belts, hosiery, gloves, scarves, hat, outerwear, sunglasses	Umbro	Sportswear, balls, accessories
Converse	Shoes, apparel	Nike Golf	Golf equipment

THE BRANDS OF LAFUMA (France)			
Lafuma	Outdoor clothing and sportswear	Le Chameau	Accessories, hunting and horse riding boots
Millet	Apparel, backpacks, gear	Charles-Dubourg/ L'Esquimau	Countryside apparel and accessories
Millet Expert Shop	Sport retailer	Oxbow	Surfwear
Ober	Jeans	Lallemand	Camping accessories
Big Pack	Backpack	Georg Schumacher	Horse riding and countryside boots
Bigshoes	Flip flops and surfing accessories	Eider	Mountaineering and ice climbing clothing and equipment

TABLE 5.1 continued

THE BRANDS OF INTERSPORT (Switzerland)

Intersport	Sporting goods retailer	Twinner Sport	Mountain sports apparel, equipment and accessories retailer and rental
Sport Leader	Sports retailer	Shooz	Streetwear retailer
La Halle au Sport	Discount and second hand sports retailer	McKinley (ME)	Mountaineering accessories
Nakamura (ME)	Bicycles	Tecno Pro (ME)	Sport bags, skiing and tennis footwear, clothing and accessories
Etirel (ME)	Skiwear, casual sportswear and swimwear	Polochon (ME)	Sport kids wear
FireFly	Snowboarding and beach lifestyle textiles	Crazy Creek (ME)	Urban surfing (skateboarding, roller skating)
Dynatour Golf (ME)	Golf equipment	Energetics (ME)	Fitness and working out equipment
Pro Touch (ME)	Team sports, boxing and martial arts		

THE BRANDS OF JARDEN CORPORATION (USA)[i]

K2 Skate	Inline roller skates	K2 Skis	Nordic and alpine skis
K2 Snowboard	Snowboards	Völkl	Skis
Marker	Ski bindings	Line	Skis
Madshus	Cross-country skis	Karhu	Cross-country and telemark skis
Ride Snowboard	Snowboards and related accessories	Atlas Snow	Snowshoes
Tubbs Snowshoes	Snowshoes	Morrows	Snowboards
5150	Snowboard, shoes and bindings	Rawling	Baseball, softball, basketball, football/soccer balls, equipment and accessories
Worth	Baseball equipment and accessories	Miken	Baseball equipments and accessories
Db Gait Lacrosse	Baseball equipment and accessories	K2 Licence Product	Licensee of Marvel, Disney, NBA . . . for toys and merchandised products
Zoot Sports	Triathlon shoes, apparel, wetsuits and accessories	Sevylor	Water floats and inflatables, boats, kayaks
Coleman	Outdoor and camping equipment	Marmot	Outdoor equipment and sleeping bags
Skis Rossignol	Alpine, snowboard and Nordic equipment (Jarden Corp. owns 17% of the shares)		

TABLE 5.1 continued

THE BRANDS OF HTM (HEAD TYROLIA MARES) (Austria)

Head	Ski equipments and tennis racquets	Head Snowboard	Snowboards
Head Protection	Helmets and dorsal protections	Penn	Tennis balls
Tyrolia	Ski bindings	Mares	Scuba diving equipment
Dacor	Scuba diving gear		

THE BRANDS OF BILLABONG INTERNATIONAL LIMITED (Australia)

Billabong	Surfwear	Element	Skateboarding textiles and shoes
Von Zipper	Sunglasses	Honolua	Surfwear
Kustom	Shoes	Surf Company/ Nixon	Sport watches

THE BRANDS OF TECNICA GROUP (Italia)

Nordica	Ski shoes	Tecnica	Skiwear, climbing, hiking and ski shoes
Dolomite	Climbing and hiking shoes	Think Pin	Outdoor clothing
Rollerblade	Inline roller skates	Marker	Ski bindings (in collaboration with Völkl, a skis and tennis racket manufacturer)
Moon Boot	Snowshoes	Völkl	Skis and skiwear (Technica Group owns the distribution network in Europe)
T Shoes	Footwear	Nitro	Snowboards
Blizzard	Skis	Lowa	Mountain sports equipment

THE BRANDS OF SPORT AUTHORITY (USA)

Alpine Design	Alpine and outdoor apparel and accessories	Aspire	Women sportswear
Golf Day	Golf accessories	Tour Collection	Golf accessories
Estero	Football studs and equipment	Parkside	Trampolines
Bodyfit by Sports Authority	Fitness accessories		

TABLE 5.1 continued

THE BRANDS OF VF CORPORATION (USA)

The North Face	Alpine, outdoor and casual sports	JanSport	Backpack and lifestyle accessories
Lucy	Women Lifestyle	Vans	Skateboarding footwear, clothing and accessories
Kipling	Footwear and lifestyle accessories	Majestic Athletic	Baseball, American football, ice hockey and basketball textiles
Nautica	Casual water sports	Napapijri	Outdoor and sportswear
Reef	Surfwear		

THE BRANDS OF PATAGONIA CORPORATION (USA)

Beneficial T'S by Patagonia	Outdoor textiles	Lotus Design	Watersports and kayak equipment and accessories
Rhythm	Women lifestyle	Water Girl	Women swimwear and sportswear textiles
Point Blanks	Surfs		

THE BRANDS OF COLUMBIA SPORTSWEAR (USA)

Columbia	Sportswear and outdoor clothing	Mountain Hardwear	Mountain and outdoor clothing and equipment
Sorel	Outdoor		

THE BRANDS OF SUMITOMO RUBBER INDUSTRY (SRI Sport Limited) (Japan)

Srixon	Golf equipment	Cleveland Golf	Golf equipment
Dunlop Sport	Tennis rackets and accessories		

THE BRANDS OF FOOT LOCKER INC. (USA)

Foot Locker	Sportswear and footwear retailer	Lady Foot Locker	Women sportswear and footwear retailer
Kids Foot Locker	Kid sportswear and footwear retailer	Foot Locker International	Retailer
Champs Sport	Footwear, apparel and sporting goods retailer	Foot Action USA	Athletic footwear and apparel retailer
Eastbay	Athletic footwear, apparel and equipment direct retailer	CCS	Skateboarding equipment retailer

TABLE 5.1 continued

THE BRANDS OF THE FORZANI GROUP LTD. (Canada)

Sport Chek	Sporting goods retailer	Sport Mart	Discount sport retailer
Fitness Source	Fitness equipment retail franchise	National Sports	Team sports and « active family » retail stores
Sports Experts	Sporting and fashionable goods retail franchise	Intersport North-American	'Neighbourhood' sport retail franchise
Atmosphere	Outdoor sports retail franchise	RN'R	Walking retail franchise
Econosports	Discount sport goods retail franchiser		
Nevada Bob's Golf	Golf franchise retailer	Hockey Experts	Ice hockey equipment retail stores
Athletes World	Athletic and urban fashion footwear and apparel retail franchise	S3	Snow, Skate and Surf retail franchise
The Tech Shop	Running and walking retail stores		

Note:

i   It is difficult to precisely identify all the brands of the group because it does not communicate much about them.

USA but also reinforced its worldwide presence as well as extending its target segments. If Adidas holds a European and technical image, Reebok holds a more feminine positioning and is also well established within the North American markets and major North American sports such as basketball and baseball. The same extension strategy was planned by Amer Sports with Salomon. This acquisition created a better complementarity in terms of market share with the other skiing and outdoor brands of the groups such as Dynamic, Atomic and Volant. Specifically, Salomon is more well known and better positioned in South European markets although Atomic is well established in German-speaking countries. This complementarity allowed a better geographical netting of the European markets as well as creating economies of scale between the Romanian and Spanish factories of Salomon and the Austrian factories of Atomic. Table 5.1 presents the main sport brand portfolios.[2] The brands' lists are not exhaustive and focus on sport brands. For instance, many non-sport brands have been omitted such as Lee Jeans, Wrangler, Eagle Creek or Eastpak for VF Corporation.

Similarly to what happens in other industries and sectors (for example food, cars, IT), corporations and groups from the sport sectors adopt two kinds of strategy in terms of brand portfolio management: either their growth is focused on a single brand or various brands. Single brand growth strategies characterise corporations which own a single brand on a single market such as the sunglasses brand Cebe sport sunglasses and the retail brands Foot Locker and Decathlon. According to this strategy, the products, services and retail stores either use the same brand or parts of the brand name such as Decat and Trocathlon for Decathlon. The strength of the single brand growth strategy is to invest and gather all resources, energies, innovations, and exposure around the same name (Kapferer, 2006). Marketing, publicity and communication costs can then be significantly reduced. It is usually adopted by companies which use the brand as a guarantee, therefore all the products and brands can benefit from that reputation and the brand's awareness levels. This strategy was historically widely used by brands which represented the name of the firm and/or brand's founder. That was for example the case for François Salomon who launched in the fifties wooden ski lines because he was a cabinetmaker. In this specific case, the rationale is justified by showcasing a specific skill. For sport athletes, it can be expertise but also performances as well. For instance the French skiing champion Jean-Claude Killy launched his clothing line thanks to his victories in the 1968 Grenoble Olympic Games. In this case, the sporting excellence is used to provide legitimacy for the brand. There are plenty of examples of sporting champions who launched their own brand using their name such as the Swedish tennis champion Björn Borg (clothing, swimwear, shoes, bags and accessories), the German handball legend Bernhard Kempa (handball shoes, clothing and equipment), the American windsurfer Robby Naish (kite-surfing, windsurfing and windsurfing gear), or more recently the Chinese gymnastic champion Li Ning (sportswear and sports equipment).

The multi-brand growth strategy, however, characterises corporations which exploit various brands to cover a single or several markets. For an international or multinational group, this strategy allows each of its components to put forward its competitive advantages for specific sectors and segments. This strategy aims for brands that will fit as well as possible to markets' characteristics and consumers' expectations via different positioning. This corresponds to a differentiation orientation strategy with each brand being independent, or almost independent. Quiksilver Inc, Jarden Corporation and Amer Sports follow this economic model which is generally speaking a relevant strategy within sectors that have reached a maturity stage such as those of ski, surf, outdoor or bike. It also embraces covering very different segments from the same sector either in terms of positioning or distribution channels. A firm which adopts this growth strategy can lead various development strategies corresponding to the characteristics of each brand, which cannot be done with single brand growth strategies. This strategy is not without its downside and the main one concerns the risk of cannibalisation if brands of the same group are not differentiated enough and target identical or overlapping consumer segments. Another negative lies in the fact that marketing and publicity investments have to be supported individually for each brand. Differentiated distribution channels and networks for each category of products also encourage corporations to adopt this strategy. For instance the premium and specialised niche segments (for example snowboards, skateboards, surfboards) can hardly function with discount sport shoes and clothing segments. Technical products such as for sailing cannot really be presented and sold in the same selling points as football and running shoes and equipment. These products and brands do not hold the same identities, development factors and consumers. For each distribution channel, consumers have their own purchase habits and brands universe which imposes an important segmentation and therefore demands a multi-brand strategy. In this regard, the growth of sport equipment dedicated to females is a good illustration. Because females have different needs and expectations, it becomes difficult for a single brand to satisfy both gender groups through a single identity, discourse and set of promises. It is for this reason that Quiksilver created Roxy, a brand dedicated to females within the surfwear, skiwear and lifestyle sectors. The brands Lacoste by women, Lady Foot Locker and Nike women were created for the same purpose.

The choice between single brand and multi-brand growth strategies strongly depends on the firm's level of netting or covering of its markets. While Shimano, Oakley and Arena, which are present on a single market segment, have adopted a single brand strategy, other brands such as Adidas, Rossignol, Salomon, Nike and Lafuma are present on several marketing segments and have adopted a multi-brand strategy. Sporting event and league brands adopt single brand strategies as their reputation is essentially based on their name even if they target different segments whereas groups such as Quiksilver Inc, Amer Sports and VF Corporation target multiple segments with various brands. Multi-brand strategies have strongly benefited international groups in a globalised context and reinforced their dominant positions within the most profitable markets, but it seems that the trend has been reversed within several sectors. Since the nineties, maturation, structuration and concentration in the main markets have forced companies to reduce their portfolios of brands to focus on the most profitable brands and the ones with the biggest potential.

Covering the whole market: the Amer Sports' strategy

Similarly to VF Corporation which now owns about ten brands specialised in the outdoor sector (including Jansport, The North Face, Napapijri, Nautica, Kipling, Reef), the Finnish group Amer Sports owned at first only one sport brand. The original field of expertise of the group was the fabrication of cigarettes under licence for Philip Morris (Amer is the short name of American Tobacco). At the end of the nineties, the group partners decided to radically change their strategy because of the competition of South Asian countries whose reduced prices threatened the group's margins. The group therefore opted for markets with high growth and then the change happened very quickly. In 1989, the group acquired Wilson, the American giant for US$200 million. Then followed the acquisition of Atomic (skis), Suunto (sport watches) and Percor (fitness equipment). The integration of Salomon, including Kema (ski poles), Marker and Look (ski bindings), and Mavic (bicycle equipment) completed the group's sport brand portfolio.

All the later acquisitions covered sectors and markets where the group was not well established: snowboarding with Bonfire, skateboarding with Cliché, mountain biking with Mavic, and high-end clothes with Arc'Teryx. The main objective of the group in acquiring these new brands was to obtain ten per cent of profitability for each of them.[3] To reach this objective, radical decisions were made: when the group acquired Wilson which was in deficit, 85 employees from the 500 working for the brand were made redundant. The golf division was the principal target for changes and its commercial strategy which focused on professional players with high-end and technical products was significantly reoriented. This strategic reorientation appeared successful because three years later the brand represented EUR 13 million of profits although it lost €2 million when acquired. A year later, the tennis division received the same treatment. However, because of the increasing competition from South Asian countries, Wilson had to reduce its production costs. Amer Sports then relocated the production in Thailand and Indonesia in parallel with the closing of its factory located in South Carolina (USA). Atomic then followed. Acquired for US$84 million in 1994, ski sales were stagnating worldwide and the brand was close to bankruptcy. The number of employees from the Austrian production site of Altenmarkt was then reduced by half. The financial results then became positive again, with a market share growing from 13 to 20 per cent from 1998 to 2002.

Thanks to an audacious shift of strategy which focused on the acquisition of sport brands well established in their markets and sectors and with a good reputation, Amer Sports became in a few years one of the main corporations in this industry. Nowadays, the group is now competing with global brands such as Adidas and Nike within the sporting goods industry, these two giants being world leaders in terms of footwear and sportswear but not in terms of sporting goods. However, even if Amer Sports claims to be number one for sporting goods, its turnover is about five times less than Nike's turnover.

Single versus multi-brand strategy: the case of Oxylane Group

Contrary to Amer Sports which follows a multi-brand strategy and Nike which mainly follows a single brand strategy, Oxylane Group follows a strategy combining both single and multi-brand strategies. This choice relies on the creation and the development of its own brands named Passion brands to cover the different sport and leisure sectors (running, hiking, skiing, board sports, fishing, and equestrian sports). While covering various niche markets through these specialised and generalist sport brands, Oxylane Group also has its own retail brand Decathlon which is developed following a single brand strategy as its identity is kept for all the different forms of distribution.

This mixed strategy is, however, a recent one. For about twenty years, the group conducted a single brand strategy to cover the whole market and its different sectors. This had an unexpected outcome: the brand was perceived as 'soviet' to use the term of Kapferer (2006). By 'soviet', this author meant that because everyone was wearing or having Decathlon's products, the brand became synonymous with uniformity. The group then decided to modify its growth strategy and created its own brands corresponding to different sport sectors. For instance the brand Tribord covers the whole water sports sector and presents an image attracting an undifferentiated public. Nevertheless, this broad positioning does not hinder the brand from offering technical products which satisfy demanding consumers and even competitors. As Tribord is one of many brands it clearly corresponds to a multiple brand strategy. However, because this brand covers many different sub-sectors within the water sports sector (for example diving, swimming, body boarding, surfing, and windsurfing), promoting the same message and promise, it can be seen as a single brand strategy within the multi-brand strategy. This appears to also be the case for foreign markets as Tribord and other brands of the group (for example Quechua, b'Twin, Wed'ze) seem to be managed autonomously. From this perspective, it is possible to find Decathlon's own brands in independent stores and competing with retail brands such as Intersport.

Until now, Oxylane Group has always led with a growth model focusing on the creation of its own brands. However, in July 2008, the group acquired Simond, a brand specialising in mountaineering and climbing equipment. This acquisition represented the first step towards external growth orientation. In the future, it is probable that the expansion of Oxylane Group mimics those of Amer Sports and Jarden Corporation which are based on building sport brands portfolios. Oxylane Group's portfolio would then comprise its Passion brands and its new brand acquisitions which would likely focus on specialist brands known for their expertise, history and tradition, to complete its segment netting. This strategy should allow the group to get new technological skills (for example Simond is well known for individual protection equipment) as well as extending its international scope, benefiting from the existing brands' distribution channels.

Sport brands innovation

With their market penetration and growth strategies, sport brands must face the difficult challenge to innovate to remain competitive. For them, the first challenge is to express in words and narratives their innovations and the new products and services they launch while the second one is to sustainably position them into markets (Semprini, 1992 and 2005). However, within markets characterised by numerous innovations and new products (for example skiing and footwear sectors), consumers do not only become more demanding but also more sceptical. Too much innovation kills innovation because new products cannot be noticed any more. Moreover, brands can create their own loss by creating unrealistic consumer expectations. They should therefore be careful about the gap they create between what they currently do and what they plan to do. If sport brands have very often managed to impose their innovations, which were sometimes very significant and groundbreaking, they have also created addictions towards them. With them, they indeed increase their attraction and seduction power but they also create the limits for their own development because they may not be able to follow the pace of technological progress, which represents a major risk.

Innovation in the marketing relationship

Innovation is a strong feature of sports brands and thanks to it they can imprint their mark in consumers' minds and lives. Innovation, reputation and brands are inseparable. Brands offer the possibility for new products and services to be easily accepted and sustainably remain in consumers' memories. Innovation always constitutes a consumer focal point. It also creates fascination and desire. In creating surprises, emotions, and sometimes clutter and transgression, which can be more risky, innovations set up a privileged relationship with brands' consumers. Therefore, innovation increases brands' image and consumer loyalty, making brands' efforts and investments profitable on a long-term perspective. With an efficient and well mastered communication strategy, sport brands are able to maintain a permanent curiosity state among consumers. Finally, innovation represents a relevant way to increase media exposure, word-of-mouth and create buzz.

Innovation is overall well perceived by consumers who always look for differentiating values. A brand known for innovating holds then a true asset as consumers implicitly establish a hierarchy of brands with regard to their capacity to regularly offer new products. According to branding experts, innovation seems to be the third most important criterion behind price and proximity. However, innovation is not equally perceived among consumers. For instance, due to its history and traditions, Adidas seems to be more associated with innovation than for instance Nike, which seems more associated to fashion. Adidas has always sought to maintain a competitive advantage over Nike through its constant innovation policy. The German brand has never stopped developing advanced products such as the 'Adidas 1' shoe model and in exploring new concepts such as the Adidas Sport Cafés. This concept of café-restaurant (a kind of sophisticated sports bar) was developed in partnership with Kronenbourg, a French beer brand, and relied on the provision of live TV sporting events and sport magazines and journals.

Without innovation brands take the risk of aging prematurely and having their consumers detaching themselves from them. In the sport sectors, the pace of innovation is important because most products and services are not consumed in a long-term frame and their consumption is highly influenced by fashion and trends. It is not rare to observe the lifetime of a sport brand product not exceeding a few months. Consequently, we can easily understand why sport brands increasingly offer vintage or restyled products to overcome this issue. These tactics aim to make consumers' memories resurface from positive and significant moments of their lives associated to specific products such as the Reef and Stan Smith shoes for example. It often appears to be a winning strategy because postmodern consumers seem to increasingly search for authenticity and express nostalgic feelings (Bodet, 2009), in particular towards disappeared brands. This is particularly the case for sport club brands because of the strength of attachment and bonds consumers had with them. This is illustrated for instance with the case of Quebec Nordiques, the professional ice-hockey franchise of the city of Quebec (Canada), which was relocated to Colorado in 1995 and became Colorado Avalanche, and for which it is still possible to buy merchandised products in Quebec city.

Nevertheless, contrary to 'originals' or 'lifestyle' product lines, vintage, restyling and replica tactics do not allow markets' renewal. No sport brand became a vintage and re-edition specialist by commercialising only one single line of products. This should not be confused with the re-launching of brands such as Puma and Converse thanks to the re-edition of successful and cult models, Speedcat and All Star respectively. In the year 2000, Converse was almost forced to reedit its famous models because the brand was in a bankruptcy situation. It was in observing the behaviours and the trends initiated by young consumers in Asia who were wearing its old models that the brand decided to launch its first vintage collection. Puma's comeback among the most successful and profitable brands has followed the same path. Since 1994, the brand has re-established its status spectacularly: close to bankruptcy the brand then showed massive growth rates for its sales, more than 30 per cent in 2001 and more than 53 per cent in 2002.

Improving productivity through innovation

For sport brands, innovation has also a negative impact on the number of lines developed and on economies of scale. Fewer operational economies are possible and so profitability becomes more difficult to achieve. This is why almost all firms have relocated their production sites in South-East Asia. As a comparison, in 2006, a worker in the USA was paid about US$14 per hour whereas a worker in China was paid about US$0.4 per hour. In order to increase its productivity and stop its decline, the tennis brand Wilson, as we saw in section 'Covering the whole market: the Amer Sports' strategy', page 109 dealing with Amer Sports' strategy, relocated its production to Thailand and Indonesia and closed its factory in the USA provoking 300 redundancies. If each Amer Sports' brand has its own research and development team, the fact they belong to the same group allows the creation of production synergies in terms of engineering and research on one hand, and marketing and communication on the other hand. From these strategic collaborations several innovations have been developed: carbon rackets, hybrid golf clubs, composites and aluminium made baseball bats, tennis shoes with improved bounce-back, extra traction and enhanced lateral support, etc. Wilson's researchers have started to use hyper carbon to create lighter and more resistant rackets and then suggested to Atomic to use this material for its skis, and this was a true success. Atomic is also indebted to Suunto, another brand from Amer Sports, for the technology they used to make intelligent bindings with pieces communicating to each other via radio frequencies. Suunto initially developed this technology for its watches. Acquired by Amer Sports in 1999, Suunto constituted a real bet for the future. Sporting metrology (the science of measurement) and instruments are indeed a fast-growing sector with high potential profit margins. Suunto's watches are a true concentrate of innovation and design which provide runners with information about their heartbeat and training tools, hikers with Global Positioning System (GPS) location, altimeter, barometer and compass functions, golfers with efficiency information about their swing, and divers with dive characteristics, etc.

With the markets' dominant trends such as subsidising and relocating production units in countries with cheap labour cost, few sport brands have chosen to take the opposite direction and invest in different productivity and economic models. Contrary to its main competitors, New Balance has for instance never followed these trends without altering its competitiveness. The brand is proud to be the only company that still manufactures athletic shoes in the USA and this is expressed via their shoe label 'Made in USA' indicating at least 70 per cent of domestic value.[4] New Balance shoes therefore hold a positive reputation and are perceived to be of quality without being necessarily more expensive than the main competitors such as Nike, Reebok and Asics, whose products are all made outside the USA. What is thus the secret of New Balance? One response to this question relies on the brand's capacity to quickly react and adjust to the variations in terms of fashion and market trends in constantly offering innovating products. Associating local production and innovation orientation seems to be a successful strategic mix, as the brand is perceived as young and dynamic, and seems to contradict all current productivity models. Its success seems to stem from a constant creativity in terms of design in addition to a constant search for improving the production process. New Balance is indeed always on the lookout for technological advances to achieve productivity gains and to improve its production machines, which strongly rely on the integration of advanced computer-aided manufacturing processes and knowledge. The brand's other secret concerns a crucial type of company resource: human resources. Again, contrary to the models of production based on relocations in cheap-labour cost countries, employees' professional development and training seem to constitute a key to its strategic orientation. The main consequence of such a focus is that the brand's employees become more versatile and competent, making them more efficient. The manufacturing management is also important and relies on small teams of five or six employees which make them more dynamic and flexible. Finally, although it requires three hours of work to manufacture one pair of shoes in Guangdong (China), this manufacturing organisation reduces the production process to 24 minutes in the factory of Norridgewock (Maine, USA), which creates a production cost of $4 for one pair of shoes; a massive reduction in comparison with the previous cost of $24 (Bontour and Lehu, 2004). Of course, the cost is still higher than the Chinese factory's unit cost of $1.40 but the difference is not so big when considering the final selling price, logistic and transport costs and constraints as well as speed of supply.

Groundbreaking technological innovations

The list of sport brands which have initiated groundbreaking innovations is very long because the sectors concerned are very often micro niches and markets. This, however, does not make these innovations either less relevant nor their success less deserved. Most of the time, these radical innovations create new markets in bringing new solutions to problems and situations faced by consumers. Once established within a market, innovations help brands to maintain a distance with their main competitors. With its revolutionary LZR Racer suit, Speedo created for itself (for a while) a clear, dominant position within the market and kept away other competitors such as Adidas and Arena. These groundbreaking innovations represent then an important trigger for brands to reach high levels of awareness and positive images. As noted by Lewi and Rogliano (2006), a new brand becomes legitimate thanks to the creation of a new market or new segment targeted, or via a brutal arrival and penetration of the market, creating a rupture in the existing structure. This is what the brand Geox has tried to do within the footwear industry with its new 'Geox breathes' patented system which favours feet perspiration to respond to sport participants' important feet sweating. This concept relies on micro-holes in the rubber outsole allowing feet perspiration and a breathable membrane absorbing sweat while keeping water out. This innovation required several years of research and development. Until then, innovation in terms of sport shoes was essentially focused on the performance issue, whereas now the brand wants to emphasise on the comfort issue thanks to its patented system. Radical innovations are also strategically interesting. When Quechua launched its '2S' instant tent ('2S' because it takes two seconds to set it), the objective was twofold (see Figure 5.1).

FIGURE 5.1   Quechua's 2S tent

On one hand, the brand aimed to fix an image deficit within the French market and in particularly towards young consumers in showing a dynamic and innovating image. On the other hand, it aimed to penetrate the North American market from which the brand had been absent so far in creating a point of attraction and arousing an immediate curiosity for the product. With a new line of tents and the

'2S' model as flagship associated to a large scale promotional campaign, the brand's intention was to create a buzz and they succeeded in their enterprise. Finally, radical innovations are recognisable because they change markets' rules and structure in fixing new landmarks and references. Its consequence is to influence the strategies of all the markets' actors including competitors. It is therefore easy to understand why sport brands seek to develop and launch innovations quite frequently, because they can shape markets' dynamics in their favour. The fierce competition between sport shoe brands (for example Nike, Adidas, Asics, Reebok, and Puma) is a good illustration of this aim. With a worldwide turnover of US$14.15 billion in 2006, the stakes are gigantic and within this context it appears clear that if a brand benefiting from a strong innovation reputation does not launch enough new concepts and products compared to its main competitors, this reputation will not last and it will lose its credibility. In turn, this will make it lose its forefront position and prematurely age. However, it can be noted that in some aspects sport markets and organisations can be quite reluctant to change and therefore adopt innovations. The long-awaited introduction of video technology in football is an example of this. Consequently, in many cases, innovations will have to face a change of mentality which is not easy to do. Marketing will then be an essential ally in this enterprise.

If sport brands are strongly involved in innovation processes, they are not the only ones, and innovations can also come within the field from non-sport companies and brands. As illustrated with the Geox example, some brands can positively and significantly influence sport practices in terms of comfort and nutrition for instance. For instance, in France the mineral water brand Vittel launched in 1998 75 cl bottles with a 'sport cap' to allow sport participants to drink while moving and running. This system, which already existed on cyclists' water bottles, was at the origin of the success of the product which was quickly adopted by young sporting consumers. For the Perrier-Vittel company which had bought the commercial rights to an American firm this represented both a marketing innovation responding to sport participants' and consumers' demands and nomadic lifestyle and a technological innovation increasing the water flow-out while reducing losses.

Ethical and responsible sport brands' practices

Social responsibility, ethical and citizen behaviours as well as sustainable practices are nowadays tightly associated with brands and sport brands' development and growth. Social responsibility should be understood as the contribution of companies to sustainable development which includes the voluntary integration of social and environmental concerns in their business operations and in their interactions with their stakeholders who can be consumers, suppliers, shareholders, employees, public organisations, non-governmental organisations and charities or professional unions and associations (Commission of the European Communities, 2001). Two features characterise a social and responsible corporation: growth which is both socially fair and sustainable (Combes, 2005). However, brands play an ethical role which goes beyond their economic, social and professional purposes. If it is now largely recognised that Corporate Social Responsibility (CSR) comprises several dimensions, it seems that three main ones can be identified and concern the relationships between CSR schemes and three particular stakeholders who are society at large, employees and suppliers (Turker, 2008). Such as their non-sport counterparts, sport brands realised the importance of corporate social responsibility as soon as their behaviours and practices were criticised by media, public and civil actors. Brands such as Nike, Adidas and Reebok have been probably the ones who received the most criticism for their inappropriate behaviours in terms of ethics regarding the working conditions and pay of sweatshop employees in South-East Asia, as illustrated by the international bestseller *No logo* written by Naomi Klein. Despite the acknowledgement of this CSR role by almost all sport brands, it does not prevent unethical practices. The recent scandal about the Adidas Great Britain kit designed for the 2012 London Olympics which was manufactured in abusive Indonesian sweatshops shows that there is still a gap between awareness, discourses and practices.

Environmental considerations, such as the reduction of polluting waste, recycling, carbon footprint, energy savings, and employees' working conditions have indeed become topical subjects but economic considerations, globalisation, consumer expectations and competitors' behaviours are probably more powerful triggers to translate them into practice. For instance, the cost of investment and revision of production and manufacturing processes can very quickly discourage companies with the best intentions. Therefore, behind strong statements and discourses, companies and organisations' efforts are sometimes minimal and then results disappointing. This is particularly the case as consumers' and societies' expectations in terms of change are often high and/or disconnected from the brands' reality.

Sport brands' commitment in sustainable development

Arguably, consumers but also employees and suppliers are increasingly sensitive to brands' ethical commitments and practices. This is expressed for instance through growing demands in terms of safety, transparency, information and image. At a time when environment preservation and human respect are more than ever praised by consumers, they become more and more interested in the behaviour of their favourite brands regarding these issues and other related ones such as fair trade. Citizenship, ethics, social responsibility, environment preservation are therefore parts of brands' commitments towards their consumers in the same way they are committed to them in terms of delivering their commercial promises and maintaining their values. These factors contribute to brands' valorisation but also take part in their communication and promotional messages. After having made sure their first commitments in terms of price and quality and immediate responsibility in terms of performance and trust were fulfilled, companies and organisations have to make a gift, an additional gesture in supporting external charitable and sustainable actions and activities which are in line with the companies' values as well as visible and appreciated by the companies' or organisations' targets. Each time a brand is involved in these kinds of schemes and initiatives, it will see its awareness increased and its reputation enhanced. For this reason, these activities and programmes hold a strategic dimension and significantly influence brands' perceived equity.

Consequently, it seems predictable that sport brands will become more and more active in terms of sustainable development, particularly if they are positioned in the sector of outdoor products and equipment. Various brands have already launched concrete initiatives although a few others have placed environmental issues at the core of their economic and management models, which often require the partnership of non-governmental organisations and the creation and/or use of labels. In terms of sustainable development the American brand Patagonia certainly appears as a pioneer in terms of eco-consciousness via waste reduction and recycling. From the start, Patagonia has produced clothes with fleece made of recycled plastic soda bottles and is even now able to produce textiles that are 100 per cent recyclable. The brand also set its own programme, the 'Common Threads Recycling Program', aiming to make every item it sells recyclable and also recycled. The programme encourages consumers to bring back any Patagonia clothing items with the 'Common Threads' label which is then sent to recycling and manufacturing units which produce new clothing with them. Since 1985, the company has also committed itself to give one per cent of sales to the restoration and preservation of the natural environment (through its scheme 'One Percent for The Planet'). It has therefore awarded over US$46 million in cash and in-kind donations to domestic and international grassroots environmental groups.[5] In 1993, the company also launched a programme targeting its own employees named 'Patagonia Employee Internship Program'. Thanks to this programme employees can leave their job for up to one month to work for an environmental group while keeping their salary and benefits. This scheme, which was undertaken by about 50 employees in 2010, has now benefited about 850 employees in total.[6] Showing a strong activism, the company runs various environmental initiatives as broad as the protection of trout fish via the funding of protection groups, the creation of a national park in Chilean Patagonia, the creation of The Conservation Alliance which gathers other companies and brands to give money to environmental organisations, and the achievement of green labels for some of its buildings.

Fair trade was probably one of the earliest organised ethical initiatives which raised the awareness of sustainable development issues among the general public. After obtaining its reputation via the certification of food products (for example coffee, chocolate, tea, rice, sugar, banana, juice), Max Havelaar has been the first international label to offer fair trade certifications to other product ranges. For instance, it certified the Dagris group whose cotton products were supplied to many sportswear companies and brands. Among these sport brands, Eider proposed three T-shirts made of fair trade cotton for the 2005 Summer collection of its Gravical line dedicated to climbing. The snowboarding, skateboarding and surfing brand Picture Organic Clothing is another example as its products only use organic cotton certified by well-known quality labels (for example Global Organic Textile Standard – GOTS, EKO Sustainable Textile Standard) and come from factories which are all ethically certified (Flo Cert and GOTS labels). Nike has started to use a mix of conventional and organic cotton for the production of some of its T-shirts and Max Havelaar has started to certify sporting goods such as the football balls sold by the Swiss sport retail brand SportXX.

Perhaps more exposed than others as the cases of Nike and Adidas show, sport corporate brands are fully conscious and aware of social responsibility and sustainable development issues. Nike has for instance launched the 'ReUSE-A-SHOE' programme which collects old trainers as well as Lance Armstrong Foundation LIVESTRONG wristbands, and recycles them in 'Nike Grind', a raw material used to make new Nike products but also courts, running tracks, playgrounds and synthetic turf infill. In this example, it can be seen that sport brands can be as active as other brands and actors in sustainable development initiatives, but they also rely on their consumers who have to behave responsibly in bringing their old trainers to drop-off locations. In the same vein, in 2008, Nike created the 'Nike Trash Talk' shoe, a performance basketball sneaker, only made of manufacturing waste. So sport brands are expected to have and show their commitments to social and environmental issues. They have to develop a 'clean' or 'green' image if they still want to be loved and purchased by their consumers. However, it seems to be also a necessity if they do not want to be exposed in the media, local communities and society at large. Sporting event, club and league brands are also involved in community development schemes and according to Walker and Kent (2009), team corporate social responsibility mainly includes initiatives such as athlete volunteerism, educational initiatives, philanthropic/charitable donations, community development, community initiatives, fan appreciation, health related initiatives, and community-based environmental programmes. All these CSR can be categorised in four main types which are: 1. philanthropy, 2. community involvement, 3. youth educational initiatives, and 4. youth health initiatives (Walker and Kent, 2009). As an example, the Leicester Tigers rugby union club conducts several community programmes. Their programme 'Inside Sport' offers opportunities to schools and college groups to take part in education days comprising theoretical seminars about sport nutrition, injuries or psychology and practical workshops about fitness and rugby skills. They also conduct programmes aiming to improve children's numeracy (MBNA Tackling Numbers), to promote healthy lifestyles (Healthy Schools Programme, Playing 4 Health, Mend), to improve social inclusion for young people in need (Dynamite Programmes) and promote citizenship (as a partner of the National Citizen Service).

Sport brands' social and environmental initiatives

Because they are, or their consumers are, in direct contact with natural environments (for example rivers, seas, mountains) more and more sport brands consider the preservation of the environment as one of their priorities as well as a marketing and competitive argument. Through its program 'Rip Curl Planet', the

Australian surfwear brand for example encourages the use of natural ingredients in its textiles. For each T-shirt with the World Wild Fund for Nature (WWF) panda logo sold, three euros are given to the WWF to protect coral reefs in the South Pacific and Indian Oceans. For Rip Curl, the environmental cause is also a means to reach young and committed consumers. Similarly, because it uses natural fabrics (organic cotton, merino wool, and recycled cotton) for its T-shirt, the British brand Howies also aims to have ethical practices and its products even display environmental and political slogans (for example 'love bikes', 'work hard ride home', 'big brand defector'). In the same vein, the Swiss brand Switcher, which supplies kits for the Swiss Olympic team, has developed a range of sportswear items which are both organic and ethical, holding the Max Havelaar label. The whole production chain is concerned as air transport is not used as it is considered to use too much energy and the label has even implemented a monitoring system named 'Respect Inside' to trace the origins of its products. The French surfwear brand Kanabeach offers a full range of eco-designed products named Biologik using natural fabrics and the Spanish brand El Naturalista has set a fully responsible chain which goes from the first steps of the production process to the support of Peruvian non-governmental organisations. Quiksilver launched the 'Quiksilver Initiative', which is an internal unit within the company whose goal is seeking for areas needing improvements to be compliant with environment protection. Through this specific initiative associations and environmental groups are also supported and funded. Since 2000, Quiksilver has invested several hundred thousand euros to support coast protection initiatives. The brand also chartered a ship to travel to various surfing spots on the planet with surfers and scientists to study ocean bottoms and reefs. Like Quiksilver, other surfwear brands are committed to the protection of coasts and reefs and many of them display their support to the Surfrider Foundation. According to Rouvrais-Charron and Durand (2004), surfwear brands distinguish themselves from other sport brands in regards to their action towards the protection of the environment because the link between outdoor and environmentalism is obvious enough to be associated with these values. These sector's brands have indeed clearly acknowledged that this strategy corresponded to a win–win–win–win strategy, which means that it is beneficial for the company and the brand, beneficial for consumers, beneficial for activist groups and beneficial for the planet.

Far before ethical fashion, in 2003, Timberland created a monitoring system to measure the impact of each of its products on the environment. A few years later, it created the 'Green Index' visible on their shoe box and which provides an indication of the product's footprint. This index comprises three main impact categories: climate impact, chemicals used and resource consumption including the weight of organic and renewable materials. With more than 50 eco-designed products, Timberland has the ambition to become the first outdoor brand in terms of sustainable development contribution. Moutain Equipment Co-op (MEC) which is a consumers' cooperative and Canada's largest supplier of outdoor equipment has from its origin tried to reduce its environmental footprint in commercialising only products responding to high environmental norms and standards. MEC does not consider sustainable development and social responsibility as constraints but as interesting opportunities. In 2006, the cooperative was even ranked number one by the Report on Business magazine in terms of corporate social responsibility in Canada. This is for instance expressed in the fact that sporting goods which have a negative footprint such as those associated with alpine skiing are not sold because of the pollution produced by ski lifts and snow grooming machines and the excessive water use of snow cannons. A member of the Fair Labour Association to improve the working conditions of its employees, the cooperative did not hesitate to cease collaborating with two of its Asian suppliers which did not follow their standards. Like Patagonia, MEC donates one per cent of its revenues each year to environmental causes. Also at the forefront of these issues can be found the New Zealand brand Icebreaker which commercialises outdoor clothing, baselayer long underwear and socks. Deeply involved in the protection of the merino breed of sheep, ethics seem to be everywhere: in the way they treat animals, in the way they treat lands, in their production and supply chains. Icebreaker have set a range of ethical manufacturing standards their contractors have to follow: their fabrics are certified to Oeko-Tex standards which is an independent certification system; their textile and garment manufacturers are all accredited to ISO 14001: 2004; their sheep stations are accredited 'Zque' which is an ethical wool program; and they are also member of The Conservation Alliance. The brand has also implemented a tracing system named 'BAACODE' allowing consumers to see the living conditions of the sheep which provided the wool for their products, to meet the farmers and to follow every step of the supply chain. More than just marketing and communication strategies, many sport brands, and in particularly small ones, have integrated sustainable development and eco-design in their brand DNA, for example Picture Organic Clothing (France), Howies (United Kingdom), and Sebola (Spain).

These orientations and strategies seem nowadays favoured by regulations and norms such as managerial and environmental norms encouraging companies to do more in terms of sustainable development. They rely on three main principles which are:

1. respect of environmental rules and legislation;
2. pollution prevention;
3. enhancement of environmental impact studies.

In order to fix the paradox of a consumer society where outdoor activities and sport enthusiasts create environmental pollutions, winter sport good manufacturers increasingly seek to behave more responsibility and to make their consumers aware of this via the certification ISO 14001 about eco-design. This is for instance the case of the sector's world leader, Rossignol whose main French production site has been certified since 2003. The brands' managers are now working on the issues of waste, liquids (for example gluing process liquid wastes and cleaning water) and air rejections which are either treated and cleaned on site, or sent to certified recycling units. The company wants to go further in using industrial methods relying on high-technology processes. Rossignol's main competitor Salomon is also involved in such processes in close partnership with the French Agency for the Environment and Energy Management (ADEME) for its main French production site. Among its main objectives are the total reduction of use of polyvinyl chloride and the reduction of energy consumption, and electricity in particular. However, even if norms and regulations are increasingly considering these environmental issues, the voluntary and non-constrained dimension of these initiatives is essential to consider them as corporate social responsibility initiatives according to McWilliams and Siegel's (2000) definition.

Lafuma's environment preservation initiatives

A pioneer in Europe in terms of environment protection is certainly the French group Lafuma with its three main brands Lafuma, Millet and Le Chameau. Thanks to an eco-design approach, which aims to design products respecting the environment, the group adopted, in the middle of the nineties, an environmental friendly policy for its products. For each product, the policy consists of assessing the environmental impact of its manufacturing, transport, packaging, usage and destruction according to a set of specific criteria. The goal of the brand is to offer a full range of footwear, clothing and equipment (for example sleeping bags, tents, backpacks) which are eco-produced.

Beyond its intrinsic and usage values, an eco-designed product has to be desired without being perceived as a sacrifice by consumers. It has to be associated with an act of citizenship and responsibility. From this ambitious aspiration were born the 'Eco 40' backpack made of hemp and recycled polyester, the 'Fidji Eco' table made of wood waste, the entirely recyclable 'Sablier' seat, the 'Sherpa' T-shirt made of organic cotton, and the 'Djebel Hemp', 'Kankor' and 'Khumo' shoes. For Lafuma, this commitment appears logical because the brand is associated with nature in consumers' minds. Fishing, horse riding, hiking, camping or surfing all represent product areas where environmental protection naturally fits. The brand logo reinforces this dimension as it represents a poplar leaf. The creation of the 'Pure Leaf Project', a sustainable development label specific to Lafuma, responds to the same objective. This label constitutes an internal charter which sets the company's objectives and standards that must be strictly followed and which should benefit the brand, consumers and stakeholders. It gathers all the brand's commitments which summarise Lafuma's social responsibility and represents a promise made by the brand to its consumers which almost defines their relationship. Within this overall orientation, Millet, one of Lafuma's brands, initiated a large scale programme of climbing ropes recycling which consists, as for Nike's 'ReUSE-A-SHOE' programme, of collecting old ropes, even from competitors, and then transforming them, with the help of Rhodia Company, into raw material used in the car industry or to make various plastic accessories. It is for example possible to read 'I was a rope' on the clothing hangers in Millet's specialised retail stores.

For Lafuma, this orientation relies as much on philosophical considerations as strategic and economic. It is philosophical because the group aspires to move towards responsible production and consumption modes. It is strategic because the brand aims to get benefits from this commitment in displaying an environmentally conscious brand image. Without being patronising and moralising, the brand wants to send a strong signal to its consumers by applying, on a voluntary basis, conception norms and constraints which may be those of tomorrow. Last, it is economic because Lafuma aims to create a strong differentiating feature with its main competitors by setting very high standards which might be difficult to reach by others, at least rapidly. Partner of the WWF since 1999, the Lafuma group has been driven by the conviction that it is possible to produce differently to 'offer more with less': more versatility, more resistance, more technicalities, and more ergonomics with less material, less energy, less waste and finally less cost and less impact on the environment. To fulfil this goal, the group has invented a consistent framework around its commitment expressed at a conception and design level, at a promotional and operational level with the support of nature protection initiatives and at an industrial level with the evolution of its production and logistics processes. At the production level, the group aims to significantly reduce its energy consumption and its eight production units based in France, Morocco, Tunisia, Hungary and China are closely monitored in terms of water and energy consumption as well as waste production. Using the same idea, all the products sent to North America are water-transported within France which reduces air pollution by the equivalent of 200 lorries per year, corresponding to a 17 per cent reduction of products' air pollution.[7]

Through the years, the sustainable development issue has become more and more important for the group and eco-design is taking a bigger part which is manifest through the group's global educational and pedagogical policy. For instance, it is done via clothing tags which explain with the contribution of the WWF how the group is better preserving and respecting the environment. Similar to Patagonia and its 'One Percent for The Planet program', Lafuma implements what it calls a 'promotion-sharing' programme aiming to give a percentage of the selling price of eco-designed products to non-governmental organisations whose goal is, for instance, to plant trees in areas damaged by storms and fires.

6

SPORT BRANDS' GROWTH STRATEGIES

Brand experts often analyse brand strategies based on their competitive positioning which consists of looking at the target markets as well as the space they occupy in the markets (for example leaders or followers, major or minor actors). This approach is interesting because according to brands' ambitions, objectives and means available to achieve them, brands' challenges and organisations, in terms of positioning and architecture, can be very different. Objectives in terms of growth, the focus on research and innovation and price policies also represent significant distinctive features and variables.

Brand positioning and strategy

Positioning-related strategies

Four types of strategies can therefore be identified, each of them implying different modes of governance and economic behaviours.

The leader strategy

This strategy concerns brands dominating their market and/or market segments in terms of sale volumes and/or turnover. Generally speaking, these leader brands have succeeded in initiating a new sector's directions and trends, in creating and exploiting a new niche market via for instance the launch of a new concept, or in doing both simultaneously. These brands play an 'animating' role within the markets. From a consumer perspective, these brands often show the highest levels of awareness and perceived quality. They also were able to create a gap with the other competitors and are able to anticipate future consumers' tastes and needs (Kapferer, 2006). In terms of sport product brands, Nike is probably the most iconic example. Gatorade in terms of sport drink brands and ESPN for sport media brands are other examples of leader brands. In terms of club brands and athlete brands, on-field successes and history are probably the main drivers for the market domination as illustrated by the New York Yankees, Manchester United, Real Madrid, Tiger Woods and Roger Federer.

The challenger strategy

This strategy characterises the will to take the dominant position from the leader brand. However, it does not necessarily mean that these challenger brands do not benefit as well from high level of awareness or perceived quality. In terms of awareness, they often show the same levels as leader brands, as with Adidas versus Nike or Salomon versus Skis Rossignol. The challenger brands have to demonstrate a constant dynamism, particularly in terms of innovation, and adopt differentiating pricing and product strategies. These brands are often slightly more specific in terms of target segments in comparison with leader brands which tend to be more generalist. Their strength is to know where they want to go and that they are able, such as in car racing or cycling, to follow the way of leader brands while continuing looking for their own directions. In terms of club and athlete brands, on-field successes are crucial but a distinctive style and charisma can help to close the sporting gap with leader brands.

The specialist strategy

This strategy relies on the targeting of niche markets and segments made of experts or frequent users and consumers. Without necessarily being the reference within its market, the specialist brand possesses a strong identity. This is generally the brand preferred by experts because it provides technical and advanced features such as Aigle (outdoor and sailing boots), Helly Hansen (sailing and kayaking clothes), Columbia (mountain and outdoor materials), Airwalk (skateboard), Hummel (handball), Canterbury (rugby), AND1 (basketball) and Panzeri (volleyball). Following its inclusion within the Adidas group, the re-positioning of Reebok on the fitness sectors can be seen as the adoption of a specialist brand strategy, corresponding to its origins as well. To legitimise their offers, these brands often put forward their experience, history and tradition. In terms of club and athlete brands this concept is less applicable because they primarily compete on the sporting fields. However, some cases such as the Athletic Bilbao FC in Spain can be assimilated to this type of strategy. The peculiarity of this football club is that it only has Basque (a region with parts in Spain and France) players in his team. From a sporting perspective, it limits the number of players they can recruit and limits then their sporting potential but it has a very strong identification with its fans that prefer having a less competitive team but representing the region and resisting the globalisation of football (Castillo, 2008).

The follower strategy

This strategy consists of not trying to compete with or mimic leader, challenger and specialist brands. The follower brands only try to follow the fluctuations of the markets' demand and to avoid the pitfalls set by the other competitors. Nevertheless, they know how to recycle and use the recipes and ideas of their competitors. Without a strong identity and a strong research and innovation appetite, these brands maintain aggressive pricing policies which often position them at the low-end range. Their products are basics and without an important differentiation and often illustrate mass marketing orientations. This strategy corresponds to many retailers' own sport brands.

Companies' main growth strategies

Alongside this classification relying on competitive positioning, sport brands can also be categorised based on the strategy they follow to conquer their markets. From this perspective, five main strategies can be identified, without being exclusive as brands can switch from one strategy to another based on tactical reasons, or over time.

The product brand strategy

The brand's offer relies on a single, star product whose name and properties will drive the company in its development and growth choices. This strategy consists of giving an exclusive and consistent name to a product with a unique positioning. The whole growth strategy then relies on a single name and promise. The company progressively disappears behind the brand to fully support the strategy. This type of strategy is for instance adopted by sport brands aiming to become international and global in a given sector (for example board sports, running shoes, outdoor sports) in valorising their know-how and skills. Typically this would be a strategy adopted by league and club brands.

The range brand strategy

For this strategy, consistent and complementary products or services are offered under the same brand and promise. The company commercialises several products within the same category or in different but very close categories. This type of strategy is often found with products with a short or very-short lifecycle such as skis and snowboards for instance. Numerous sportswear brands offering boots and clothes can be associated to this strategy, such as Umbro.

The umbrella brand strategy

With this strategy, companies commercialise many different and heterogeneous products, corresponding to different functions, utilities and promises. These offers often result from a diversification process from a core successful product which allowed then the brands to be extended. Sport brands such as Adidas, Lacoste, Oxbow, Roland Garros as well as numerous famous sporting event and club brands can be associated with this strategy. Licensing, which allows an organisation to purchase the right to use a brand, is often associated with this type of brand strategy and is very common in the context of sports merchandising.

The guarantee brand strategy

With this strategy, the brand provides a guarantee for the products in putting forward its name and reputation. For consumers, this represents a safe choice due to an implicit quality promise. This type of strategy is usually implemented by major brands. It can take the form of dual branding and co-branding. One example is provided by Decathlon, a major European sport brand retailer, which has created diverse offers using declensions of its name. For instance, its high street stores are named Decat (see Figure 6.1) and its concept of second-hand sport material sale and purchase is named Trocathlon. Sports Direct with SportDirect.com and Foot Locker with Lady Foot Locker and Kids Foot Locker are other examples.

FIGURE 6.1   The guarantee brand strategy of Decathlon with Decat

The global brand strategy

With this strategy, brands aim to cover the whole production chain from conception to commercialisation via production and distribution. In adopting this strategy, the objective is simultaneously to be present in different markets as well as increase the level of control of the value chain. Concretely, it can imply either a vertical upward or downward integration, or target and brand extensions. From many aspects, the Oxylane group is a good example of this strategy with its constituent brands (for example Equarea, Essensole, Novadry), its product brands (for example Artengo, b'Twin, Domyos, Kipsta, Quechua), its store and online retail brands (for example Decathlon, Koodza, Ataos), and its other activities such as Oxylane Research, Oxylane Village, Oxylane Foundation, Oxylane Art Foundation, Alsolia financing solutions and Ogea Sport insurance.

Differentiation orientations

Four main differentiating orientations allowing brands to be more competitive and successful can be identified. The first orientation is named 'differentiation through simplification' and consists of offering less complex and cheaper products and services than competitors. This orientation can be compared to low-cost or cost-cutting strategies. That was for example the strategy followed by BIC and its windsurfing boards. The second orientation is named 'differentiation through sophistication'. This orientation is the exact opposite of the previous one and consists of providing more complex and more technical offers, which are more expensive as well. This was for instance the strategy used by Salomon with its high-end skis. The third orientation is named 'differentiation through innovation'. This strategy consists of offering new products and services to consumers and is for instance the strategy adopted by Petzl, the world leader in its segment, with its range of climbing headlamps using LED technology. Thanks to this strategy, sport brands will look for setting new rules, standards and usage norms. The fourth orientation is named 'differentiation through specialisation' and consists of further segmenting products and services to target upper or lower segments, or completely new segments, tribes and subcultures (for example by using diversification, line extension).

Vertical integration strategies

Within the sport industries and the sport goods sector in particular, we can observe many collaborations and rapprochement between firms from the same domain which can take the form of integration processes (from upward to downward firms and conversely – either from the top of the supply chain with manufacturers down to the distributors at the bottom of it, or the opposite). Initiated in the nineties, there are two types of vertical integration. The first type categorises downward strategies where major and international sport good brands and their groups have sought to become specialised retailers as well. The second type categorises upward strategies and concern sport retail brands which have sought to become producers and manufacturers. These two within-sector strategies have significantly modified the structure of the concerned markets. Specifically, power balance, stakeholders' roles, leadership and interactions between market agents have particularly been modified. New collaboration and partnership relationships have been established and new actors and rules have appeared as well.

Intra-industry downward vertical integrations

In France, sport good distribution is largely dominated by the leader Oxylane Group. This status allows the group to carefully select the brands they want to distribute in their stores. Looking for instance to the tennis racquet sector, Oxylane offers Artengo, one of its own brands, and only few major and international brands, often the most known ones, such as Head, Wilson, Babolat and Prince. This dominant position allows the group to identify only the major international brands that will provide the highest margins while putting forward its own brand which brings more profits. In this situation, it can happen that retailing groups stop offering certain brands which are seen to compete too much with their own brands. This is for instance what happened to the brand Lafuma. This example shows that with such a group controlling most of the sport specialised retailing, negotiations become harder for international sport brands. Only their reputation and exclusive products can prevent them from being excluded in these major networks. The major retailers' strategy is to reduce the space allocated to corporate brands with the constraint of offering enough diversity and still offering the most-known brands in order to attract consumers in their stores.

In such contexts, where very few but powerful sport specialised retailer brands dominate, major and international sport brands have been forced to develop their own distribution and sale networks in order to better control sale prices and their margins. This downward vertical integration strategy has been for instance implemented by sport brands such as Nike, Adidas, Lacoste, Le Coq Sportif, Arena and Quiksilver. For these brands the goal is to better control their merchandising and the whole value chain, from the first products' designs and drawings to their display in stores. In many countries, retailers' dominant positions have created difficult relationships and negotiations and sport corporate brands had to accept that they were in direct competition with retailers' own brands to continue being offered by them (Lebrun, 2006). These relationships incited sport corporate brands to shorten their distribution channels in creating single brand networks and developing sales via the Internet, to be closer to consumers.

Sport corporate brands' responses to the increasing competition of sport retailers' own brands were of two types. They created some associations with other brands in the same situation and enhanced vertical integrations to better control the commercialisation process. Specifically, major and international brands have created their own distribution networks made of their own stores, named single brand stores. This strategy was for instance followed by many sport brands from the outdoor sector such as Patagonia, Aigle, and Timberland. As they were not all able to develop their own network some of them created partnerships with other brands such as the associations Quiksilver–Rossignol–Andaska (although this association does not exist anymore), Lafuma–Oxbow and The North Face–Helly Hansen, for the last two associations are essentially in the USA. For all these brands, vertical integration has become an obligation, in particular because of the broadness of the products they offer requiring vast dedicated surfaces which cannot be found in sport specialised stores. Major and international corporate brands also consider that sport retailers do not stage enough dramatisation and storytelling which is a key component for their products. However, to avoid upsetting sport retailers, they state that these strategies do not replace classical distribution channels but complement them. Specifically, they say that these stores are essentially flagship stores or pilot stores where they can test new concepts and ideas and where they can provide new experiences to consumers such themed entertainment and themed flagship brand stores (Kozinets et al., 2002). It can be noted that some international sport corporate brands have invested in some sport retailers' brands in order to grow and enhance their overall turnover. This is for instance the case for Billabong which acquired in 2008 Kirra Surf, a Gold Coast retail store, and Quiet Flight's fourteen store chain, one of its partners in the USA, expecting a turnover increase of three per cent.[1] Its main competitors such as Rip Curl are following the same strategy. If corporate brands seek for new distribution channels and alternatives it is also because they consider that the conditions set by the retailers are judged inappropriate (for example the constraints of set prices, and short supply durations). Furthermore, they do not always have the same views in terms of trend evolutions and new segments to target. Retailers can indeed be reluctant to target new segments which represent a financial risk for them and sometimes an opportunity cost because store surfaces are limited and the allocation of space to a new, uncertain segment would be to the detriment of an existing, established one.

Intra-industry upward vertical integrations

Like sport corporate brands, sport retailer brands seek to increase their control on value chains and this makes them develop new sets of skills far from their original sale functions to become producers as well. They are changing their status but also extending their power in becoming their own suppliers and then reducing their number of existing suppliers. The first reason they put forward stems from their will to offer products manufacturers did not want to place in their stores, because they preferred other more profitable specialised networks (Kapferer, 1991). The second reason they put forward was the lack of dynamism of sport goods' manufacturers. For a sport retailer brand, offering its own brands presents several advantages. They can better control their margins in controlling the production costs, ordering big volumes and targeting low-end products which have the highest profitability rates. Sport retailers then have more strength to negotiate with corporate brands and reduce their selling prices in pretending their own brands are more popular among consumers. With their own brands, retailers can also put forward the fact that they are the only ones to offer certain brands and products representing a significant advantage in terms of loyalty. Last, they are guaranteed a certain legitimacy thanks to their existing brand awareness and transfer of positive associations. In terms of communication they also kill two birds with one stone as retailers' own brands are automatically associated with the store and because the publicity made about them also benefits the store brand. The link between retailers' own brands and store brands increase consumers' trust because they think that retailers could not afford to sell bad products in their stores due to the strong negative impact it would have on their reputation.

If power balance seems to give a strong advantage to sport retailers, several elements should, however, be considered. Sport corporate brands also take advantage of the increasing strength of sport retailers. In order to offer products with comparable quality, numerous retailers have chosen to sub-contract their production to industrial leader brands. For suppliers the benefit is clear: they accept to produce sport retailers' own brands, even if they can represent future competitors to their brands, in exchange for exclusivity and guaranteed high volumes. The links, which are then more complex than simple competition relationships, are positive because they also develop the innovation focus of major and international brands (Lewi, 2003). Sport retailer brands also know that they cannot do without corporate brands because of their history, tradition and reputation, and they acknowledge it by using them intensively in their publicity and promotional campaigns. If corporate brands firstly offer technical products and a quality image, sport retailers' brands firstly offer products with good quality–price ratios, and consumers make a clear difference between them. In terms of technicality and innovation, consumers tend to favour sport corporate brands which better respond to their expectations in terms of performance. Engineering costs have remained a strong barrier to overcome for sport retailers even if things are changing. Some sport retailers' own brands are now able to develop and launch products as technical as those of corporate brands as illustrated for instance in Europe by the brands Tribord, Artengo, Quechua, Domyos or Wed'Ze of Oxylane Group and McKinley and Etirel for Intersport.

A new phenomenon in the sport industry in terms of upward integration is the arrival of clothes and food retailers which are attracted by the potential high profitability rates. In France, Carrefour, the second biggest generalist retailer worldwide in terms of revenues, launched in 2007, the year the rugby union World Cup was organised in France, a sportswear brand named Ovalattitude (oval being a reference to the rugby ball shape) to compete with brands such as Eden Park and Serge Blanco. For sport corporate brands, these new competitors represent real threats because of their capacity to offer cheaper prices and to reach very large numbers of consumers. In Switzerland, SportXX Migros, the sport retailing brand of Migros, the retail brand leader in the country, is another example of this phenomenon. Migros launched its own sport brands: Trevolution (trekking, outdoor, camping), Obscure, Extend (shoes), Cronics (mountain bikes and accessories) and Crosswave (bikes and biking clothes). Furthermore, the group also launched its own sport service brands such as Golf Parc, Fitness Parc and Parc Pré Vert, a leisure and recreation park.

Cooperative strategies between manufacturers and retailers

While sport corporate brands try to reinforce their competitive advantage over sport retail brands, they also try to improve their relationships with them and create cooperation and partnership links. They can for instance share their resources to develop new products and lines by exchanging information and sharing data, also known as category management, or by investing in strategies with reciprocal benefits such as trade marketing for instance. Within stores for example, corporate and retailer brands both have interests in staging a nice and appealing physical environment. Packaging, merchandising, shelves' vertical and horizontal organisation, scenery, and lighting all contribute to the reinforcement of the intangible component of sold products (Ohl, 2003).

Category management, which is a common tactic in the grocery and food sectors, is increasingly used in sport industries. For international corporate brands this tactic allows them to collaborate with retailers to enhance merchandising, activation and promotion. During the 2008 UEFA European Football Championship, Adidas created in partnership with Sport 2000, the retail store chain, specific corners dedicated to the French football team's official kits. This is a common practice during major sporting events. Sport retailers can also take the initiative in the creation of new products and submit specifications and proposals to potential industrial partners. Another form of category management can take its origin from a manufacturer which wants to sell an innovating and unique product and seeks a specific retailer's help.

These partnerships usually concern the creation of a unique product such as running shoes. Foot-Locker for instance had the exclusive distribution in Europe of the 'Nike Tuned' (Nike Air Max Plus) model which had a great success among youth generations. This was also the tactic used in France by the retailer Courir with its shoe models signed by Adidas, Asics, Nike, Puma and Reebok. About half of the shoes offered by a particular retailer are exclusive models coming from partnerships with international corporate brands. These partnerships which often represent exclusive products for retailers can involve the adaptation of significant features, or basic ones such as a product's colour. Other types of partnerships result in the creation of a new brand. This can involve either sport retailers or generalist retailers (see Figure 6.2). In the USA, the brand C9 is the fruit of the collaboration between Champion USA and the retailer Target. The mass market brand Starter was born as well from the collaboration between Nike and Wal-Mart, the retail world leader, and a common will to offer very cheap sport shoes. In 2008, Nike sold Starter after a review of its Exeter Brands Group Subsidiary because it offered less growth prospects than its other subsidiaries. In investing in discount markets,

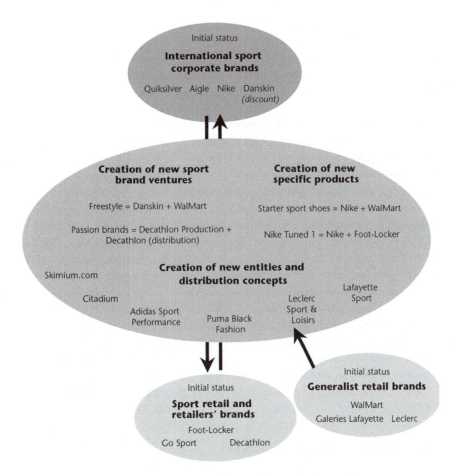

FIGURE 6.2 Upward and downward extensions of sport retail and manufacturer brands

Nike demonstrated its ambition to become a significant actor of sport retailing. On one hand, the absence of the swoosh signature on the products did not alter the image, values and promises which made the reputation of the brand. On the other hand, it limited new competitors as retailers and discounters can develop their own sneaker brand which would compete with Nike's products. Staying in the USA, the discount brand Danskin launched Freestyle, a brand positioned on the fitness sector and whose products are commercialised by generalist retailers such as Wal-Mart. Another strategy for retail brands consists of extending their market by targeting new segments such as the discount, high-end and premium ones. In Europe, this is the strategy adopted by Oxylane Group with its Passion brands which were initially positioned at the bottom end and middle range and are now investing in high-end segments while maintaining their presence in the lower ones. On the contrary the group even seeks to reinforce its position in lower-end segments by finding new models for discount retailing. The group created the retail store Toboggan, whose scenery is similar to discount retailers such as Costco warehouses, and Geologic, a discount store targeting hunters and fishermen. Since, 2009, Oxylane Group has created Skimium.com, a franchise retail brand which allows independent stores, particularly those located in skiing resorts, to commercialise the group's brands alongside the brands they already offer.

It can be estimated that brands' tendency to simultaneously position themselves as manufacturers and retailers results from the will to extend their target markets as well as to modify their original role and function. When a major or international sport corporate brand decides to open its own stores, its intention is clearly to expand its brand territory and conquer new markets and segments through a direct distribution and encounter with consumers. This brand will implement marketing and communication tactics which are out of reach for many retailers and are often very successful in their enterprise, as illustrated by the examples of Dorotennis and Roxy. This strategy of having stores dedicated to specific segments, such as women with Dorotennis and Roxy (Quiksilver Group), seems also justified by the fact that men and women have different shopping behaviours. Contrary to men who seem to mainly shop in suburban shopping centres, women seem to have their own specific shopping circuits. Style, price, merchandising and publicity then need to be adapted to this segment. Women seem used to cheap clothing retail franchises and contrary to men, seem less sensitive to technical products and performance features which are important sport brands' sale arguments and promises. Sport brands need to develop a marketing customised to women and as the Oxbow marketing director once said, 'a brand does cannot become trustworthy with women overnight'.

Sport brands' extension strategies

Using their reputation and positive associations to invest in new landscapes and markets represents a common practice for sport brands. They rely on their strong brand equity to target new markets and segments which are generally peripheral to their basic or core sectors of activity. Brand extension objectives aim to both consolidate and increase turnovers in exploiting tangible and intangible brand values in new growing markets to benefit from a significant and unique competitive advantage (Kapferer, 2006). Four main forms of extension can be identified corresponding to different growth objectives (see Table 6.1).

Geographical extensions simply correspond to the will to target foreign markets and consumers although line extension corresponds to the broadening of offers in categories where brands are already present. This consists then of creating new items in the range of products and services already offered by the brand (Aaker, 1996). When Adidas commercialises a new model of shoes for a sport activity which was not covered yet, it represents a line extension. However, when the same brand decides to offer energy drinks, this will be a brand extension. There are several ways to justify brand and target market extensions. First, new products are launched to stay in contact with demand evolution in terms of taste and expectations. Second,

TABLE 6.1 The different forms of sport brands' extensions

Extension forms	Characteristics	Examples
Brand extension	Extending the brands with new products and services in new sectors	Rossignol Skis extended its offers with roller skates; Lacoste extended its offers with cologne, glasses, watches and luggage; Nike and Airness extended their offers with glasses, luggage, MP3 players and even mobile phones for Airness; Nascar offered grape tomatoes and potatoes; Real Madrid launched an island resort complex in Dubai.
Target market extension	Broadening the target markets with new products and services in sectors or segments where the brand is already present	Nike extended its offers with football boots; Adidas, the football specialist, extended its offers with basketball shoes to invest the North American market; Reebok which first offered fitness shoes extended its offers with football boots and now lifestyle shoes; Intersport now offers skiing rental services; ASICS will introduce in 2013 a complete line of baseball goods.
Line extension	Launching a new type of product in a sector already invested by the brand	Salomon extended its offers to new skiing and snowboarding segments such as free-riding and carving; Oakley is looking at developing smart glasses; in 2012, Under Armour recently launched the new Spine RPM footwear collection; In June 2012 Vans launched the LXVI, a new athletic footwear line.
Geographical extension	Investing new regions and countries to reach new markets for its products	This is the case of almost all international sport brands which mainly invest in developed or in-development countries; in 2010 Li Ning, the Chinese brand, opened its first store in Portland, Oregon; NBA and NFL organise each year a game in London; Most European professional football clubs such as Real Madrid and Manchester United organise pre-season tours in South-East Asia and North America.

the parent brand uses its brand equity to increase its financial income due to additional money spent by current consumers as well as new consumers. Third, brand extensions allow the spreading of different costs such as research and innovation, and marketing and communication over several products to maximise their margins. Fourth, they represent a response to the increasing threats coming from other competitors to maintain aggressive strategies. The global level achieved by Nike is a relevant example of the importance of extensions in sport brands' growth strategies. At first, the brand focused on athletic shoes which were progressively used for casual purposes. The growth towards other sports was done through line extensions and the penetration of distribution circuits that reached mass markets and general TV audiences. Then, thanks to many innovations, creative publicities, large scale sponsorship deals, Nike went into many other markets such as golf, football, basketball, creating each time new links and emotional connections between consumer groups, tribes and communities (Kapferer, 2006).

Horizontal line extensions

For sport brands, the best current example of horizontal line extensions is the development of offers specifically targeting females and Roxy is a perfect illustration as its turnover is now bigger than its parent brand Quiksilver. Lacoste is another good example. At first very masculine, the brand launched its first female line in 1997 for golf and tennis by adjusting its style and colour codes. Since then, major international sport corporate brands such as Adidas, Nike, Reebok, Puma and Asics have followed the trend in developing new clothes and shoes whose design, shape and comfort have been adjusted to females' bodies and tastes. It is probably in the shoe sector that line extensions have been the most noticeable and female models have generated huge profits in particular in the high-end segments. Women runners no longer seem to be reluctant to purchase expansive technical models. Just in the USA for instance, 70 per cent of runners are female and the dynamic of the running shoes sector is widely due to them. They do not hesitate to spend significant amounts of money on products which are well-designed and which better fit to female body shapes; in this case the price issue seems secondary. Therefore, after having invested a lot in the soccer market, Nike has placed females at the heart of its strategy with its main target segments being females between 12 and 18 years old who frequently wear sports clothes and those between 20 and 22 years old who practice individual sports.[2]

Females seem more sensitive to elegance and style than males. Marketing experts talk about style guarantee. If males seem to be more interested in technicality and innovation, females seem to be more attracted to colours and shapes corresponding to current fashion styles. For these reasons, sport brands propose complete kits and accessories. Collections, such as in the fashion industry, are created using tendencies and trends which encourage a female to purchase new items from one season to another. Roxy for instance has adopted this collection strategy which allows women to mix, combine and adapt styles and usages. To attract females, sport brands do not hesitate to get help from well-known fashion designers. As an example, Converse launched in 2006 a winter collection signed by John Varvatos. The goal was to mix classic American clothes with sexy androgynous models with punk influences. Puma did the same with designers such as Neil Barret, Christy Turlington with her fitness line named Mahanuala, and Philippe Starck who designed a shoe line made of three models. In the same vein, Stella McCartney partnered Adidas to create Adidas by Stella McCartney, a special line for females, and recently designed the Great Britain team kits for the 2012 London Olympics. Line extensions targeting females were also accompanied by changes in terms of distribution channels, with the creation of dedicated stores and corners in specialised retail stores such as Adidas Woman. Even aisles displaying these products were specifically designed to fit with the brand's lines.

Benefiting from its commercial successes in the sportswear sectors, Lacoste is another good example in terms of horizontal extensions. This brand quickly extended the scope of its offers in developing new clothes and underwear lines before implementing a broad diversification. Extensions started with tennis racquets, and then followed with glasses. However, the main challenge the brand successfully managed was establishing its legitimacy and perceived competence in the extended areas. To avoid failure in this area, the brand sought the help of other brands; brands with strong brand equity and seen as legitimate. Therefore, its first tennis racquets were made in 1963 by Dunlop Sumitomo, its glasses have been made since 1981 by L'Amy, one of the oldest and most famous eyewear brands, its shoes has been made since 1991 by Pentland, its watches by Roventa-Henex (1993) and Tag-Heuer, and its luggage by Delsey. Nevertheless, in 1993, Lacoste launched new products which were quite far from its original territory which were male underwear and female and male fragrances. From an economic and growth perspective, these moves were justifiable, however, as a sport brand, it had started flirting with the boundaries of its brand territory (see Figure 6.3). There is indeed a theoretical threshold beyond which brands cannot go if they want successful extensions and if they do not want to damage the brand in the long-term because of dilution. However, many examples have showed that the stronger the brand equity is, the further the limit is. Looking at Lacoste's values, which mainly correspond to a high-end positioning and the classic and almost aristocratic tennis traditions, some extensions can appear risky. Similarly, it can be estimated that the extensions in the perfume industry targeting young urban consumers with nomadic and zapping behaviours represent a sustainable orientation.

Another successful example in terms of horizontal extension but for a non-sport brand is the case of BIC. Specialised in plastic injection, this brand offers numerous products such as pens and razors and was one of the earliest to diversify and extend its targets. While innovating in its original industry, BIC invested in the sport and leisure industries by commercialising windsurfing and surfing boards under the name BIC Sport. Following these successful extensions, the brand launched in 2004 its first collection of surfwear, rapidly followed by a line of neoprene suits and tops as well as a line of bags and luggage.

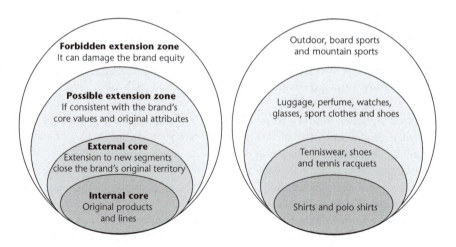

FIGURE 6.3 Lacoste's extension boundaries

Alongside sport manufacturers' brands, sport clubs and leagues have widely used brand extensions. Manchester United, one of the most famous football clubs in the world, has been conducting numerous line and brand extensions. The brand has offered fashion clothes and accessories for adults and babies, football and golf accessories, luggage, bags and wallets, mugs, bed furniture, fragrances, stationery, car accessories, toys and games, computer accessories, confectionery, calendars, frames, DVDs, books, jewellery and watches. The club has also developed MU mobile providing news and goal alerts, wallpapers, animations, videos and games. MUTV and MU Finance provide, in collaboration with various partners, insurance and debit and credit cards for UK based fans as well as South-East Asian fans (those in Malaysia, Indonesia, Singapore, and South Korea) and it has opened several restaurants in South-East Asia. In the same vein, Olympique Lyonnais (OL) football club launched extensions in other sectors with its OL travel agency, OL Taxis, OL hairdressing, and OL driving school.

Vertical line extensions

Two types of vertical line extensions can be identified. Downward line extension involves extending the brand to lower-end ranges whereas upward line extensions correspond to the opposite dynamic.

Downward vertical line extensions

This strategy consists of introducing, within the same category, a product comparatively different in terms of function, design and performance. For brands, the goal is to operate a differentiation through lower quality products within the same range

(Randall, Ulrich and Reibstein, 1998). This often corresponds to a will to democratise a brand. This also represents a relevant tactic when market competition becomes intense (Aaker, 1991). The goal is to create new usage opportunities and increase the size of the consumer base. Profits do not come via attractive margins but via sale volumes. That was for instance the strategy followed by Adidas in India with its shoes sold for €1. It can be a long term strategy which consists of hooking up new consumers, hoping they will remain brand loyal, or will purchase higher range products.

Downward line extension strategies also bear some risks. Providing cheaper products can create a depreciation of the other products offered as they can be perceived by consumers to have lower quality and can then damage the reputation of the brand as a whole (Kirmani et al., 1999). The consequences can therefore take the form of a cannibalisation of upper segments as well as a diminution of the brand's perceived added value (Nijssen, 1999; Lomax and McWilliam, 2001). In many countries, sport shoe brands offer cheaper models by using another brand from their group positioned on lower segments. For instance, Nike created, before selling it a few years later, the brand Starter in collaboration with Wal-Mart to be sold within the discount stores. In this way, brands traditionally positioned on upper segments can appear more accessible to consumers. In Europe, Tribord (Oxylane Group) offered swimming goggles named X-base for between €3 for juniors and €4 for adults, although the main brands on the segments proposed their products for about twice these prices. This product was not only cheaper but also had an interesting innovation in allowing the length adjustment of the nose bridge, creating a double competitive advantage as even more expensive goggles positioned on upper segments did not offer this.

When the perceived distance between sport brands' vertical extension and their current offers is too short, there is a risk of depreciation either for the category concerned or for the worth of the whole brand. This is what happened for instance to the American streetwear brand Airwalk. After a rapid and tremendous popularity rise thanks to a highly successful viral communication, the brand faced a decline resulting from a strategic positioning change. Airwalk started to offer more and more basic shoe models, which in turn were not differentiated enough from competitors' models any more. The brand then became progressively less popular despite audacious advertising campaigns. Its models were sold in major retail chains such as Kinneys, Champs Sports and Foot-Locker and, as a consequence, specialised retail stores started to be less interested in the brand because they felt that it did not correspond enough to their demand's tastes and needs, essentially made of passionate and non-mainstream consumers. The brand was not primarily targeting a consumer minority group any more because it was probably financially less attractive than the mass market. However, that minority group was also made of trend makers. This downward vertical extension created a negative feedback loop on its brand image damaging its reputation and making it lose market share as well.

Upward vertical line extension

With this strategy, brands seek to create and commercialise within the same categories products and services targeting higher-end segments. This extension allows (from a short term perspective) access to profitable segments but can also (from a long term perspective) enhance brand image and brand equity. This is what Randall et al. (1998) demonstrated in analysing the product lines of ten mountain bike brands (among them Conejo, Klein, Cannondale, Marin, Trek) in the USA. These authors found that new products from upward line extension have to demonstrate an overall better perceived value, expressed via better attributes, quality, design and technological performances, to justify higher prices. Price is therefore seen as a direct indicator for quality.

When sport brands decide to offer premium products such as Dynastar with its skis 'Premium 40', Adidas with its shoe 'Adidas 1' or Nike with its model 'SB Dunk Black', they are rather responding to a line strategy and orientation. Whereas when sport brands offer super premium or hyper premium products they are rather responding to an image orientation aiming to develop a prestigious reputation. These super premium lines are generally limited and sale volumes are significantly lower than other products from the same category. The premium or super premium products will be widely used in promotional and marketing campaigns as well as displayed in stores to attract curious consumers who are unlikely to buy them but may be incited to buy other products from the brand.

These premium products are often created by famous designers as in the cases of Converse, Puma and Adidas. This is also what Lafuma did with a skiing clothes line designed by Thierry Mugler and Rossignol with its luxury clothes signed Emilio Pucci and Jean-Charles Castelbajac. These premium products can also result from a co-branding strategy such as in the case of Dynastar which launched a ski line signed Hugo Boss and Dior. For Rossignol, the skiing market's world leader, an upward extension was seen as a strategic obligation to maintain its market shares and fix its image deficit. This upward line extension aimed to rejuvenate its image while offering products that were slightly less performance oriented but had more attractive designs, risking a decrease in sale figures.

Geographical extensions

Geographical extensions correspond to the broadening of the brand presence outside its original territory. In investing in new territories brands can either keep their identity, promises, values and narratives or on the contrary modify and adjust them to the different territories and cultures concerned. This was the strategy adopted by Adidas in the 60s for its globalisation and diversification strategy. At first, the German brand was specialised in sport shoes but invested in new markets with sport ball lines, rapidly followed by tracksuits lines. The Adidas logo was then created to appear on the tracksuits it provided for the Munich Olympic Games (80 per cent of the athletes were equipped by Adidas) alongside the three parallel bars logo. Nevertheless, two products highly contributed to the worldwide brand expansion: the famous 'Stan Smith' shoe model which was bought by millions and Yvan Lendl's argyle shirt. The worldwide reputation acquired by Adidas is mainly due to its dynamic geographical extension policy set up by Horst Dassler, the brand founder's son. Another example of geographical extension can be seen with Lacoste, which in 1951 created three coloured models of its famous white shirt to accompany its world extension. From 1963, the geographical extension became the heart of the brand's strategy under the direction of René Lacoste's son when he became chairman of the group. The company began rapidly exporting to Japan and the USA. The group now represents 35 million products sold per year comprising six million shirts, 600 stores and 1,200 points of sale, with 20,000 employees worldwide.

While increasing their profitability by opening new markets, geographical extensions present several financial and industrial advantages for brands. This strategy allows them to benefit from economies of scale in producing more to supply these new markets, using the same production chains, decreasing the cost for each unit produced. Furthermore, it allows the absorption of research and development costs. Nowadays, the research and development costs and efforts are so high that geographical extensions are almost required to absorb them. In this context, it can be noted that sport goods present the significant advantage of being more universal and adaptable from both functional and cultural perspectives in comparison with other goods. For instance, football/soccer balls and tennis racquets are uniform and standardised all around the world. However, this standardisation may not be applicable for the marketing and packaging of these products. For instance, violet is not a colour universally used because in many countries and cultures it is associated with bereavement and funerals. The colour green is often associated with health and freshness in western countries although in South-East Asia it is often associated with sickness. Brands have also to make sure that there is no important cultural obstacle requiring a strong adaptation of the products and brand names. Adaptation to local markets should not require important modifications concerning the product's intrinsic characteristics (for example design, colours, shape, size, and packaging). It is crucial to understand the importance of each attribute or characteristics as it may vary depending on the geographical market; the criteria may change but so might their importance as well.

The worldwide success of Quiksilver – the American brand is leader in the boardsports and sportswear sectors – can be explained by its mastery of these different parameters. Besides its own brands such as Roxy, the brand integrated DC Shoes and Skis Rossignol (now sold) to better cover promising markets. Originally, the brand was embedded within the surfing subculture, but engaged in an active diversification strategy within snowboarding and skateboarding sectors. Finally, in most countries, Quiksilver has been able to seduce young urban consumers and not only boardsports' fans who represented smaller markets within countries but this also varied between countries.

Licensing and co-branding

One effective strategy to reach a wider range of markets through the exploitation of brand image and reputation is the licensing of industrial partners. Thanks to the products commercialised under licence, sport brands can better cover their targeted markets as well as increase their exposure. Licensed products are also highly profitable, in particular when they are distributed via major generalist retail chains, as are glasses, watches, exercise books and shoes. Many sport brands use this strategy. For instance, thanks to its subsidy LafProm, Lafuma produces school bags, and Adidas licensed the company Coty to produce its toiletries sold in major retail stores. However, licensing has recently faced many changes in its scope in order to conquer new marketing territories. At first, it essentially relied on commercial licences to develop merchandised products. Nowadays, it does not only control the product issue but the communication as well through sale promotion, event sponsorship, and athlete and celebrity endorsement.

Another means to increase brands' profits is co-branding. It represents an advanced marketing tactic relying on a strong partnership between brands that gives birth to a new product or service. For Aaker (1996), co-branding is an important strategic option because it corresponds to a form of brand extension bringing an additional guarantee and legitimacy to the product or service thanks to the partner. However, if the partnership does not imply a co-creation or co-design and only consists of associating and marking the product or service, or its packaging, with another brand, this represents a brand alliance or a form of licensing but not a co-branding process. The use of the Olympic rings is a classic example of this brand alliance but this contractual usage of a logo, a name or a symbol cannot be considered as co-branding.

Successful sport brands licensing

Licensing represents nowadays an unavoidable marketing strategy for sports brands aiming to reach new territories, in particular in fields which are far from the brands' original domains. Intrinsically, the exploitation and management of a license is similar to those of classical brands involving the identification of criteria such as target markets, brand territories, promises, price, distribution networks, packaging and colours. This strategy is particularly interesting in contexts where communication and media costs are high and the general creation costs remain an obstacle. Another motivation to use licensing is linked to the reduction of products' life cycles in many categories which make new products and brands' investments more risky. Brand congestion and clutter make the markets difficult to read for consumers; this factor also encourages the use of co-branding strategies. A brand license presents a double advantage. First, it provides the owner with royalties and second, it avoids losing brand's rights due to commercial inactivity by maintaining a constant exploitation of a brand. Through a contract specifying the conditions and rights of usage, a person or company is authorised to use the brand with the owner's agreement and against the payment of royalties.

Within sport markets, brand licensing has been increasingly used and this trend does not seem to slow down because it provides significant profits to brands' owners. Among many, Jean-Claude Killy, the famous former French skier, successfully managed his strategy to develop a high-end mountain sports brand with its products licensed by Eider, a brand benefiting from a strong perceived equity. In another sector, Umbro, the English clothes and shoe brand, relied on a wide network of licensed partners around the world. The same strategy was followed by the English brand Grays International which has developed since the eighties offers in sport shoes, clothes, and protection equipment (Barrand *et al.*, 2004). Airness, another sport clothes brand, extensively used licensing to cover many growing markets and sectors. For its lifestyle products, Airness licensed JAJ Group; Uhlsport for team sports clothes; Asian Footwear for shoes; Olympia for socks; Afflelou for glasses; Hamelin Group for school bags and exercise books; Marlay for pens and leather accessories; Ambre for watches; MCT for linen; L'Oréal for perfume; ModelLabs for mobile phones. For Airness, licensing was at the core of the brand's strategy and provided a lot of growth starting with a turnover of €20 million in 2003 and growing to €144 million in 2007.[3] When a brand is successful, there is fierce competition between manufacturers to obtain licences, which is a comfortable situation for brands. Sport brands' owners who want to provide a license can do it for any kind of products or services, even in categories far from the brand's original territory, as demonstrated with the Airness example. The Austrian group Head Tyrolia Mares (HTM) is another example of a sport brand which invested in many different sectors via more than 80 licences granted for the textile, sport bags, mountain bikes, glasses, sport shoes, gloves, golf clubs, luggage, caps, online rollers, socks, toiletries, perfume, watches, underwear and sport balls sectors.

For license holders, selling products and services from an international sport brand allows access to markets where the brand's fame and notoriety constitute strong assets and factors of attraction for consumers. This also provides a kind of guarantee and, even if benefits are shared between licensors and licensees, risks are shared as well. On this specific point, brand licensing differs from franchising because, besides a brand, the franchisor also provides know-how, services, managerial and communication tools or procedures in terms of human resources management. Furthermore, in the sport sectors, franchising generally associates a selling point and a manufacturer brand whereas brand licensing generally associates a manufacturer brand and a supplier which is often a manufacturer too. Quiksilver, Lacoste and Aigle have all developed a network of franchised stores and at the same time they also granted licenses to several of their suppliers. These brands then generate revenues from both streams but licensing appears the most profitable strategy by far. For instance, Lacoste gets most of its revenues from its licence royalties as this brand never manufactured its own products. From 1963, the firm Devanlay have been producing Lacoste's shirts. Devanlay now possesses 35 per cent of the brand shares, produces between 30 and 35 per cent of Lacoste's clothes, and supplies about 90 per cent of the European market (Logié and Logié-Naville, 2002).

Licensing widely benefits sport club and sport event brands. When it concerns sporting events, licensing grants the right to other firms and organisations to exploit the event name, logo and image to commercialise either products and sport goods or services (for example insurance, transport, hospitality and catering). For instance, major tennis tournaments such as the Australian, American, French and British opens have become true brands with extended ranges of products and services produced under licence. In 2000, the Roland Garros French open's tennis range comprised balls, video games, books, watches, towels, clothes and accessories. The line Roland-Garros Sportswear comprised toiletries, glasses and sunglasses, cosmetics, swimwear, clothes and accessories. Last, the line Roland Garros Art de Vivre (lifestyle) comprised motorised scooters, mobile phones, cars, clothes and accessories. With a network of more than 10,000 selling points worldwide, the Roland Garros brand possesses more than 600 referenced items in collaboration with many other brands such as Ericsson (mobile phones), Adidas (sport shoes), Lanvin (Panama hats and ties) and Longchamp (luggage). In the same vein, the All England Lawn Tennis and Croquet Club (AELTC), which holds each year the Wimbledon Championships, started its licensing programme in 1979 which now comprises about 30 licensed companies worldwide in eight international markets.[4] Clothes are categorised into four ranges ('Classics', 'Performance', 'Lifestyle' and 'Authentics') and concern successful and prestigious companies to fit with the Wimbledon brand image such as Christy (towels), Links of London (jewellery), Prince (rackets and bags), Rodenstock (sunglasses), Ralph Lauren (clothing) and Fila (footwear). Wimbledon products can be found on-site, in department stores and airports around the United Kingdom, in 35 Wimbledon shops in China and in 95 Wimbledon shops with Polo Ralph Lauren at key USA retailers such as Bloomingdales, Macy's and Lord and Taylor, and in Polo Ralph Lauren stores and key polo department store accounts in Europe and Japan.

Another sport brand licensing case is the one of the National Basketball Association (NBA). The main target segments for licensed products are the eight–24 year-olds for whom the NBA represents a dream for both spectators and basketball players. In the year 2000, NBA licenses were present in video games (Acclaim, Electronic Arts, Microsoft, Nintendo, Sega, Sony), sportswear, caps (Champion USA), sport bags (Champion USA, Lafuma), balls and tiny baskets (Spalding), toys and games (Mattel), stickers (Panini), school material (Hamelin), linen (SDE) and pens (Stypen). The NBA is not a unique case and licensing also concerns numerous sport club and league brands. In the United Kingdom, Brandco management Ltd is a business dedicated to provide clothes and accessories (rugby jerseys, polos, hooded tops, caps, bags, and pins) for many licensors such as England Cricket, England Rugby, Fulham FC, Scottish Rugby, University of Oxford, RBS Six Nations and Thomond Park.

The different forms of co-branding

Several forms of co-branding can be identified depending on the type of brands involved (for example sport and non-sport brands) and the nature of the relationship.

Horizontal and vertical co-branding

For a horizontal co-branding configuration, both partner brands do not initially have a strong link and are positioned in two different sectors. The specific Peugeot car models signed Roland Garros, the French tennis open, are an illustration of this collaboration. The partnership is limited because the sport event brand does not have any particular skills or know-how in terms of car production. However, Roland Garros brings a reputation and strongly contributes to the marketing and promotion of the new models. This can be considered as a minimal co-branding because it mainly concerns communication and aesthetic dimensions. The partnership between Eider and Nouvelles Frontières, a French travel agency and operator, also falls within this category and consists of supplying co-branded products to the travel operator's trekking guides. In this case, the partnership is justified as both brands have the same target segments and markets. On the one hand, with this partnership, the travel agency brand seeks to get some credibility from the sport brand which acts as a technical guarantee as well as providing cheap and up-to-date apparel and materials for their employees. On the other hand, Eider seeks to test new products, benefiting from the expertise and advice of experts. The sport brand also benefits from an important level of exposure through its presence on the promotional tools (for example books, leaflets, trade shows) of the travel agency.

With vertical co-branding, there is a direct link between the partner brands within the same industry or sector. It is particularly the case when one brand supplies the other, when a constituent brand is for instance associated to a sport brand. This is the case with the partnership between Gore-Tex and the Italian brand Trezela, which produces climbing and hiking boots, and between Lycra and the swimwear brand Arena. With vertical and horizontal co-branding, there is an exchange and a sharing of competences and techniques resulting in a competitive advantage for both brands they could not have otherwise.

Promotion and new product/service project alliances

This type of co-branding aims to get promotional and awareness boost for both brands at a specific moment. Both brands' name and logo are shown as this association has to be made visible to consumers. This linkage can sometimes take the form of a sponsorship agreement and consists in associating a brand image with a sporting event. The only difference with a sponsorship agreement is that it results in the creation of a new product or service. In this case, the creation of the 'China-Mac' sandwich by McDonald's during the 2008 Beijing Olympics falls within this category. A second form corresponds to the sharing of specific skills and know-how to increase brands' legitimacy. The outcomes of such associations are new co-signed products or services which in this case receive a new brand name. This strategy is increasingly used in sectors requiring important research and development investments. This second type of partnership is therefore more complex and deep because it concerns the whole design to production and commercialisation.

The partnership between Michelin, the world leader in terms of racquet heads, and Babolat to create a range of tennis shoes is a good illustration of this co-branding link. Michelin went into the same kind of partnership with the German brand Kempa focusing on shoe soles' innovation and performance; Michelin's main competitor Goodyear entered in a co-branding partnership with Adidas to commercialise a collection of sport shoes; and Quiksilver partnered Olympus to imagine the TC-610 waterproof camera commercialised on the Australian market.

Functional and affective/symbolic co-branding

This form of close collaboration seeks to conceive new physical attributes for products and services. Within this format, an 'invited' brand modifies and brings new features to the 'inviting' brand's offer. This is an efficient strategy that shares the costs of design and creation to achieve significant competitive innovations. This archetypal co-branding relationship comprises an ingredient brand (the 'invited' brand) which allows an international sport brand (the 'inviting' brand) to develop new products and product categories due to its competences, industrial properties and technological know-how. This partnership is sometimes known as ingredient branding (Norris, 1992). Within the sport industries, alliances between Gore-Tex and Aigle for outdoor clothing or between Lafuma and Millet for hiking jackets are relevant examples. Brands' efforts and contributions are not necessarily equal in terms of research and development but the invited brand guarantees a certain level of quality and technicality helping consumers to clearly identify the specific and unique offer's characteristics. With its brand Cordura, Invista is strongly involved in sport bags and luggage. This firm collaborates with Eastpak to create backpacks for sport participants and skaters. With its brand Winstopper, Gore & Associates collaborate with numerous sport corporate brands (for example Puma, Scott, Galvin Green, Chiemse, Arc'Teryx, The North Face, Peak Performance, and Columbia) to develop technical textiles. Nevertheless, the uncontested champions of functional co-branding seem to be Shimano and Vibram. The former collaborates with almost all biking brands providing breaks and derailleurs whereas the latter is associated with almost all mountaineering brands providing special soles for their shoes.

Affective or symbolic co-branding relies on a different logic because it mainly consists of associating an inviting brand to an invited one to generate additional symbolic, psychosocial, and experiential attributes. This type of partnership mainly concerns promotional activities and operations relying on a double exchange of brand associations and image elements. In order to be fully justified, brands should not initially share the same tangible characteristics. This co-branding relationship remains superficial in the sense that it mainly seeks to create a new synergy between brands and concerns marketing operations, creative communication and publicity, and exclusive services. For instance, they can imagine and commercialise products more rapidly (with a shorter distribution time due to economies of scale) and more efficiently (using a broader distribution channel and network). In theory, brands' benefits should be equal but in reality, it seems that one brand frequently gets more benefits than the other. When Michelin and Babolat co-branded a range of tennis shoes, the partnership principally benefited the manufacturer (Michelin) because it holds a better brand reputation and image allowing the brand to show the masses that its expertise in terms of rubber and plastic is transferable to shoe soles. Even if Babolat did benefit from Michelin's reputation, the risks of failure would not similarly impact the brands. If the co-branded product is not a success in terms of sales, it will not have an important impact on Michelin as it will not be affected in terms of finances and image. On the contrary, for Babolat, a failure would be damaging because there is a direct link between its tennis products and these shoes. The negative consequences of poor sales can even be serious in terms of image and credibility if consumers make a transfer between the co-branded product's failure and the brand's own product ranges.

Events co-branding and technological co-branding: the case of Peugeot–Roland-Garros cars and the case of Nike–Apple

Co-branding initiatives are frequently accompanied by sponsorship deals to increase the scope and impact of the partnership and its return on investment. The partnership between the car brand Peugeot and the sporting event brand Roland Garros is in this way a very good example. Since 1989, Peugeot have been sponsoring the French tennis open which holds an international reputation. The car brand takes care of the transport of athletes, celebrities, clients and VIP persons during the tournament. It also offers a limited edition of Peugeot cars signed Roland Garros showing the official colours (green and terracotta) of the sporting event. At first the car manufacturer contacted the French Federation of Tennis (FFT) to initiate a co-branding partnership for one of its oldest models (the 205 convertible) which had reached the decline stage of its lifecycle. Thanks to this co-branding strategy, they managed to sell several thousand models. Nowadays, a successful and recent model is co-branded (the 207 CC) because it fits very well with tennis which is urban, trendy and associated with the middle and upper classes. This corresponded well with the prestige image of Roland Garros as the car product is a significant social object people like to personalise and use to reflect their identity (Bayle, 2001). Based on this success they extended the co-branding programme to other car models such as four-door saloons and seven-seater models. For these models targeting family segments, tennis also presents a good fit as it generally interests all family members as spectators and participants.

Either for co-branding or sponsorship strategies, the level of fit or congruence is crucial to their success. For this reason, it is not surprising to see limited editions of skis associated to a ski resort brand such as the ranges developed by Dynastar and co-branded with Val d'Isère and Courchevel (both famous French ski resorts). The co-branded product or service should always hold the same values defended by both stakeholders, as for sponsor and sponsee relationships.

After having conducted co-branding operations with Audi, BMW and Volvo, Nike successfully implemented technological co-branding operations with Apple in order to design MP3 players allowing runners to be able to get some information about their speed and distance run thanks to a small device integrated into the 'Air Zoom Moire' shoe sole.

With this partnership two major global brands brought together their knowledge to create an innovating product. The 'iPod nano' is a true micro control centre allowing casual and regular runners to check and monitor the parameters of their physical activity and performance such as distance, speed and burnt calories. It can also provide experts' advice coming for instance from Alberto Salazar, the American athletics champion, besides music tunes. Through this co-branded new product, Nike demonstrated its intention to conduct a growth strategy based on diversifications and target extensions. As stated by Nike's CEO Mark Parker, the Nike-iPod represents a partnership between two iconic brands sharing the same passion for the creation of innovative and meaningful goods. It aimed to strongly improve people's running experience by being more than a training device and act as a coach or running partner surrogate. When launched, the product was sold at US$29 and was located within the sole of the Nike 'Air Zoom Moire' model sold at about US$100. The idea was simple but innovative: the sole pedometer recorded parameters which were transmitted to the iPod nano which would display them. During the running, a feminine voice would communicate the main parameters through the headset while the main key sets off the 'Power song', a rhythmic song aiming to motivate runners. Apple also offered running song selections via iTunes Music Store. The MP3 player can be synchronised with nikeplus.nike.com to upload run characteristics and compare them with other consumers and runners.

This partnership was not the first attempt of the American brand in the technological field because it previously signed with Motorola the 'Commjacket' and the 'Commvest', two skiing jackets (one was designed for rescue professionals) with integrated Bluetooth communication devices. Before collaborating with Apple, Nike worked with Phillips on a Portable Sport Audio (PSA) which was a CD-MP3 player (see Figure 6.4).

FIGURE 6.4 The Nike–Philips Portable Sport Audio

It was specifically designed for runners and bike riders. Mobile and resistant, it comprised a remote control and a screen. Three main parameters had been taken into consideration: ergonomics, resistance and audio quality. Furthermore, athletes could assess their progress as data were recorded and could be uploaded within a training book accessible on www.nikerunning.com.

7

SPORT BRANDS' THREATS

Nowadays, brands seem to be at the centre of many criticisms and are increasingly considered to be directly or indirectly responsible for the current economic, health, environmental and societal turmoil. Some people indeed consider that brands control their everyday life almost like George Orwell's Big Brother whereas others blame them for fixing economic rules, for making children obese or for breaching human rights. Already mentioned in a previous chapter, the book *No Logo* (Klein, 2001) is a good example of such criticisms. In developed countries, economic growth reached such levels that it would be difficult and biased not to recognise the benefits brands have had on people's lives, health, workplace, leisure and well-being as a whole. However, as any system, it has its downsides embedded within the consumerist phenomenon. Offer abundance, globalisation, relocation and some shareholders' and managers' greed and indifference have indeed provoked direct and indirect social, environmental and human damages in the form of pollution, work-related illness, appearance tyranny and massive household debts. Opposition and resistance movements and groups have been set up to publicly criticise and counter brands' interferences and growing importance and demonise their constant performance and profit objectives. Resistance behaviours can take various forms on a continuum from avoidance and minimisation behaviours to active rebellion such as complaining, boycotting and dropping out (Fournier, 1998), and it is now impossible to ignore them. From this early classification, it seems that resistance forms have been extremely diverse, using methods such as counter-publicity, parasitism or website hacking. These consumers and activists are obvious brand threats but other threats coming from the market itself and brands' main competitors can also hinder growth and development. First of all is the aging phenomenon but other threats dealing with marketing and communication erosion phenomena such as product and brand name trivialisation and upward extension towards premium products are becoming serious. A final threat that is particularly concerning for sport brands is counterfeiting.

Countering sport brands' aging

Every sport brand will face the aging issue, from the most prestigious and power-ful to the oldest and eventually the most recent ones. If the phenomenon is unavoidable, the questions are then: why does it happen and how can sport brands counter or cope with it? For some experts, aging occurs because of the creation of a gap between consumer expectations' evolution and brands' strategies and messages, which are too much embedded and attached to their own histories, tradi-tions and culture. A brand will start aging when its offers do not correspond to what consumers want any more and make them increasingly disinterested (Lewi and Rogliano, 2006). For other experts, this phenomenon can be explained by the fact that brands were not able to break out from the contexts and configurations that made their success. Particularly, this seems to be the case for brands whose awareness and reputation levels are due to a product or service innovation and fell into the 'milking' strategy pitfall. This pitfall consists of maintaining a market posi-tion by relying on the competitive advantage obtained with past products and services without making sufficient investments and/or marketing efforts. Finally, for other experts, this phenomenon can be precipitated if the company's culture is too focused on products instead of brands. In this case, aging brands are those who failed to embrace a branding logic by giving a meaning and a specific image to their objectives and strategies, to their values and promises.

Anticipation and prevention before it is too late

As mentioned in this chapter's introduction, the aging phenomenon concerns or will concern all brands, which require pro-action in terms of strategy and policy. For instance, Lacoste did not escape from this phenomenon despite its strong repu-tation and notoriety. More than 60 years after its creation and after a fantastic commercial growth, the brand had to rejuvenate itself. After three decades of success until the end of the nineties, the managers got carried away, in particularly by the counterfeiting issue which was a significant problem for the brand, and stopped monitoring closely enough the evolution of their core target markets. Indeed, a generational gap was being created and it became imperative for the brand to do something to fix this issue. However, a brutal rejuvenation was not the solution as it would have primarily concerned the Generation Y, which was known for its volatility (Noble, Haytko and Phillips, 2009; Benn, 2004), and would have created a too big gap between these young consumers and the older historic ones. Lacoste had indeed an upper-class image which corresponded to older generations and there was a risk that these consumers would not accept being associated with very young ones. Moreover, against its will, the brand became in the middle of the nineties very popular among French teenagers and young adults living in big city neighbourhoods and council estates. This 'neighbourhood' image was in total contrast with its bourgeois image and represented a major risk for the brand. Consequently, in order to maintain its image and keep its core segment targets, the brand had to be very active and sinewy, and launched a large scale communication and promotional campaign. The logo was also changed with a more discrete, coloured, elegant and minimalist crocodile which seemed to correspond to the trend of that period. A slogan ('become who you are') was for the first time associated to the brand emphasising the authenticity and independence which were reflected in the brand's identity. While this reinforcement may have only concerned the French market, it represented a quarter of the brand's turnover worldwide. The German brand Puma faced the same kind of aging situation. At the beginning of the nineties, the brand did not hold a strong positive image and had become dated in consumers' eyes. Close to bankruptcy, the brand's managers initiated an original brand repositioning. Although Nike and Adidas tried to reduce the price of their sneakers, Puma chose the opposite strategy and targeted upper segments. The brand commercialised a trendy urban collection inspired by its models designed for sport competition. Available in many colours, these models were very quickly successful. The 'Mostro', which looked like a climbing shoe, the 'Speed Cat' which looked like Formula 1 footwear, and the 'H Street', which copied an athletics footwear model designed for the 1976 Olympics, were among the best successes of the collection. In order to promote its trendy and fun image, Puma did not only rely on its new product lines but also on sport sponsorship and creative marketing campaigns. The brand commercialised an original sleeveless shirt for the Cameroon football team and created a dress specifically designed for the tennis player Serena Williams. During the Atlanta Summer Olympics, the brand also created a buzz with the sprinter Linford Christie who wore contact lenses with the brand logo. Thanks to its repositioning towards fashion, and sometimes luxury and scarcity (for example some models were produced in limited editions), but also by using very selective distribution channels, Puma passed its rejuvenating challenge and has become one of the younger generations' favourite brands.

In some cases, the change or death of the brand's founder can accelerate the aging process even if the financial situation is healthy. The transmission to heirs or more frequently to financial and industrial investors is always a challenge. As long as the new owners and managers keep some links with the founders, either because of familial ties or because they hold the same values, the brand does not face major risks. However, a sudden transmission, whether it is provoked or not, can create an instability and difficult managerial situation, particularly when the values and the know-how of the brand's founder are not transferable. This will be particularly the case for brands created by former athletes such as Björn Borg, Fran Cotton (Cotton Traders), Robby Naish or Li Ning when their founder dies. The brand Killy, which was created by the former skiing champion Jean-Claude Killy and now belongs to Eider, will probably face the same situation due to the close link existing between the brand's values and images and the former champion's personality. For these sport brands, the main challenge is not to live in the past but move on because younger generations very often do not know who they are or are not aware of their sporting performances. Therefore, to counter aging these sport brands will need to reinvent themselves and their identity: an identity which combines authentic but also contemporary values and meanings.

Another premature aging risk is linked to markets' evolutions towards new tendencies, modes and sport practices. The ski brands Rossignol and Salomon, which are closely associated with competition, the Olympics and traditional skiing values, did not anticipate the trends initiated by the tribes of young snowboarders and which very quickly spread among many different groups and segments. Snowboarding was developed in opposition to skiing and its dominant culture, which was seen as a disciplined, bureaucratised, rationalised, uniform and bourgeois sport, impregnated with a 'must win mentality' whereas snowboarding was synonymous with entertainment, spectacle, camaraderie and fun (Heino, 2000). In the snowboarding segments these two brands have been overtaken by other brands such as Quiksilver, Oxbow and Billabong which have their identity embedded in the boardsports and free-ride culture. Obviously, repositioning a brand does not necessarily mean setting it apart from its current targets and segments. It means that brand values have to be transformed to go along with the level of identity changes.

Finally, brands' aging can be more simply linked to the aging of its consumers, products or communication and marketing techniques. In this regard, the Stade Français Paris professional rugby club is quite illustrative. The club which was no longer successful and popular in the second part of the twentieth century was taken over in the nineties by Max Guazzini, a former director of a popular French radio station. This new president completely changed the club's image by implementing innovative marketing strategies in a sport usually associated with rural values and traditions (Bodet, 2009). He changed the club's logo, anthem and symbols and introduced new creative and provocative rugby jerseys with lightning, with lily flowers, with camouflage pattern, with historical characters and with pink colours. He also organised big shows around games with stunts, concerts, parades and celebrities targeting and attracting new spectators, launched a semi-naked players' calendar and a moisturiser brand extension (Bodet, 2009). Thanks to these marketing changes, he totally changed the brand's image making it popular, trendy, vibrant and provocative; a perfect fit with the city of Paris.

The cases of Nike and Adidas

Nike, the sport brand world leader, also had to face this erosion and aging phenomenon. Despite a significant growth (seven per cent from 2007 to 2011) and massive annual revenues (the company reported US$16,326 million in 2007, US$19,176 million in 2009, and US$20,862 million in 2011[1]) some experts consider that the American brand has been stagnating since the end of the nineties. Its core segment targets are aging and the fact that the brand did not anticipate or did not want to follow the development of outdoor clothing and the evolution of footwear towards more stylistic, fashionable and urban models should have decreased its attraction power.[2] Even with massive promotional campaigns about football and basketball which often create a buzz, it seems that the brand did not manage to attract young non-mainstream sport consumers such as skateboarders and surfers. Consequently, it did not appear legitimate to this particular segment where brands such as Vans, Carhartt and Airwalk were getting a strong reputation. These brands did not hesitate to get involved in close sponsorship partnerships with well-known professional skateboarders as well as sponsoring music festivals and famous exhibitions within the boardsports world. These brands have now become references within this sector. It can be then questioned whether Nike's strategy corresponded to the vision a world leader brand should have.

Within the highly fluctuating and changing sports markets, consumers' tastes, needs, expectations and desires have dramatically evolved and if during the eighties and nineties promotional campaigns featuring the best world champions were enough, it seems that this strategy is no longer applicable to all segments. It seems that Nike did not listen enough to its consumers but instead focused on technological performances targeting athletes, when it should have further integrated fashion and pricing issues in its strategy. Therefore, constantly innovating is not sufficient. Moreover, increasing costs have forced the brand to move its products towards high-end segments where profits and return on investments are bigger. However, this upward extension, which will be later discussed in section 'The pitfalls of excessive marketing', page 160, is efficient only if the brand is still present in the middle range segments gathering most consumers. What was first a relevant strategy to counter other competitors progressively became a handicap. Nike's offers became less attractive in comparison with its main competitors who offer cheaper prices and elaborated designs. It is also true that at the same time, the brand faced many attacks and criticisms regarding its soft attitude towards the working conditions in its Asian sweatshops and took some time to react in an appropriate manner which seriously damaged its reputation. It was probably the lack of communication and reaction to these accusations which harmed the brand most and for this its co-founder and former chairman Philip Knight was reproached. If there is a lesson to be learnt from this example is probably that a sport brand cannot indefinitely follow the strategy which made its success and that brands' positioning and values have to constantly try to adjust and adapt to markets' evolution, even if they are sometimes very difficult to predict and anticipate.

The rejuvenating strategy adopted by Adidas is in many aspects similar to the case of Nike. At the end of the eighties, when the founder Horst Dassler died, the brand did not want to pursue the urban, jogging and fitness trends in order to extend its lines focused on competitive sports (Bontour and Lehu, 2004). Progressively, the brand was distanced from competitors such as Nike, Reebok or Fila. In 1993, when Robert-Louis Dreyfus became chairman, he rapidly realised that the brand was aging considerably despite high perceived quality levels. Particularly, the brand did not respond to the aggressive marketing campaigns conducted by Nike and Reebok to conquer major international markets. At that time, Adidas was used to competing with Puma which was less aggressive from a commercial and marketing perspective than Nike and Reebok. Therefore, Adidas had to adapt. The brand decided to rejuvenate its image and to conquer new segment targets. This strategy relied for a large part on focusing on the football sector. In 1994, Adidas opened a football dedicated store in Paris and launched a new, innovative model, the 'Predator', supported by the 'Earn them' promotional campaign designed by David Lynch which enhanced the brand's image. Boosted by its success at the 1996 Atlanta Summer Olympics where 220 of its sponsored athletes won a medal including 70 gold medals, Adidas became the official sponsor of the 1998 FIFA World Cup which saw the victory of the French team, sponsored by Adidas. Alongside this new marketing orientation the company also adopted a new industrial approach to compete with Nike and Reebok and relocated its main production units in South-East Asia. A new operational division for each sport was also set up while the brand was repositioned and production processes reviewed to be able to efficiently manage smaller collections better adapted to market trends (Bontour and Lehu, 2004).

The British agency Leagas Delaney was entrusted with its rejuvenating mission and came up with a very specific mix of marketing and communication. They tried to create a deep emotional link with the public instead of focusing on rational and cognitive elements such as technologies and medals as they had before. The strategy also focused on younger consumer segments in exploiting television and Internet media. For instance, a large scale campaign was set on the television music channel MTV whose audience is mainly younger generations. The football and the young and trendy strategies were quite successful and are symbolised for instance by Adidas' collaboration with David Beckham who stands at the crossroads of these two universes.

Brand name change

The need and sometimes the obligation to change a brand name often comes from the fact that the name has become dated and old-fashioned. With time, a brand name can become obsolete because of out-of-date phonetic, verbal or semiotic characteristics. A big generational gap can also be a factor encouraging such a change. When the younger generations start considering that a brand is firstly associated to their parents or sometimes grandparents, a name change may be considered as an option. However, for brands whose reference to past and authentic values is an asset, an old-fashioned image should be kept. It seems, however, that this is not often the case for sport good brands as consumers primarily look for contemporary and trendy brands, except for a few examples and/or limited lines such as Converse or Champion USA. For club and sport organisation brands it is, however, the contrary as their age and history are signs of legitimacy. Even if they can sometimes rejuvenate their logos or colours, they actively try to keep their name and symbols especially when they associate them to a glorious past such as Real Madrid (football and basketball), FC Barcelona (football, basketball, handball), New York Yankees (baseball), and Chicago Bulls (basketball). In some cases, the name is so important and embedded within a local history and community that fans and members of the local community want it back such as in the case of the

Canadian ice-hockey franchise Winnipeg Jets. In 1996, the Canadian franchise was relocated to Phoenix (Arizona) and became Phoenix Coyotes. But in 2011, the Atlanta Thrashers franchise was relocated to Winnipeg and due to strong local support the franchise was renamed Winnipeg Jets, just as the old franchise. Very few cases of name change can be identified such as the New York MetroStars (football) which was changed to New York Red Bull because of the takeover by Red Bull GmbH. The same thing happened to other clubs taken over by Red Bull such as the Austrian football club FC Red Bull Salzburg, previously named SV Austria Salzburg. However, for the latter, this name change created a lot of resistance from diehard fans who saw in this change the negative impact of the commercialisation and commodification of football. Some of them refused this name change so deeply that they ultimately formed a new football club using the club's former name (SV Austria Salzburg).

A brand name can be changed because it has become out-of-date but also for strategic reasons: when the brand is acquired by another brand or corporation, when there is a merger, when there is organisational culture's change, when range, brand or geographical extensions are considered, when a new promise is promoted, or when the brand portfolio has to be rationalised. In 2007, Decathlon Group changed its name to become Oxylane Group essentially for strategic purposes. 'Oxy' was chosen to refer to oxygen, 'lane' was explicitly referring to path, and 'x' and 'y' symbolise both male and female. The final name was meant to become a symbol of conviviality, communication, and pleasure in collective practices. This change not only reflected a new internal organisation but also an identity change. Specifically, Oxylane Group was going to fulfil two roles: manufacturer of sporting goods and brands and click and mortar retailer of sporting goods. Although Decathlon remained the brand name of the retail stores, Oxylane was meant to integrate both activities as well as providing an international dimension to the group by being intelligible in many languages and in particular in English.

In the context of mergers and acquisitions, four methods of strategic brands merging can be identified (Basu, 2006):

1. only one brand, often the one with the strongest brand equity, is kept (either A or B);
2. both brand names can be merged creating a 'joint brand' (A-B, such as Adidas-Salomon);
3. both brands can be associated creating a 'flexible brand' (A and B);
4. a new brand is created.

Most of the time, a change of name is a risky strategy which is not without consequences from a financial, marketing and strategic perspective (Kapferer, 1998). As the links are close between corporations and their brands, it can harm corporations' interests which makes this decision very difficult to take. A new name will go along a new set of meanings, a new style and a new identity for the brand. Consequently, recreating high levels of awareness and a good reputation without losing consumers remain a tough challenge (Lewi and Rogliano, 2006). Consumers may not be able to recognise their usual product or be sceptical about the reliability of the standards and level or quality which can be directly translated into market share losses. Furthermore, a name change is also expensive as all communication supports have to be changed as well as formal documents. Sometimes the change is part of a bigger strategy involving introducing an unknown brand to a specific market. In that case the change aims to rapidly transfer reputation and consumers to the new brand. This transfer can be brutal (for example if the name is changed overnight), this is what happened in the food sector to 'Raider' when renamed 'Twix', or progressive, taking successive steps in order not to disorientate current consumers. These steps can for instance include a double branding for a temporary period and/or a new communication campaign announcing the change. The brutal change is more appropriate when the initial brand does not have very high aware- ness levels or a strong reputation. Another strategy consists of transforming the name of a successful line or product into a new brand. This is for instance what Oxylane Group did with few of its brands, when b'Twin, which was the name of one bike line, replaced Decathlon to become the brand name for all bikes and related products. In this case it was a progressive change. The same strategy was applied when Wed'ze, which was initially the name of a ski range, became the brand name for all the company's snow products and accessories. Brand name changes are quite common for club and league brands especially when two clubs merge. It is a tricky exercise because names often represent more than just a brand but also a specific geographical location. Therefore, it is often difficult to satisfy everyone, from spectators and fans to public authorities. In 1999, the London Irish rugby union club merged with London Scottish and Richmond to form a new company to support a professional team and the structure kept the name London Irish RFC. Catalans Dragons, the only French club of the English Super League (rugby league), is another example as the club was formed by a merger of XIII Catalan and AS Saint Estève, two clubs based in the city of Perpignan. These types of brand name change are increased by the naming right practice where stadiums and leagues are renamed by the name of a sponsor as for Arsenal FC's Emirates Stadium, Newcastle United's Sports Direct Arena, Colorado Rockies's Coors Field, Pittsburgh Steelers' Heinz Field, the Aviva Premiership (English rugby union premiership) and the RaboDirect Pro12 (Celtic rugby union league). It has to be noted that if these naming rights strategies provide significant financial incomes, they create mixed reactions with fans and spectators.

The pitfalls of excessive marketing

In some cases the difficulties and threats brands face come from an economic or commercial logic which is pushed too far. Although initiated by brands to conquer new markets and segments and to enhance their reputation and increase their growth they can also become counterproductive and produce unexpected negative outcomes. Two main pitfall types can be identified. The first pitfall category relates to product or brand trivialisation whereas the second category relates to brand positioning and particularly their upward growth extension towards premium and ultra-premium products. Finally, a particular focus is given to club brands and fans' resistance towards commercialisation and marketisation.

Branductisation and trivialisation

Brand owners are often advised to make sure that their brand and/or product names do not become trivial and that they are not used to designate a category of products. A product which represents an entire category is named a 'branduct' (Kapferer, 2008), a portmanteau term made of brand and product. Numerous brands and products have become branducts such as Lego, Malibu, Kleenex, Bailey's, Jeep, Polaroid, Fenwick, Mars, Velux, Post it, Nutella or Nylon. Becoming a branduct is a paradoxical situation as it is simultaneously the best and the worst that can happen to a brand (Lewi, 2004). It represents the best because it corresponds to the climax of commercial success. It can appear positive at first because it gives the impression of a monopolistic position if consumers designate all the products of a category to one brand name, but it has also several negative consequences. It is particularly problematic if the name integrates into dictionaries because it appears to be public and can be used by other competitors to sell their own brands and products. In this case, brand owners have to be very careful and systematically pursue those who illegally use their name to protect it. As noted by Kapferer (2008), branducts have also to invest twice as much in advertising as they have to compete at a category level and not at a product level. However, the clear advantage is that when one thinks of the category, the brand appears automatically among the purchase options, when it is not the only one. In the sport context, 'Snowblade', which is a brand owned by Salomon, has become a branduct for the whole ski-board category. In rock climbing, 'Spit' has also become a branduct designating a type of anchor and fixing. 'Hydrospeed', which designates all kinds of water sledges, 'Zodiac', which designates all kinds of inflatable boats, Helly Hansen which can designate all kinds of baselayers, are other examples of this phenomenon.

Brands' trivialisation also occurs when one brand or one of its products is used by another consumer segment which was not initially targeted by the brand. This is for instance what happened to Aigle whose '1983 Copeland' sailing jacket became trendy as an autumn lifestyle jacket. More than 100,000 units were sold although this model was only sold in specialised sailing stores. This outcome was clearly unexpected when the jacket was designed for such a small niche segment. If these unexpected sales represented a positive thing, the possible drawbacks on the specialist brand image and the perceptions of the core initial segments could be negative and have long-term consequences. One adequate strategy to avoid this trivialisation is to regularly launch new products to reinforce the cutting-edge dimension of the brand and avoid any hijacking from other brands; the competitors should not be able to use reputation of other brands' products for their own advantage. Three main strategies seem possible to minimise this risk. The first one relies on product innovation and this is the strategy Nike adopted in 1979 with the 'Tailwind' high-tech shoes, its first model with an air cushion. This model launch was also strongly supported from a promotional perspective with the use of Michael Jordan, from 1984 to 1999, and aimed to convince consumers that they needed this model for their everyday life. For this specific case, Nike created its own label, the 'Nike Alpha Project', which gathered all its innovative products. The second strategy consists of remaining a reference for experts and specialists particularly in satisfying these demanding consumers in terms of performance and technicality. This is the strategy adopted for instance by Timberland which continues targeting lumberjacks offering them safety shoes and jackets adapted to cold working conditions while offering new shoe models targeting a large public. Finally, the third strategy relies on displaying and affirming its history and values. This is for instance what Quiksilver tried to do by promoting its surfing anchorage and transferring those values to all its lifestyle lines. The strong reference to its surfing roots allows the brand to regularly launch new collections which appear legitimate: the products explicitly refer to the surfing world through their colours, symbols and models while referring as well to a creative and innovative spirit which is embedded within the sport.

Another form of trivialisation can occur when a product becomes so successful that it shadows the brand's other products, reducing the brand to a single famous product. This is what happened to Lacoste with its shirts which became inseparable from the brand name. This had its downsides because the brand became too dependent on a single product and limited its diversification opportunities. This trivialisation risk can be extended to all brands whose name was given by a famous founder and/or athlete. In this case the founder's reputation and personality could limit the brand's development, or at least its emancipation and autonomy. Because of the notoriety of the tennis champion Jean Lacoste between 1930 and 1950, the brand's managers decided to add the term 'shirt' to its brand name (Chemise Lacoste) but it became a problem later when the brand was only associated to shirt products.

Brand trivialisation does not only happen through their products but also through their symbols and logos. Badging, which represents the fact that people consume and display brands to have a confirmation of their self-image that they present to others (Kapferer, 2008), is one function that brands use to attract and keep consumers, especially young consumers. Many brands from the textile sector have for instance actively tried to integrate their brands, logos and symbols in a street culture in order to become identity and group indicators. However, in some circumstances, their symbols can be diverted from the meanings wanted by the brands and re-appropriated by groups and tribes who confer on them other meanings, which may not satisfy the brands any more. Becoming too popular can then sometimes mean that the brands do not belong to their managers any more but to their consumers, with all the risks conveyed. Burberry, which tried to rejuvenate its image by offering baseball caps, faced this issue when these caps became popular among hooligans. The brand was then forced to stop offering this product. The same kind of phenomenon happened to brands such as Helly Hansen, Le Coq Sportif, Pro-Keds, Sergio Tacchini and Lacoste which became very popular in hip hop and gangsta fashion. For instance, for many young French people from citiy neighbourhoods and council estates, Lacoste had become a synonym of financial success and wealth which led Becker (2002) to say that Lacoste became a brand which allows people to say where they are from and where they belong (for example bourgeois or rebel, wealthy or poor, young or old, trendy or dated, ignorant or expert). Lacoste's strategy was almost schizophrenic because although they did not officially target these segments, specific products were created with bigger crocodile logos for these consumers!

The pitfalls of upward trends toward premium and ultra-premium products

For the last few years, sport brands have been engaged in a highly competitive race towards high-end segments called premium or ultra-premium segments because of their potential high benefits. Furthermore, some brands estimate that it is more interesting to target more demanding consumers who are willing to pay more for selected products than competing on bottom-end segments where success seems more unlikely. The Nike skating model 'Braat LR Low Premium ID', Le Coq Sportif's lifestyle model 'Sapporo Premium' and Asics' running model 'Gel-Kinsei 4' are examples of these premium products. Therefore, brands will try to add more value to their products through sophistication, higher technology, better quality and design. Generally speaking, it can be said that consumers get more value for what they pay, but this relationship is not continuously linear. Specifically on the sport goods markets, after a certain ceiling the products' technical advantage is marginal when it concerns non-elite athletes. As these sport participants are not unconditionally looking for performance improvements, the perceived added value of such premium products becomes limited. This clearly represents a handicap for sport brands as the more technical the products are, the smaller the number of target sport participants. The limits here are predominantly those of consumers before becoming those of products, even if the symbolic dimension also plays a significant role which is difficult to estimate financially. Offering products which potentially increase performance, promoted by celebrity athletes, constitutes an excellent selling argument which is sometimes enough to justify pricing differences, especially big ones between high-end and middle range items. In the ski sector, most brands offer racing models for competitors (for example 'Radical World Cup' from Rossignol) used by endorsed elite athletes (for example 'Blizzard S-Power Full Suspension', 'Völkl TigerShark 11 Feet Power Switch', and 'Dynastar Speed Limited'). Some brands even offer prestige models: Lacroix commercialises a ski model, the 'Cruiser Titane', which is worth €3,500. The dream and prestige dimension of these products is always difficult to accurately evaluate.

From an economic perspective, sport brands have a lot to win by targeting high-end segments. As prices are higher, profitability is often higher. For this reason it attracts many brands which are positioned in other lower segments. This strategy was adopted by Oxylane Group in Europe with its retail brand Skimium.com where consumers can rent the 'Ski Premium Pack' comprising high-end skis such as Dynastar's 'Outland 80 XT' or Atomic's 'Nomad Black Eye 82' models. However, the main problem of this strategy is that many brands target these segments only for their potential benefits or because they feel they have to, and not necessarily in response to a consistent and rationalised line strategy. Part of brands' motivation seems to be the rising costs of raw material, research and development, logistics and distribution. Globalisation also seems to play a moderating or accelerating factor in the sense that more models are being imported and offered to consumers for very competitive prices against which brands struggle to cope. They are therefore prompted to offer more developed and advanced products to make a clear differentiation with these low-price products. This can be then considered mainly as a defensive strategy from brands but the danger is that consumers do not perceive any justified added value for the premium products. Ultimately, this could create a drawback which would increase consumers' scepticism and would make them focus more on bottom-end and middle range products.

Resistance to sport clubs' commercialisation

Since the nineties, the commercialisation of European football driven by national leagues and professional clubs has significantly increased and intensified to reach a current stage where its role is seen as crucial in the success of professional clubs or even the survival of some of them. This process has undoubtedly produced some positive consequences for professional football clubs but its intensity and its expansion have also seemed to provoke some dissatisfaction and resistance from some fans and supporters and even some disaffection in the worst cases. Several current examples can be highlighted as illustrations of the risks incurred. In the English Premiership, there has been increasing fan complaints about the frequent change of home kits which supporters cannot afford to buy so regularly. As an example, in 2010, Tottenham Hotspur had changed its home jersey design in each of the previous six years and Chelsea FC had done it four times in the previous five years. Although nothing legally prevents these clubs making these changes so frequently, it has been recognised that supporters are increasingly dissatisfied with this practice.[3] Similarly, supporters have increasingly complained about other practices such as the sale of naming rights (supporters of Newcastle United FC fiercely opposed the renaming of St James' Park stadium as the 'sportsdirect.com @ St James' Park Stadium' for the 2009–2010 season), the renaming of their clubs, the change of colours (in 2012 Cardiff City fans complained about the colour change from blue to red), the extensive use of brand extensions and the increasing targeting and compliance to foreign markets and demands (many pre-season tours are organised overseas and the English Premier League even considered organising some fixtures abroad).

According to several authors (for example Giulianotti, 2005; Oppenhuisen and van Zoonen, 2006), European football is facing major changes in terms of commercialisation or marketisation. Besides the motives of the professional football clubs and their stakeholders, this noticeable evolution can be explained by the globalisation and Americanisation of sport, of which McDonaldisation (Ritzer, 1993) and Disneyisation (Bryman, 2004) are two aspects. For Duke (2002), the principles of McDonaldisation, which can be seen as a systematic rationalisation process such as in McDonald's restaurants, have been evident in English football since the nineties and are represented in many changes and practices. Relocation to new stadia, ground sharing schemes and multiple sport usages are examples of the 'efficiency' principle. 'Bigger and better' leagues, altering fixtures to suit TV and targeting more affluent audiences are examples of the 'calculability' principle. More predictable 'product', introduction of artificial turf (now less fashionable) and penalty shoot outs are examples of the 'predictability principle'. Finally, increased stewarding, all seated stadia and button control of crowd noise in some corporate boxes are examples of the 'control' principle. Disneyisation can be seen as the transfer or the application of Disney theme parks' principles to other parts of society and seems also to apply to English football. The introduction (or use) of mascots, the renaming of clubs and leagues are examples of the 'theming' dimension. The introduction and standardisation of pre-game shows, the standardisation of football grounds and the lack of atmosphere in relocated or restructured grounds are examples of the 'dedifferentiation of consumption' component. Franchised products, replica shirts and naming rights practices are examples of the 'merchandising' component. Finally, excessive cheerfulness and friendliness, the development of executive boxes and hospitality functions and the ejection of partisans with unwanted and dysfunctional attitudes and behaviours are examples of the 'emotional labour' component. This concept seems highly relevant as it is well understood by football stakeholders as illustrated by St Pauli's (Germany) chairman who stated that he did not want to transform the stadium into 'a Disneyland full of ads'.[4] Even if parts of this commercialisation process are accepted by many spectators and fans it has created much resistance from within traditional football fan culture which can be expressed in many different ways (for example through petitions, protests, campaigns, boycotts) and can lead to disaffection and non-attendance on a long-term basis.

If this issue seems to have primarily arisen in European football, two interconnected explanations can be put forward. The first one is cultural and relies on the level of tolerance and acceptance of marketing practices which may vary according to cultures and subcultures. For instance, marketing practices are extensively used by North American, Australian and New Zealand franchises and leagues and they do not seem to create much resistance among fans and spectators. Therefore, strong variations should be observed between countries and cultures. The second issue relies on the commercialisation level of football which seems to be the most advanced sport in this regard in Europe. Consequently, it can be anticipated that when other European sports will reach the same level of commercialisation dissatisfaction and resistance reactions may also arise.

Resisting parasitism, boycott, social criticism and counterfeiting

Sports brands have always faced public criticisms and complaints, sometimes very aggressive, which come either from anti-brands or environmental activist groups or even consumers' associations. In the seventies, petrochemical groups had been the first ones to face opponents engaged in environment protection such as Greenpeace, but now all types of corporations and groups, international ones in particular, are under the focus of these kinds of groups. For sport brands, it was probably the focus on the poor and abusive working conditions in Nike's sweat-shops located in South-East Asia which triggered the development of a more global and collective awareness of unethical sport corporations and brand practices. Since, the variety of criticisms has also been extended, and in some cases over-extended to make sport brands responsible for all kinds of problems in contemporary developed societies and individuals' ill-being. They have for instance been accused of generating anxiety among consumers because of the overabundance of products and the proliferation of fake novelties (Cristol and Sealey, 2000).

It is probably because they stigmatise and symbolise the drifts of societies that brands are in the bullseye of criticisms and protests of 'adbusters' and 'alter-global-ists'. Brands are now targeted by individuals, groups and sometimes states which diffuse via the Internet a lot of parasite information – or counter information – aiming to harm brands or make consumers more aware about these practices, which in turn can have strongly negative impacts. In this 'war', the better known the brands are, the more widespread the information will be, particularly through a negative but very efficient word-of-mouth. Depending on the nature of malprac-tice, responses to these parasite information campaigns can be calls for boycotts and other kinds of activities which can harm brand reputation, create an unwanted notoriety and damage turnover.

Boycott to sanction sport brands' malpractices: lessons from the Nike case

Probably the first major case of boycott happened in the seventies and concerned Nestlé, which was accused of killing African babies with its powdered milk. Well used, boycott can represent a powerful weapon which can significantly affect inter-national brands, particularly in this globalised world where information is quickly diffused and competition intense between brands. This tactic certainly does not only concern non-sport related brands, and numerous sporting events such as the Olympics or the Dakar Rally (formerly known as the Paris–Dakar Rally) have faced boycott campaigns. And the reasons for boycotting are endless: the host coun-try does not respect human rights, too much pollution created by the events, too many people killed (as for the Dakar Rally), the sporting facilities are not environ-mentally friendly enough, facilities are built on sacred sites for local people (as for the Vancouver 2010 Winter Olympics and illustrated by a mural pictured in Montreal, see Figure 7.1), plus many contextual and political reasons.

FIGURE 7.1   A resistance example directed at the Vancouver 2010 Winter Olympics

Just to name a few, more than 60 countries boycotted the 1980 Moscow
Summer Olympics to protest against the invasion of Afghanistan by the USSR and
18 countries boycotted the 1984 Los Angeles Summer Olympics officially for
security reasons but for many of them it seemed to be in response to the 1980
Olympic Games boycott. More recently a boycott call for the 2008 Beijing

Summer Olympics was launched a few years before to protest against China's policy regarding Tibet. Very recently, in 2012, calls were made to F1 teams, drivers and media to boycott the Bahrain F1 Grand Prix because of the country's political troubles and to political leaders to boycott the EURO 2012 football championship in Ukraine because of the alleged bad treatment of a former Ukrainian Prime Minister Yulia Tymoshenko. With boycott tactics, the main objective is to make brands' owners and managers face their technical and citizenship responsibilities. This represents a clear threat for them as nine out of ten consumers state that they would be willing to do it to protest against child labour, polluting production processes, employees' redundancies when the companies are making benefits or when working conditions legislations are not applied (Mercier, 2004; Le Borgne-Larivière, 2005). For these reasons, ethics are now taken seriously by companies and brands. Moreover, it seems that no company is fully protected from negative counter-publicity and tough criticisms from groups and activists who are increasingly well informed. The growing importance of sport in people's everyday lives associated with sports' values, make sport an area in which boycott campaigns will increase (Drillech, 1999).

Another form of resistance, which can be associated to boycott, is the parody of brands' slogans, logos and signatures by consumers and activist groups (for example 'just break it', 'just smoke it', 'just did it' for Nike's slogan 'just do it') also known as 'subvertising' (a portmanteau term made of subvert and advertising) or 'culture jamming'. If it is illegal to use brands' logos, it is, however, not prohibited to parody them or use the colour codes generally associated to brands. However, although in most cases these tactics come from resistance and activist groups, some of these subvertisements come from profit enterprises which just want to use them to make money, without any anti-brand or anti-consumption messages.

Following the accusations of activist groups and organisations which pointed out the responsibilities of Nike, Reebok and Adidas regarding the poor working conditions in their supplying sweatshops (more than 65 hours of work per week for less than €10), Nike's stock price which had reached US$76 in 1997 went down to US$27 in 2000, following a drop in its turnover. In 1996, *Life* magazine published a picture of a Pakistani child working on an American brand's football which shocked public opinion worldwide. However, it was an audit conducted by Ernst and Young in one Vietnamese factory which had important negative consequences (Keller, 2003). In this report, Nike was directly accused of favouring child labour and slavery among its subcontracted Asian sweatshops. In response to that, the Clean Clothes Campaign, which is a garment industry's alliance of labour unions and non-governmental organisations, launched a campaign to increase people's awareness about people's stories behind their sport shoes. After this event, Nike remained under non-governmental organisations and media scrutiny for more than a decade. In denouncing malpractices from international brands, Naomi Klein (2001) was certainly a trigger for anti-brand attitudes in public opinion and Nike was one of the favourite targets. Her goal was to point out the excessive role of brands in economies and Nike was a good illustration as it generated about five per cent of Vietnam's GDP in the middle of the nineties because of its numerous factories based in the country (Kahle et al., 2000). Although Klein (2001) recognised that multinational companies contributed to emerging countries' growth and development, the author wanted to emphasise the drifts and negative consequences of the continuous search for profit which seemed to be the unique driver of brands' shareholders. However, we can wonder if Nike did not play a scapegoat role as numerous other corporations and brands had the same unethical practices at that time, and if the brand still deserves this image. In any case, it seems that Nike seems to cultivate ambiguities because it invests a lot in developing a brand image articulated around a philosophy of life and humanist values on one hand, although on the other hand it extensively uses subcontractors which are not often highly respectful of human rights and working conditions, at least from western standards. Since its origins, the brand has advocated a discourse centred on team spirit, the respect of everyone's differences, the importance of example and self-achievement (Drillech, 1999), but at the same time, Nike did not want to know what was going on in its subcontractors' factories. Beyond the case of Nike, the growth of activism can be thought to correspond to an increasing contestation and resistance against companies and brands' hegemony which invest all areas of social spaces. From many different aspects, Nike is a symbol of worldwide industrial and commercial success in the same way as Coca-Cola, Microsoft, Apple, MacDonald's and Sony are. It is therefore not surprising that the brand was at the forefront of consumers' resistance and activism because it represented numerous textile companies which had the same malpractices. Why attack small, unknown representatives when attacking the biggest, richest and most famous will have a better impact on consumers and media? Attacking Nike is attacking the giant, the leader, the number one, and the powerful one which, besides media attention, gives a romantic touch to the fight, such as David and Goliath (the biblical characters, not the brand).

If Klein (2001) pictured brands as dictators and criticised their domination over consumers, Chevalier and Mazzolovo (2004), in their book *Pro Logo* looked at it from another angle and from a more positive perspective. Even if they do not share Klein's point of view they recognise the importance of her book in triggering new practices and putting brands' impacts under the spotlight. All the justified attacks against Nike and others are at the origins of the implementation of monitoring programs to make sure that products are made under acceptable conditions. Obviously, many people will estimate that these programmes and corporate social responsibility concerns do not come from genuine philanthropy but from calculated tactical orientations and that many things can still be improved. However, from a pragmatic point of view, it cannot be denied that things have been improved. The fact that Nike got caught for its malpractices has imposed the creation of new standards either set from the companies themselves or from states. All the discussions and debates around the Nike's case have accelerated the redaction of the SA8000® certification established by Social Accountability International (SAI) and which aims at protecting workers' basic human rights, including banning child and forced labour, the respect of workers' right to form and join trade unions and zero tolerance on corporal punishment, mental or physical abuse of personel. Nowadays, it seems that only the corporations which clarified their positioning regarding these issues in accordance with societies' expectations are able to succeed. As seen in Chapter 5, corporate social and environmental responsibility have become common practices among companies and brands to satisfy consumers' expectations and society at large. However, as highlighted in Nike's behaviour–discourse gap, CSR initiatives do not prevent. On the contrary, a more pessimistic view on things would tend to believe that the more brands behave badly, the more they will implement CSR initiatives. Conversely, the fact that they increasingly engage and commit to CSR programmes would tend to signify that they are fully aware of their malpractices and that they try to re-buy public opinions through them. As illustrated in the recent scandal involving Adidas regarding Great Britain's kits for the London 2012 Summer Olympics which were made in abusive Indonesian sweatshops, this issue is not over, although it first struck Nike more than fifteen years ago. We can then wonder whether the Nike case only taught a lesson to Nike itself and that learning from boycott campaigns really works only for the brands concerned. Despite the creation of a non-governmental organisation, Global Alliance for Workers and Communities, in association with Gap and the World Bank whose aim is to audit subcontractors to control the decency of their working conditions, and despite the creation of an internal code of ethics, Nike remains one the favourite targets of human rights and environment activists. In public opinion, Nike will remain guilty for a long time and whatever it does, Nike will still be morally indebted to society.

Sport brands against parasitism and ambush marketing: the case of the Olympic brand

Parasitism, also known as reputation leeching, is a marketing term designating all types of practices and behaviours which aim to use another product or brand's reputation to enhance its own. It is a rather 'efficient' strategy to limit the benefits of some brands while increasing the parasite brand's benefits. As a comparison, if boycotting is a form of protest, parasitism is simultaneously a form of counter-publicity and a form of unfair competition. Furthermore, forms of parasitism are illegal because they breach copyrights and legal rights and can have very negative consequences for the brands concerned. Moreover, if boycott tactics stem from an opposition and resistance with the hope of modifying corporations and brands' practices, parasitism aims to benefit at the expense of the other, such as in a biological configuration. An illustration is given with Figure 7.2 representing a shop's front in a Mexican city which illegally uses David Beckham's image to sell brands who are not partners of the football player. The brands benefit from the investments and the success of other brands, mainly by using their reputation. For this reason it can be considered as an efficient strategy in the sense that it requires minimum costs, as they are borne by the 'host brand', for potential important benefits. If some legal costs corresponding to a trial defence could make this ratio far less efficient,

FIGURE 7.2 A parasitism example using David Beckham's image

one could say that publicity, even negative, generated by a court case would still benefit the 'parasite brand'. With parasitism, brands are so to speak caught in their own games because the communication they use to better influence and control consumers' tastes and desires is not entirely controlled by them anymore. Particularly with new media and information technologies, these criticisms and hijacks become easier and more frequent. Moreover, because of the importance and amplification roles of social media, even the most untrue and small rumours or boycott calls have to be taken seriously. In this context, the more brands are known, the more they are exposed to such practices.

Sport brands are particularly targeted by such parasite tactics because of their strong awareness levels and brand image, and the Olympic brand which belongs to the International Olympic Committee (IOC), is a good example of this (Sandler and Shani, 1989). For each Summer and Winter Olympics, the event's sponsors and partners benefit from exclusive rights to use the Olympic properties which are the Olympic hymn, Olympic medals, the Olympic motto (citius, altius, fortius), Olympic posters, the Olympic symbol (the five interlaced rings), the Olympic flag, the Olympic oath, the Olympic flame and torch relay, the Olympic mascot, Olympic emblems (the rings associated with the logo of an Olympic organisation or sponsor), Olympic pictograms, still images of the Olympics, moving images of the Olympics, and Olympic data (e.g. start list, finish lists, intermediary and final results, medals tables) (Ferrand, Chappelet and Séguin, 2012). However, many companies and brands which do not have a contract and then no rights with the IOC still try to confuse consumers' minds in making them believe that they are indeed official partners and sponsors. These strategies are known as ambush marketing. For Séguin and Ellis (2012), four main categories of ambush marketing strategies can be identified. The first one relies on the sponsoring of media coverage and is according to these authors among the most effective. The second category relies on the sponsoring of subcategories such as athletes, teams, national and international governing bodies. The third category concerns advertising that corresponds to the event and the fourth category concerns thematic advertising and implied association. The last two are probably the more subtle ones, and therefore probably the most difficult ones to challenge, because they make no claims about any direct association, restricted trademarks, symbols or words. Ambush marketing concerns numerous major sporting events and brands but because of their popularity, the Olympics are probably the pinnacle for such practices; the birth of this practice being traditionally associated with the 1984 Los Angeles Summer Olympics when Kodak ambushed the official sponsor Fuji (Séguin and Ellis, 2012).

Subtly conducted, ambush marketing strategies allow non-official partners and sponsors access to important benefits in terms of spontaneous awareness and image associations and it is not rare to see consumers identifying ambushers as official sponsors and sometimes to see consumers showing higher memory rates for ambushers. In some cases, the fact that brands do not hold official rights force them to be highly creative to attract spectators' and consumers' attention without being obviously illegal. Such results would tend to demonstrate the efficiency of ambush marketing tactics. However, it would also tend to highlight the lack of efficiency of sponsors' leveraging and activation strategies. Basically, they do not do enough to fully benefit from their rights. This confusion in spectators' and consumers' minds can be compared to counterfeiting. Although legal strategies to prevent ambush marketing have been recently put in place with for instance the involvement of host cities and countries' governments and the creation of anti-ambush legislation (for example the London Olympic Games and Paralympic Games Act 2006, Canada's Olympic and Paralympic Marks Act 2007) (Séguin and Ellis, 2012), suing all ambushers does not represent a sustainable solution, particularly because of the numbers of ambushers and their size and because this could have a negative counter-effect in demonstrating the legal but excessive power of brands. For this reason, other protection strategies have been set up such as education programmes targeting specific groups: ambushers, small businesses, sport federations, athletes and consumers (Séguin and Ellis, 2012). It is indeed important to differentiate real ambush marketing strategies which result from a real will and intention from ambushers to get benefits they are not entitled to and who are fully aware of copyrights and properties issues and so will try to play within legislation's grey areas, and what can be called clumsy marketing and promotion strategies often implemented by small businesses which are not aware of all these property issues and sometimes do not even know what ambush marketing is. In the first category more and more specialised advertising and communication agencies can be found trying to exploit all the gaps left by the Olympic organisers and right holders. As an example, during the 2008 Beijing Summer Olympics, ERKE, a Chinese sport brand, which was not an official sponsor, managed to show its logo and obtain important TV exposure thanks to the endorsement of Chen Xiexia, a Chinese weightlifter who won the first Chinese gold medal. For brands which are not officially associated with the Olympics and then do not benefit from any rights, the best strategy, without following a risky ambush marketing strategy, is probably to be creative and audacious. During the same 2008 Beijing Olympics, Mengniu, the dairy products' brand leader in China, was not an official partner as was its main competitor Yili, but ran an advertising campaign during the Games featuring a weightlifter, then a kid showing a drawing featuring a cow with 2008 written on, and then female fans in red cheering, creating indirect associations with the Games. KFC launched its 'I love Beijing' campaign; the sports channel CCTT5's commentators were endorsed by Li Ning; Pepsi launched a red can quite similar to those of the official partner Coca-Cola; and Nike launched a 'Run China Campaign'. These are just few examples among plenty and do not even include social media and digital ambush marketing. The final example is not properly speaking a case of ambush marketing in the sense that it does not rely on the sole responsibility and intention of the ambusher, but the fact that Li Ning, a former Chinese gymnastic champion and founder of the clothing sport brand of the same name, was the final torchbearer at the 2008 Beijing Olympics is clearly a case of parasitism which boosted massively the global awareness of the brand for free, even if he was still wearing an Adidas uniform, the official partner.

Sport brands' counterfeiting

One main threat for sport brands is certainly product counterfeiting, commonly defined 'as the unauthorised copying of trademarked or copyrighted goods' (Bloch, Bush and Campbell, 1993, p.27) and which sees efforts and investments in terms of design, research and development, marketing and communication not being financially rewarded and counterfeiters getting the benefits. According to the French Federation of Sport and Leisure Industries (FIFAS), six out of ten brands counterfeited worldwide are sport brands, providing sport sunglasses, sneakers, merchandised products and sport kits. In 2004, according to the Taxation and Customs Union of the European Commission, Lacoste and Nike were among the most counterfeited brands for textile products (estimated by the total number of seizures at EU borders) although Nike and Adidas were among the most counterfeited brands for accessories. Overall the most counterfeited sport brands for the UE markets were Nike, Adidas, Puma, Lacoste, Reebok and Umbro.[5] Recent statistics published by the European Commission tend to show an increase for the year 2010 in EU cases (about 80,000) of intellectual and property rights infringements corresponding to more than 100,000 articles with an estimated value of the equivalent genuine products at over €1 billion.[6] According to the same source, more than

26 per cent of the cases concerned the clothing category and 4.5 per cent concerned sport shoes. The principal expeditor countries involved in clothing and accessories' counterfeiting were China (about 85 per cent), India, Hong Kong, Moldova and Turkey. If it is difficult to assess with precision the financial loss to sport brands, there is no doubt that counterfeiting negatively affects brands' turnovers. It also affects retail and distribution brands. But most importantly, it negatively affects consumers who are more willing to pay the full price for authentic products. This global phenomenon does not only concern the biggest brands such as Nike and Adidas but also the smallest ones, as long as their products are of important financial value.

Within the sport industries, three main counterfeiting types can be identified. First are the copies which have the same appearance and which are difficult to notice for consumers. If most of the time consumers genuinely believe the products to be authentic, the dodgy products' origin can, however, cast doubts. However, with the increasing use of websites as distribution channels, the possibility for consumers to discover the real nature of their goods is limited. For these consumers, the badging value is probably more important than the quality or performance value. The second category gathers coarse copies which mimic the basic aspects, colours and design of the authentic products without causing any doubt about the products' inauthentic nature. They lack finesse and finishing and thus do not really compete with the original products. In this sense, it does not reduce significantly brands' turnovers as they mainly concern non-usual brand buyers. Furthermore, these copies are often meant to be sold in in-development countries where the power of purchase is generally low despite a clear enthusiasm for popular brands, and barely reach developed countries' markets. Last, the third category concerns products which do not aim to copy authentic products, but their packaging. This type of counterfeiting is mainly marketing and concerns names and logos which are very close to the original brands. Brands' logos and symbols are protected by trademarks and using a slight alteration to an original logo can be considered as counterfeiting. This is for instance what happened in 2003 in the Adidas versus Fitnessworld Trading Ltd case. Adidas' logo features three parallel stripes, and the corporation Fitnessworld Trading Ltd commercialised clothes featuring two parallel stripes. The corporation claimed that they did not infringe copyright and trademark properties because, according to them, the logo was to be considered as a design feature only. In this case, the European Court of Justice rejected Adidas' complaint stating that linking the brand's logo to another brand's logo does not necessarily mean that consumers confuse them, and that if consumers considered it as a design feature they would not infer any mistaken link to another brand. In conclusion, Adidas could not oppose the commercialisation of the products featuring two parallel stripes made by Fitnessworld Trading Ltd.

With a protected name or designated expression, sport brands can sue another part for counterfeiting but can be sued as well, which is rarer, depending on counterfeiting types. Semantic counterfeiting occurs when the names or terms used are almost identical. The words might not necessarily be identical but the overall sentence or expression can be extremely similar. Counterfeiting can also be phonetic, such as La Casta and Lcasta which were recognised as Lacoste's counterfeiters, and visual, regarding graphic elements and pictograms. Finally, counterfeiting based on pure reproduction consists of using the exact same terms which is both bold and illegal when no licence has been given. Nowadays, the Internet significantly facilitates the work of counterfeiters and conversely complicates brands' defence. After the 2004 Athens Summer Olympics, many medallists saw their Internet domain name commercially exploited by other parties. For instance a Chinese company bought the domain names of two well-known Chinese athletes (duli.cn and wanggyifu.cn just after they obtained a medal). To avoid this kind of practice during the 2008 Beijing Olympics, the Chinese government gave a full official list of Chinese competing athletes to the competent authority to protect athletes' domain names. Apparently more than ten athletes were already concerned when the list was composed.

Few options are available for brands to counter counterfeiters. The first one is to continuously launch innovations which are impossible to follow by counterfeiters. This is for instance what Petzl decided to do as two years after the launch of the 'Tikka' model (the first LED headlamps), there were already 23 Chinese copies for a price six times cheaper, with quality levels probably six times lower. Another solution is to multiply education and prevention campaigns in countries which are strongly affected by counterfeited products. Adidas launched a creative communication campaign which featured a foot with Adidas' logo made of bandages and with the following slogan 'fake hurts real'.

A third strategy requires constantly scrutinising markets and subcontractors in particular to see if copied products go out from their factories, and obtaining quality labels such as Nike did with the German TUV Rheinland. A fourth solution consists of systematically suing the putative counterfeiters or trying to find an agreement with them as court cases are expensive and can be risky as illustrated by the Adidas versus Fitnessworld Trading Ltd example. However, to get the best results, sport brands have to find support from governments and establish possible close collaborations with customs departments. Without support from public organisations and states, the likelihood of getting positive results is thin. However, it is not always possible because of the importance of mafia groups especially in eastern European and former Soviet Union countries or because of cultural differences, in particular regarding the definition of industrial and intellectual properties. If sport brands are increasingly victims of counterfeiting, they can sometimes be on the edge of becoming counterfeiters themselves either intentionally or unintentionally. Some do it intentionally in measuring all the risks involved both in terms of finance and image. The commercial stakes and potential benefits, in addition to the limited eventual damages, are sometimes more appealing than anything. Several law suits were for instance intended against Nike for plagiarism and counterfeiting in several countries including France (Sport Color vs. Nike and Texto vs. Nike in 2006). Corporate brands are not the only ones to be concerned with such practices and retail brands are also concerned. As an example, the French retail brand

Auchan was sentenced by the Chinese justice to pay US$46,000 of damages to Nike for having made and commercialised in collaboration with two local Chinese companies counterfeited Nike shoes in its Shanghai stores. These examples show that despite the fact that most of counterfeited products come from China, counterfeiting practices are not unidirectional and can come from more established and well-known sport brands. Many observers would have noticed for instance similarities between Li Ning's former logo and Nike's swoosh logo and that Li Ning's English slogan 'anything is possible' was very similar to Adidas's slogan 'nothing is impossible'. A rapid conclusion would then make us believe that Li Ning copied these two famous brands. However, Li Ning's tagline seems to have been launched before Adidas' tagline,[7] which tends to advise us not to judge apparent counterfeiters only on appearances.

CONCLUSION

It seems that all sport brands currently have a common feature which is the need to cultivate their difference to remain sustainable. To illustrate the particular identity of firms, organisations and brands, practitioners and professionals often talk about brand DNA, which integrates history, stories, memories, values and goals, its 'raison d'être'. Beyond consolidating a stature and improving an image, comparing sport brands' intrinsic and extrinsic characteristics allows us to see differences in terms of identity, positioning and communication. Moreover, it improves the understanding of possible strategic evolutions driven by the endogenous (within the firms and organisations) and exogenous (market and socioeconomic) environments. Finally, this double conceptualisation, as the double helix, contributes to the definition of sport brands' DNA, which makes each brand different. Based on the work of Ladwein (1995), two categories of sport brands' attributes can be identified and illustrated (see Table C.1). First, intrinsic attributes indicate the common characteristics of all products and services offered by the brand: field of expertise, technical characteristics, features, knowhow etc. Second, extrinsic attributes depend on the way the brand is valorised through various strategies: positioning, segmentation, targeting, communication, etc. It is possible to identify two co-existing categories of strategic orientations and actions determining the brand's future. On one hand, endogenous actions directly concern products and services and on the other hand, exogenous actions characterise the expansion and acquisition of new attributes potentially modifying consumer perceptions.

Nowadays, it seems that sport brands have been at the forefront of economic and social orientations particularly in terms of globalisation. With the development of club brands, event brands and celebrity brands we can wonder if the sports markets are not becoming the Trojan horse in the conquest of new markets. The sports sectors have indeed probably been among the first to contribute to the globalisation phenomenon in making actors from different sectors and geographical

TABLE C.1 Examples of strategic actions differentiating sport brands' DNA

	Sport brands' DNA main attributes	
	Intrinsic *(products/services' specific attributes)*	*Extrinsic* *(brand's specific attributes)*
Endogenous actions (Dependent on products and services ranges)	Efficiency (comfort, practicality, price…)	Leisure (women, seniors, babies…)
	Creation (innovation, originality…)	Heath (obese, diabetic…) Expert (competitor, elite, connoisseurs…)
	Line extension (sub-segments, premium, low-cost)	Fashion (aesthetic, style, vintage…)
Exogenous actions (Independent from products and services ranges)	Brand extension (new fields of expertise and sectors)	Social marketing (ethical, responsible, green…)
	Co-branding (internal or external)	Community/tribal marketing (generations, ethnicities, religions…)

Source: Adapted from Ladwein, 1995

areas meet each other. In this regard, sport can be seen as a global brand on its own. Consequently, our views on the functioning of the current consumer society and its links with such major sporting events as the FIFA World Cup and the Olympics and the massification of sport products and services can be questioned. After having qualified as a social fact, professional sports as football, rugby, baseball, basketball or tennis may have become universal brands in the current world village. With the multi-branding trend, which consists of owning several brands within the same product or service category, it seems that sport brands are moving towards this direction. For instance, sport video games have become bestsellers worldwide and this has encouraged sport brands to become their partners and sometimes their co-investors. In the future, it would not be surprising to see emerging brand gatherings or teams which would associate sport brands with non-sport brands from various industries. These rational marriages would certainly create new generations and families of products and services whose main characteristic would be to offer original and unseen promises. In our opinion, the sport brands' new challenges and stakes prefigure significant changes in the way products and service are conceived.

The relationships between brands and consumers will be forced to evolve towards more balancing contributions than in the past in terms of product and service creation processes (for example towards more co-production) and in terms of development of internal and external resources involved in B to C and B to B (towards knowledge marketing). The current brand literature is already discussing 'prosumers' or 'consumactors', portmanteau terms which underline the active role played by consumers as growth factors but also uncertainty factors. Moreover, the increasing integration of social and cultural promises in sport brands' strategic and mix marketing demonstrate their increasing adjustment to consumers' ecological and technological concerns. In other words, through the products and services they offer and the messages they carry, sport brands will play an increasing role in satisfying consumers' demands and their search for pleasure, sense, comfort, simplicity, personalisation, authenticity, safety and interaction. To achieve these objectives, sport brands will have to be more consumer-oriented, more creative, and more responsible. Beyond their classical functions and missions, firms and organisations will have to respond to new ambitious and sometimes unrealistic expectations: reducing inequalities, making sense of the world and its changes, respecting the environment, creating social links and interactions and increasing people's well-being overall. Facing the changes in consumer behaviours and expectations, it seems that four prospective and non-exclusive strategies can be followed by sport brands as illustrated by Figure C.1: growth actions, ethical actions, segmentation actions and consumer excellence actions. If these types of actions are meant to encourage a better differentiation, they can generate some downfalls harming sport brands' development. Specifically, we can question whether sport brands' commercial re-enchantment and marketisation of the world, particularly the sport world, will be appreciated by everyone, the majority or the most loyal consumers, or whether it will create more criticism.

FIGURE C.1 Sport brands' strategic actions to face changes in consumers' expectations

In response to the trends witnessed in developed countries (for example development of sport for health among seniors, clustering towards smaller communities, evolution towards sustainable development), sport brands should experience a similar growth to other sectors' brands. The major ones will become megabrands and the smaller specialised ones will increase the number of segments they target, including new categories of more demanding, difficult to target consumers (for example utility vs pleasure purchase, mono vs multi-channel purchase, generational vs transgenerational behaviours, priority to local vs global offers, etc.). From an industrial point of view, an increase in terms of extensions, mergers and acquisitions can be anticipated. For the major groups whose industrial and commercial reality has to go through the reinforcement of current positions and a broadening of the markets they cover, these actions will be realised to increase their capitalisation. Between November 2007 and January 2008, several significant operations were witnessed with Maus Frères (Lacoste, Aigle) launching a takeover bid over Gant, a former American but now Swedish sportswear brand listed on Stockholm's stock exchange since 2006. New Balance extended its clothing ranges by acquiring Vital Apparel, specialised in female clothing and running sectors, with the brands Vital and InSport. The group GSM which owns Billabong extended its brand portfolio with Tigerlily, an Australian beachwear brand for women. Nike acquired Umbro to intend to become world leader on the football boots sector and Oxylane Group extended its brand portfolio in acquiring the brands Nabajiji (swimming), Newfeel (sport walking) and Simond (climbing). It is likely that the trend will intensifiy and create more concentrations on the sport markets as already noticed by Desbordes (2001).

From the demand side, consumers seem more and more fragmented and heterogeneous forcing sport brands to rapidly identify prehensile and relevant indicators of new consumer segments and groups. Sport brands will have to better understand their consumers' social and cultural fields and analyse the ways consumers experience their products and services according to the consumption contexts and situations (for example in-store, at home, in the public space, on holidays, online, via social networks). In other words, they will have to better anticipate consumers' expectations in terms of sport and leisure and precisely distinguish the different forms of experience (for example corporal, spatial, social) they live. In societies where individuals increasingly look for an identity affiliation in their consumption, sport brands' products and services represent powerful and privileged expression supports. In this sense, the word recreation seems to perfectly reflect consumers' demands as they search for the re-creation of their body, their mind and their self, via the acquisition and the consumption of sport brands.

Regarding these challenging evolutions, the further inclusion of co-construction and co-design in the elaboration of offers appears pertinent. For sport brands, the challenge consists of translating, in an operational way, strategies which focus on consumers and employees' learning processes (Curbatov, 2003). In giving to consumers the power to manage their own experiences and develop their own competences, sport brands could therefore consider the development of relational programmes which valorise consumers' propositions. This is manifested through the development of mass-customisation which relies on the co-creation of experiences (for example 'NIKEiD', 'miAdidas') and upward innovation which relies on the co-creation of offers via the involvement of consumers in the design of products and mix marketing variables (Cova and Dalli, 2009). Therefore, sport brands will have to co-manage an organisational know-how by putting in place collabo-rative processes of co-production, co-innovation and co-promotion with consumers. The valorisation of consumers' ideas and creative power is essential in the realisation of tailored and customised offers, in avoiding missing great oppor-tunities and in qualitatively improving the endogenous creative capital of organisations (Berger and Piller, 2003; Franke and Shah, 2003). Sport brands will have to soon integrate the ideas, feedback and technical solutions provided by pioneer consumers, lead users and consider them as collaborators. This process is nowadays accelerated by the power of social networks and communities. Moreover, not taking into account the rituals and practices of communities would be a dangerous mistake as it could alienate them from the brands. As shown in the case of European football more and more fans tend to be dissatisfied by their club-brand which prefers new and wealthier spectators and engages in aggressive marketing strategies. On the contrary more and more club brands collaborate with supporter trusts (democratic and not-for-profit organisations of fans) and groups because they have realised the importance of the co-production process in sport.

In any case, sport brands' omnipresence in international media and economic scenes call out to numerous consumer associations and activist groups who reproach them for invading public and private spaces. In this vein, experiential and communication marketing represent strong brand pillars of reenchanted sport offers. If reenchantement strategies allow firms and organisations to partially respond to criticism about the world's commercialisation, the criticism should also be extended to non-commercial environments and activities in which sport brands are involved, as it appears that commercial exchanges and activities increasingly rely on non-commercial activities and exchanges (Sue, 1997). Responding to the social and economic criticisms by denying or diminishing the reality of commercial exchanges means sport brands try to reduce the transactional and utilitarian dimen-sions from their relations. Consequently, sport brands will have to further invest and enhance the other sides of their offers but we may wonder if this is possible. Brands will increasingly exist and rely on the emotions they provide. Sport brands are concerned by the Disneyisation of society (Bryman, 2004), regarding the commer-cialisation of life experiences, affects, sensations and feelings (Ariès, 2002). Rather than providing extraordinary experiences, Disneyisation deals with an ideological representation of the world and social relations which seems to be less and less popular as it is perceived as another form of manipulation from commercial organ-isations and marketers. In this context, it would be probably naïve to see sport brands as the great 'master of puppets' controlling everything and consumers as consenting victims. The debate therefore remains open as much from the practi-tioners and researchers side as from the consumers, citizens and politicians side.

When considering different sport brands' actions, consumers will face new choices in terms of purchase, usage, expression, and reactions. Joining Hirschman's (1983) point of view, either consumers continue trusting brands and remain loyal, voice their discontent or exit the relationships. With the development of social media (for example Facebook, Twitter), voicing one's opinion and protesting is extremely easy and powerful. Indeed, the main evolution of contemporary consumption relies on the development of an individual form of consumerism and the defence of interests linked to the consumption of brands rather than products. We believe that the consumerist focus' shift from the products and services to the brands is shaping sport brands' strategies and actions. This would also force them to take consumers' opinions into account earlier in the relationship. This consumerist pressure should not be underestimated especially as it seems to be growing. It is expressed for instance in the development of ethical and social funds which represent 10 per cent of American capital investors as well as in the debates about firms and organisations' democratisation and governance (Gomez, 2001). Via the notions of sustainable development, fair trade, social performance, corporate social responsibility, environment-friendly, consumerist pressure is increasingly affecting shareholders and stakeholders' strategic decisions. Finally, this pressure also appears in firms and organisations' tactical and operational dimensions as more and more norms and standards are edited which, in a sense, truly integrates consumers in sport brands' organisations and firms.

NOTES

Introduction: concepts, values and contextual framing

1   http://www.economist.com/node/770992 (accessed 2 July 2012).

1 The great variety of sport brands

1   Sport Goods Retailing – UK (2012), Mintel, May 2012.
2   www.about.americanexpress.com/news/pr/2011/vente_usa.aspx (accessed 18 June 2012).
3   www.fogdog.com/home/index.jsp (accessed 24 June 2012).
4   www.plunkettresearch.com/sports-recreation-leisure-market-research/industry-statistics (accessed 25 June 2012).

2 The tangible influence of sport brands

1   www.guardian.co.uk/business/2006/aug/04/football.china (accessed 29 June 2012).
2   www.businessweek.com/innovate/content/jul2009/id20090729_402556.htm (accessed 29 June 2012).
3   www.news.bbc.co.uk/1/hi/world/europe/7039772.stm (accessed 29 June 2012).
4   www.guardian.co.uk/world/2007/nov/15/football.argentina (accessed 29 June 2012).

3 The intangible influence of sport brands

1   www.ft.com/cms/s/0/bae8154c-95eb-11e1-a163-00144feab49a.html#axzz1vUv FBMns (accessed 21 May 2012).

4 Subcultures, communities and sport brands

1   www.curves.co.uk/about-curves/overview (accessed 21 June 2012).
2   www.itftennis.com/shared/medialibrary/pdf/original/IO_19613_original.PDF (accessed 21 June 2012).

3   www.youtube.com/watch?v=nMzdAZ3TjCA (accessed 21 June 2012).
4   www.microsoft.com/en-us/news/press/1999/jun99/tourneypr.aspx (accessed 21 June 2012).
5   www.virtualregatta.com/ (accessed 21 June 2012).
6   www.manyplayers.com/sitecorp/News_read/VENDEE_GLOBE (accessed 21 June 2012).
7   www.adidas-group.com/en/home/Welcome.aspx (accessed 1 November 2007).
8   www.adidas-group.com/en/home/Welcome.aspx (accessed 1 November 2007).

5 The economic and social value of sport brands

1   www.wfsgi.org/ (accessed 1 December 2009).
2   The firms' sport brand portfolios may have changed since the writing and publication of the book.
3   lexpansion.lexpress.fr/economie/amer-sports-aussi-discret-qu-intraitable_25450.html (accessed 5 July 2012).
4   www.newbalance.com/company/committed-to-american-workers/ (accessed 24 April 2012).
5   www.patagonia.com/us/patagonia.go?assetid=1960 (accessed 25 April 2012).
6   www.patagonia.com/eu/enGB/patagonia.go?assetid=9153 (accessed 25 April 2012).
7   www.groupe-lafuma.com/ (accessed 30 October 2010).

6 Sport brands' growth strategies

1   http://news.smh.com.au/business/billabong-catches-a-ride-on-quiet-flight-20080612-2pd8.html (accessed 5 July 2012).
2   Interview with J.P. Petit, *Nike* France director in 'Total look – Mix & Match', *Sport Première Magazine*, 264, March 2007, p. 51.
3   www.fashion-dailynews.com/interview/itw-kone.html (accessed 5 July 2012).
4   www.wimbledon.com/news/media-centre/merchandising (accessed 30 March 2012).

7 Sport brands' threats

1   http://investors.nikeinc.com/Theme/Nike/files/doc_financials/AnnualReports/2011/index.html#select_financials (accessed 1 May 2012).
2   The shoe sector was more profitable during the eighties than during the nineties.
3   www.guardian.co.uk/money/blog/2010/sep/21/football-kits-premier-league-cash-cow (accessed 6 July 2012).
4   www.guardian.co.uk/football/2011/jan/31/bundesliga-raphael-honigstein-st-pauli (accessed 6 July 2012).
5   www.gacg.org/Content/Upload/Documents/Transcrime_Report%20Existing%20Standards_Project%20FAKES.pdf (accessed 9 May 2012).
6   http://ec.europa.eu/taxation_customs/resources/documents/customs/customs_controls/counterfeit_piracy/statistics/statistics_2010.pdf (accessed 9 May 2012).
7   http://adage.com/article/global-news/ad-age-china-s-2009-marketer-year-li-ning/141601/ (accessed 9 May 2012).

REFERENCES

Aaker, D.A. (1996) *Building Strong Brands*. New York: The Free Press.

Aaker, D.A. (1991) *Managing Brand Equity: capitalizing on the value of a brand name*. New York: The Free Press.

Aaker, D.A. and Keller, K.L. (1990) 'Consumer evaluation of brand extensions', *Journal of Marketing*, 54: 27–41.

Aaker, J.F. and Maheswaran, D. (1997) 'The effect of cultural orientation on persuasion', *Journal of Consumer Research*, 24: 315–328.

Abdourazakou, Y. (2003) 'Les stratégies génériques des télévisions: le cas des chaînes sportives face à un environnement hyper compétitif en Europe', *Revue Européenne de Management du Sport*, 10: 47–76.

Albert, E. (1984) 'Equipment as a feature of social control in the sport of bicycle racing', in N. Theberge and P. Donnelly (eds), *Sport and the Sociological Imagination*. Fort Worth, TX: Christian University Press, 318–333.

Andreff, W. and Szymanski, S. (2006) *Handbook on the Economics of Sports*. Cheltenham: Edward Elgar Publishing.

Andrews, D. (1998) 'Excavating Michael Jordan: notes on a critical pedagogy of sporting representation', in G. Rail (ed.) *Sport and Postmodern Times*. Albany, NY: State University of New York Press, 185–219.

Ariès, P. (2002) *Disneyland: le royaume désenchanté*, Paris: Editions Golias.

d'Astous, A. and Ahmed, S.A. (1999) 'The importance of country images in the formation of consumer product perceptions', *International Marketing Review*, 16: 108–125.

d'Astous, A., Ballofet, P., Daghfous, N. and Boulaire, C. (2002) 'Comportement du consommateur'. Montréal: Chennelière/McGraw-Hill.

Barrand, D., Britcher, C. and Curtis, J. (2004) *Sport Brandleaders, an Insight into Some of Britain's Strongest Sport Brands*. London: Superbrands Ltd.

Basu, K. (2006) 'Merging brands after mergers', *California Management Review*, 48: 28–40.

Baudrillard, J. (1998) *The Consumer Society: myths and structures*. London: Sage Publications.

Bayle E. (2001) 'Le développement de la marque Roland Garros', in M. Desbordes (ed.), *Stratégies des Entreprises dans le Sport*. Paris: Economica, 231–253.

Becker, C. (2002) *Du Ricard dans mon Coca: nous et les marques*. Paris: Les Editions d'Organisation.

Belk, R.W. (2003), 'Shoes and self', *Advances in Consumer Research*, 30: 27–33.

Belk, R.W., Wallendorf, M. and Sherry, J.F. Jr (1989) 'The sacred and the profane in consumer behavior: theodicy on the Odyssey', *Journal of Consumer Research*, 16: 1–38.

Benn, J. (2004) 'Consumer education between "consumership" and citizenship: experiences from studies of young people', *International Journal of Consumer Studies*, 28: 108–116.

Berger, B. and Piller, F. (2003) 'Customers as co-designers: the miAdidas mass customization strategy', *IEE Manufacturing Engineer*, 82: 42–46.

Bernache-Assollant, I. (2006) 'Contextes intergroupes and stratégies de gestion identitaire chez les supporters', Unpublished doctoral thesis. University of Burgundy, Dijon.

Bloch, P.H., Black, W.C. and Lichtenstein, D. (1989) 'Involvement with the equipment component of sport: link to recreational commitment', *Leisure Sciences*, 11: 187–200.

Bloch, P.H., Bush, R.H. and Campbell, L. (1993) 'Consumer "accomplices" in product counterfeiting: a demand-side investigation', *Journal of Consumer Marketing*, 10: 27–36.

Bodet, G. (2009) 'Sport participation and consumption and post-modern society: from Apollo to Dionysus?' *Loisir et Société/Society and Leisure,* 32: 223–241.

Bodet, G. (2009) '"Give me a stadium and I will fill it": an analysis of the marketing management of Stade Français Paris rugby club', *International Journal of Sports Marketing and Sponsorship,* 10: 252–262.

Bodet, G. and Chanavat, N. (2010) 'Building global football brand equity: lessons from the Chinese market', *Asia Pacific Journal of Marketing and Logistics,* 22: 55–66.

Bontour, A. and Lehu, J.M. (2004) *Lifting de Marque*. Paris: Editions d'Organisation.

Borgne-Larivière, M. Le (2005) 'Le marketing éthique', in D. Wolff and F. Mauléon, *Le Management Durable, L'essentiel du Développement Durable Appliqué aux Entreprises*. London: Hermès Science Publication/Lavoisier, pp. 213–244.

Borneman, E. (1978) *Psychanalyse de l'argent*, Paris: PUF.

Bouchet, P. (2005) 'L'analyse de la "sensorialité" des magasins : approche exploratoire dans la distribution d'articles de sport', *Proceedings from the 21st International Congress of the French Association of Marketing*, Nancy (France).

Bouchet, P. (2002) 'Une nouvelle tendance de consommation chez les personnes âgées: le tourisme sportif "haut de gamme"', *Leisure and Society/Loisir et Société*, 25: 377–396.

Bouchet, P., Bodet, G., Bernache-Assollant, I. and Kada, F. (2011) 'Segmenting sport spectators: construction and preliminary validation of the Sporting Event Experience Search (SEES) scale', *Sport Management Review*, 14: 42–53.

Bouchet, P. and Hillairet, D. (2009) *Marques de Sport: approches stratégiques et marketing*, Brussells: De Boeck.

Bouchet, P. and Hillairet, D. (2008) *Les Marques de Sport*. Paris: Economica.

Bouchet, P. and Kaach, M. (2004) *Afrique Francophone et Development du Sport: du mythe à la réalité*. Paris: L'Harmattan.

Bouchet, P. and Lebrun, A.-M. (2009) *Le management du tourisme sportif: de la consommation à la commercialisation*. Rennes: PU Rennes – Broché.

Bouchet, P. and Sobry, C. (2005) *Management et Marketing du Sport: du local au global*. Villeneuve d'Ascq: Presses Universitaires du Septentrion.

Bourdieu, P. (1984) *Distinction: a social critique of the judgement of taste*. Cambridge, MA: Harvard University Press.

Bourgeon, D., and Bouchet, P. (2001) 'La recherche d'expériences dans la consommation du spectacle sportif', *Revue Européenne de Management du Sport*, 6: 1–47.

Bromberger, C. (1998) *Passions Ordinaires: du match de football au concours de dictée*. Paris: Bayard.

Bryman, A. (2004) *The Disneyization of Society*. London: Sage.

Carpenter, P. (2000) *Ebrands – Building an Internet Business at Breakneck Speed*. Boston, MA: Harvard Business School Press.

Castillo, J.C. (2008) 'The other Basque subversives: Athletic de Bilbao vs. the new age of soccer', *Sport in Society: Cultures, Commerce, Media, Politics*, 11: 711–721.

Catoera, P.R. and Graham, J. (1999) *International Marketing*. McGraw-Hill.

Cegarra, J.J. and Michel, G. (2003) 'Alliances de marques: quel profit pour les marques partenaires', *Revue Française de Gestion*, 29: 163–174.

Certeau, M., De (1988) 'The practice of everyday life'. London: University of California Press.

Chanavat, N. and Bodet, G. (2009) 'Internationalisation and sport branding strategy: a French perception of the Big Four brands', *Qualitative Market Research: An International Journal*, 12: 460–481.

Chappelet, J.L. (2006) 'The economics of the International Olympic Committee', in W. Andreff, W. and S. Szymanski (eds), *Handbook on the Economics of Sport*. London: Edward Elgar.

Chevalier, M. and Mazzalovo, G. (2004) *Pro Logo: brands as a factor of progress*', New York: Palgrave Macmillan.

Combes, M. (2005) 'Quel avenir pour la Responsabilité Sociale des Entreprises (RSE)? La RSE: l'émergence d'un nouveau paradigme organisationnel', *Management and Avenir*, 6: 131–145.

Commission of the European Communities (2001) 'Green paper on promoting a European framework for corporate social responsibility', Brussels, 18.07.2001. Available http://eur-lex.europa.eu/LexUriServ/site/en/com/2001/com2001_0366en01.pdf (accessed 25 April 2012).

Coupland, D. (1991) '*Generation X: tales for an accelerated culture*', St. Martin Press.

Cova, B. and Cova, V. (2002) 'Tribal marketing: the tribalisation of society and its impact on the conduct of marketing', *European Journal of Marketing*, 36: 595–620.

Cova, B. and Dalli, D. (2009) 'Working consumers: the next step in marketing theory?', *Marketing Theory*, 9: 315–339.

Cova, B. and Roncaglio, M. (1999) 'Repérer et soutenir des tribus de consommateurs', *Décisions Marketing*, 16: 7–15.

Cristol, S.M. and Sealey, P. (2000) *Simplicity Marketing: end brand complexity, clutter and confusion*, New York: The Free Press.

Csikszentmihalyi, M., and Rochberg-Halton, E. (1981) 'The meaning of things, domestic symbols and the self'. Cambridge: Cambridge University Press.

Curbatov, O. (2003) 'L'intégration du consommateur par le "knowledge marketing": conception, production et consommation d'un produit personnel', Unpublished doctoral thesis. Université de Nice-Sophia Antipolis.

Davidson, H. (2001) 'Future vision and values: a big opportunity for marketers?', *The Marketing Review*, 2: 267–284.

Day, G.S. (1969) 'A two-dimensional concept of brand loyalty', *Journal of Advertising Research*, 9: 29–35.

Desbordes, M. (2001) 'Innovation management in the sport industry: lessons from the Salomon case', *European Sport Management Quarterly*, 1: 124–149.

Deshpandé, R. and Stayman, D.M. (1994) 'A tale of two cities: distinctiveness theory and advertising effectiveness', *Journal of Marketing Research*, 31: 57–64.

Drillech, M. (1999) *Le Boycott, le Cauchemar des Entreprises. . . et des Politiques*. Paris: Presses du Management.

Duke, V. (2002) 'Local tradition versus globalisation: resistance to the McDonaldisation and Disneyisation of professional football in England', *Football Studies*, 5: 5–23.

Duménil, G. and Lévy, D. (2011) *The crisis of neoliberalism*, Cambridge, MA: Harvard University Press.

Eco, U. (1985) *La Guerre du Faux*. Paris: Grasset.

Ferrand, A. (2007) 'Contribution à l'analyse de la relation à la marque au sein des systèmes sportifs', Habilitation à Diriger les Recherches, Université Claude Bernard Lyon, 1 November.

Ferrand, A., Chappelet, J.-L. and Séguin, B. (2012) *Olympic Marketing*. London and New York: Routledge.

Ferrandi, J.M., Merunka, D. and Valette-Florence, P. (2003), 'La personnalité de la marque: bilan et perspectives', *Revue Française de Gestion*, 145: 145–162.

Floch, J.M. (2001) *Semiotics, Marketing and Communication: beneath the signs the strategies*. London: Palgrave Macmillan.

Fournier, S.M. (1998) 'Consumers and their brands: developing relationship theory in consumer research', *Journal of Consumer Research*, 24: 343–373.

Fournier, S. (1998), 'Consumer resistance: societal motivations, consumer manifestations, and implications in the marketing domain', *Advances in Consumer Research*, 25: 88–90.

Fournier, S. (1994) 'A consumer-brand relationship framework for strategic brand management', Unpublished doctoral thesis, University of Florida.

Franke, N. and Shah, S. (2003) 'How communities support innovative activities: an exploration of assistance and sharing among innovative users of sporting equipment', *Research Policy*, 32: 157–178.

Frith, K.T. and Mueller, B. (2010) *Advertising and Societies. Global issues*, 2nd edn. New York: Peter Lang Publishing.

Garnier, J. (2002) 'Les femmes et le sport : sachez reconnaître leurs spécificités, *LSA*, 1788: 46–50.

Garnier, J. and Guingois, S. (2003) '13–20 ans: les champions du mixage culturel', *LSA*, April: 48–52.

Giulianotti, R. (2005) 'Sport spectators and the social consequences of commodification: critical perspectives from Scottish football', *Journal of Sport and Social Issues*, 29: 386–410.

Gomez, P.Y. (2001) *La République des Actionnaires: le gouvernement des entreprises entre démocratie et démagogie*. Paris: Alternatives Economiques, Syros.

Gratton, C. and Taylor, P. (2000) *Economics of Sport and Recreation*. London: Taylor and Francis Books.

Heino, R. (2000) 'New sports: what is so punk about snowboarding?' *Journal of Sport and Social Issues*, 24: 176–191.

Hillairet, D. (2006) 'Etats des connaissances dans les industries d'articles de sport aux niveaux stratégiques (les firmes) et technologiques (les produits et les process)', in P. Bouchet and C. Pigeassou (eds), *Management du Sport: actualités, développements et orientations de la recherche*, Montpellier: Editions AFRAPS, 315–346.

Hillairet, D. (2005) *Sport et Innovation: stratégies, techniques et produits*. Cachan: Hermes Science Publications.

Hillairet, D. (2003) *Economie du Sport et Entreprenariat*. Paris: L'Harmattan.

Hillairet, D. (1999) *L'innovation Sportive. Entreprendre pour Gagner*. Paris: L'Harmattan – Broché.

Hirschman, A.O. (1983) *Bonheur Privé, Action Publique*. Paris: Fayard.

Hirschman, E. (1981) 'American Jewish ethnicity: its relationship to some selected aspects of consumer behaviour', *Journal of Marketing*, 46: 102–110.

Hofstede, G. (2001) *Culture's Consequences: comparing values, behaviors, institutions, and organizations across nations*, 2nd edn, Thousand Oaks, CA: Sage.

Holbrook, M.B. (1999) *Consumer Value: a framework for analysis and research*, London and New York: Routledge.

Holbrook, M. and Hirschman, E. (1982) 'The experiential aspects of consumption: consumer fantasy, feelings and fun', *Journal of Consumer Research,* 9: 132–140.

Holt, D.B. (2004) *How Brands Become Icons: the principles of cultural branding*, Boston: Harvard Business School Press.

Holt, D.B. (1995) 'How consumers consume: a typology of consumption practices', *Journal of Consumer Research*, 22: 1–16.

Horney K. (1945) *Our Inner Conflict*. New York: W.W. Nortin.

Hunt, K.A., Bristol, T. and Bashaw, R.E. (1999) 'A conceptual approach to classifying sports fans', *Journal of Services Marketing*, 13: 439–452.

Kahle, L.R., Boush, D.M. and Phelps, M. (2000) 'Good morning Vietnam: an ethical analysis of Nike activities in Southeast Asia', *Sport Marketing Quarterly*, 9: 43–52.

Kapferer, J.N. (2008) *The New Strategic Brand Management: creating and sustaining brand equity long term*, 4th edn. London and Philadelphia: Kogan Page.

Kapferer, J.N. (2006) *FAQ – La Marque*. Paris: Dunod.

Kapferer, J.N. (2005) *Ce qui va Changer les Marques*, 2nd edn. Paris: Editions d'Organisation.

Kapferer, J.N. (2003) 'Réinventer la marque?', *Revue Française de Gestion*, 29: 119–130.

Kapferer, J.N. (1998) *Les Marques: capital de l'entreprise*, 3rd edn. Paris: Editions d'Organisation.

Kapferer, J.N. (1997) *Strategic Brand Management*, 2nd edn. Dover, NH: Kogan Page.

Kapferer, J.N. (1991) *Les Marques: capital de l'entreprise*, Paris: Editions d'Organisation.

Kapferer, J.N. and Laurent, G. (1998) *La Sensibilité aux Marques*, 3rd edn. Paris: Editions d'Organisation.

Kates, S.M. (2002) 'The protean quality of subcultural consumption: an ethnographic account of gay consumers', *Journal of Consumer Research*, 29: 383–399.

Keller, K.L. (2003) *Best Practice Cases in Branding: lessons from the world strongest brands*. Upper Saddle River, NJ: Prentice Hall.

Keller, K.L. (1998) *Strategic Brand Management: building, measuring and managing brand equity*. Upper Saddle River, NJ: Prentice Hall.

Keller, K.L. (1993) 'Conceptualising, measuring and managing customer-based brand equity', *Journal of Marketing*, 57: 1–22.

Kern, S. (2012) 'Islam conquers European football', Gatestone Institute, International Policy Council, 5 May. Available www.gatestoneinstitute.org/2994/islam-conquers-european-football (accessed 30 May 2012).

Kerr, A.K. and Gladden, J.M. (2008) 'Extending the understanding of professional team brand equity to the global marketplace', *International Journal of Sport Management and Marketing*, 3: 58–77.

Kim, J.-B. (1993) 'For savvy teens: real life, real solutions', *New York Times*, 23 August, p.S1.

Kirmani, A., Soods, S. and Bridges, S. (1999) 'The ownership effect in consumer responses to brand line stretches', *Journal of Marketing*, 63: 88–101.

Klein, N. (2001) *No Logo*. London: Flamingo.

Koebel, M.N. and Ladwein, R. (1999) 'L'échelle de personnalité de la marque de Jennifer Aaker: adaptation au contexte français', *Décisions Marketing*, 16: 81–88.

Kopytoff, I. (1986) 'The cultural biography of things: commoditization as process', in E. Appadurai (ed.) *The Social Life of Things: commodities in cultural perspective*. Cambridge: Cambridge Unviersity Press.

Kotler, P. and Dubois, P.L. (1997) *Marketing Management*, 9th edn. Paris: Publi-Union.

Kozinets, R.V. (1999) 'E-tribalized marketing: the strategic implications of virtual communities of consumption', *European Management Journal*, 17: 252–264.

Kozinets, R.V. (1997) '"I want to believe": a nethnography of the X-Philes' subculture of consumption', *Advances of Consumer Research*, 24: 470–475.

Kozinets, R.V., Sherry, J.F., DeBerry-Spence, B., Duhachek, A., Nuttavuthisit, K. and Storm, D. (2002) 'Themed flagship brand stores in the new millennium: theory, practice, prospects', *Journal of Retailing*, 78: 17–29.

Ladwein (1995) 'Catégories cognitives et jugements de typicalité en comportement du consommateur', *Recherche et Applications en Marketing*, 10: 89–100.

Lai, C. (2005) *La Marque*. Paris: Dunod.

Landowski, E. (2004) *Passions sans nom*. Paris: PUF.

Laurent, G. and Kapferer, J.N. (1985) 'Measuring consumer involvement profiles', *Journal of Marketing Research*, 22: 41–53.

Lebrun, A.M. (2006) 'L'évolution des recherches sur la distribution: conséquences pour le secteur des articles de sport', in P. Bouchet and C. Pigeassou (eds) *Management du Sport: actualités, développements et orientations de la recherche*, Montpellier: Editions AFRAPS.

Lehu, J.M. (2001) '*Stratégiedemarque.com, concevoir, protéger et gérer la marque sur l'Internet*'. Paris: Les Editions d'Organisation.

Lehuédé, F. (2003) 'Les seniors: des consommateurs accomplis', *Enquête Consommation 2001–2002*. Paris: Credoc.

Leroux-Sostenes, M.-J. and Rouvrais-Charron, C. (2008) 'Le marché des seniors: une approche marketing adaptée à une nouvelle offre de services sportifs', *Revue Européenne de Management du Sport*, 23: 15–24.

Lévi-Strauss, C. (1976) *Structural Anthropology*. New York: Basic Books.

Lévi-Strauss C. (1968) *Totemism*. Boston: Beacon Press.

Levy, S.J. (1980) 'The symbolic analysis of companies, brands and customers', *Twelve Annual Albert Wesley Frey Lecture*, Graduate School of Business. Pittsburgh, PA: University of Pittsburgh.

Lewi, G. (2006) 'Le développement international des marques "France ou connotées France"', in O. Challe and B. Logié, *Marques française et langue*, Paris: Economica, pp. 65–68.

Lewi, G. (2004) *La Marque*, 4th edn. Paris: Vuibert.

Lewi G. (2003) *Les Marques, Mythologie du Quotidien: comprendre le succès des grandes marques*. Paris: Pearson Education France.

Lewi, G. and Rogliano, C. (2006) *Memento Pratique du Branding. Comment gérer une marque au quotidien*. Paris: Pearson Education France, Village Mondial.

Logié B. and Logié-Naville, D. (2001) *Leur nom est une Marque*. Paris: Editions d'Organisation.

Lomax, W. and McWilliam, G. (2001) 'Consumer response to line extensions: trial and cannibalisation effects', *Journal of Marketing Management*, 17: 391–406.

Loret, A. (1995) *Management du Sport: de l'éthique à la pratique*. Paris: Revue EPS.

Maillet, C. (2005) *Le Marketing Adolescent: comment les marques s'adressent a l'enfant qui sommeille en vous*. Paris: Pearson Education France.

Malaval, P. (2001) *Strategy and Management of Industrial Brand: business to business – products and services*, London: Kluwer Academic Publishers.

Malaval, P. and Bénaroya, C. (1998) 'Les marques de distributeurs dans le contexte industriel', *Décisions Marketing*, 15: 59–68.

Marion, G. (2003) 'Apparence et identité: une approche sémiotique du discours des adolescentes à propos de leur expérience de la mode', *Recherche et Applications en Marketing*, 18: 1–29.

Marshall, R., Dong, X. and Lee, C.K.C. (1994) 'The development of basic values of a sub-culture: an investigation of the changing levels of individualism exhibited by Chinese immigrants to New Zealand', *Asia Pacific Advances in Consumer Research*, 1: 91–96.

McCracken, G. (1986) 'Culture and consumption: a theoretical account of the structure and meaning of consumer goods', *Journal of Consumer Research*, 13: 71–84.

McWilliams, A. and Siegel, D. (2000) 'Corporate social responsibility and financial performance: correlation or misspecification?' *Strategic Management Journal*, 21: 603–609.

Mercier, S. (2004) *L'éthique dans les Entreprises*. Paris: La Découverte.

Merunka, D. (2002) 'Recherches sur les marques: quelques dangers, quelques directions', *Recherches et Applications en Marketing*, 17: 1–6.

Moles, A. (1969) *Théorie des Objets*. Paris: Editions Universitaires.

Nash, J.E. (1977) 'Decoding the runner's wardrobe', in J.P. Spradley and D.W. McCardy (eds), *Conformity and Conflict: reading in cultural anthropology*, 3rd edn. Boston, MA: Little Brown and Company, 172–185.

Nijssen, E.J. (1999) 'Success factors of line extensions of fast-moving consumer goods', *European Journal of Marketing*, 33: 450–469.

Noble, S.M., Haytko, D.L. and Phillips, J. (2009) 'What drives college-age Generation Y consumers?', *Journal of Business Research*, 62: 617–628.

Norris, D.G. (1992) 'Ingredient branding: a strategy option with multiple beneficiaries', *Journal of Consumer Marketing*, 9: 19–31.

Ohl, F. (2003) 'Comment expliquer le succès des marques sportives auprès des jeunes consommateurs', *Revue Française du Marketing*, 191: 33–47.

Ohl, F. and Tribou, G. (2004) *Les Marchés du Sport*. Paris: Armand Colin.

Oppenhuisen, J. and van Zoonen, L. (2006) 'Supporters or customers? Fandom, marketing and the political economy of Dutch football', *Soccer and Society*, 7: 62–75.

Park, C., Jaworski, B. and MacInnis, D. (1986) 'Strategic brand concept-image management', *Journal of Marketing*, 50: 135–145.

Park, C. and Srinivasan, V. (1994) 'A survey-based method for measuring and understanding brand equity and its extendibility', *Journal of Marketing Research*, 31: 271–288.

Pelsmacker, P. De, Janssens, W., Sterckx, E. and Mielants, C. (2005) 'Consumer preferences for the marketing of ethically labelled coffee', *International Marketing Review*, 22: 512–530.

Pereira, J. (1988) 'The well heeled, pricey sneakers worn in inner city help set nation's fashion trend, *Wall Street Journal*, December: A1–A6.

Pernès, G. (2000) 'Marques, qualité de la vie et bien-être', *La Revue des Marques*, 29: 6–7.

Petry, K. and Schulze, B. (2011) 'Germany', in M. Nicholson, R. Hoye and B. Houlihan (eds), *Participation in Sport: international policy perspectives*. Abingdon: Routledge.

Pigeassou, C. (1993) 'La labellisation des activités sportives de loisir', in A. Loret (ed.) *Sport et Management: de l'éthique à la pratique*. Dunod: Paris, 309–331.

Pine II, B.J. and Gilmore, J. (1999) *The Experience Economy: work is theatre and every business a stage*. Harvard, MA: HBS Press.

Pons, F., Laroche, M., Nyeck, S. and Perreault, S. (1998) 'Role of sporting events as ethnoculture's emblems: impact of acculturation and ethnic identity on consumers' orientation toward sporting events', *Sport Marketing Quarterly*, 10: 231–240.

Porter, M. (1982) *Competitive Strategy*. New York: The Free Press, Macmillan Publishing Co.

Quart, A. (2004) *Nos Enfants Otages des Grandes Marques*. Montréal: Village Mondial.

Quester, P., Beverland, M. and Farrelly, F. (2006) 'Brand-personal values fit and brand meanings: exploring the role individual values play in ongoing brand loyalty in extreme sports subcultures', *Advances in Consumer Research*, 33: 21–28.

Randall, T., Ulrich, K. and Reibstein, D. (1998) 'Brand equity and vertical product line extent', *Marketing Science*, 17: 356–379.

Ransdell, E. (2000) *The Nike Story? Just tell it!* Fast company, January–February, p. 44.

Ritzer, G. (2010) *Enchanting a Disenchanted World: continuity and change in the cathedrals of consumption*, 3rd edn. Thousand Oaks, CA: Pine Forge Press.

Ritzer, G. (1993) *The McDonaldization of Society*. Thousand Oaks, CA: Pine Forge Press.

Robinson, L., Chelladurai, P. Bodet, G. and Downward, P. (2012) *Routledge Handbook of Sport Management*. Abingdon, Oxon: Routledge.

Rogers, E. (1995) *Diffusion of Innovations*, 4th edn. New York: The Free Press.

Rogers, E. (1983) *Diffusion of Innovations*, 3rd edn, New York: The Free Press.

Rouvrais-Charron, C. and Durand, C. (2004) 'Le rôle des héros de tribus sportives dans l'offre des équipementiers de la "glisse"', *Revue Européenne de Management du Sport*, 11: 57–90.

Sahlins, M. (1976) *Culture and Practical Reason*. Chicago, IL: University of Chicago Press.

Sandler D. and Shani, D. (1989) 'Olympic versus "ambush marketing": who gets the gold', *Journal of Advertising Research*, 29: 9–14.

Schmitt, B.H. (1999) *Experiential Marketing: how to get customers to SENSE, FEEL, THINK, ACT and RELATE to your company and brands*, New York: The Free Press.

Séguin, B. and Ellis, D. (2012) 'Ambush marketing', in L. Robinson, P. Chelladurai, G. Bodet and P. Downward (eds) *Routledge Handbook of Sport Management*. London: Routledge.

Semprini, A. (2005) *La Marque, Une Puissance Fragile*. Paris: Vuibert.

Semprini, A. (1992) *Le Marketing la Marque: approche sémiotique*. Paris: Liaisons.

Sheth, J.N. (1968) 'A factor model of brand loyalty', *Journal of Marketing Research*, 5: 395–404.

Schouten, J.W. and McAlexander, J.H. (1995) 'Subcultures of consumption: an ethnography of the new bikers', *Journal of Consumer Research*, 6:43–61.

Sicard, M.C. (2001) *Ce que Marque Veut Dire…*. Paris: Editions d'Organisations.

Sitz, L. and Amine, A. (2004) 'Consommation et groupes de consommateurs: de la tribu postmoderne aux communautés de marque: pour une clarification des concepts, *3rd Journées Normandes de la Consommation*, CD-Rom.

Skinner, J., Zakus, D. and Edwards, A. (2008) 'Coming in from the margins: ethnicity, community support and the rebranding of Australian soccer', *Soccer and Society*, 9: 394–404.

Solomon, M.R. (2005) *Comportement du consommateur*, New Jersey: Pearson Education France.

Solomon, M.R. (2003) *Consumer behaviour*, 6th edn. New Jersey: Pearson/Prentice Hall.

Solomon, M.R. (1988) 'Building up and breaking down: the impact of cultural sorting on symbolic consumption', in J. Sheth and E.C. Hirschman (ed.) *Research in Consumer Behavior*. Greenwich: Jai Press.

Solomon, M.R. (1986) 'The missing link: surrogate consumers in the marketing chain', *Journal of Marketing*, 50: 208–219.

Solomon, M.R. (1983) 'The role of products as social stimuli: a symbolic interactionism perspective', *Journal of Consumer Research*, 10: 319–329.

Solomon, M.R., Bamossy, G., Askegaard, S. and Hogg, M.K. (2010) *Consumer Behaviour: a European perspective*, 4th edn. London: Prentice Hall FT.

Solomon, M.R. and Englis, B.G. (1994) 'Reality engineering: blurring the boundaries between marketing and popular culture', *Journal of Current Issues and Research in Advertising*, 16: 1–17.

Stanbouli, K. (2003) 'Marketing viral et publicité', *Revue Française du Marketing*, 192–193: 97–106.

Sue, R. (1997) *La Richesse des Hommes*. Paris: Odile Jacob.

Toffoli, R. and Laroche, M. (1998) 'Cultural and language effects on the perception of source honesty and forcefulness in advertising: a comparison of Hong-Kong Chinese and Anglo Canadian', *Proceedings from the Multicultural Annual Conference of the American Marketing Science*, Montreal.

Turker, D. (2008) 'Measuring corporate social responsibility: a scale development study', *Ethics*, 85: 41–427.

Underwood, R., Bond, E. and Baer, R. (2001) 'Building service brands via social identity: lessons from the sport marketplace', *Journal of Marketing Theory and Practice*, 9: 1–13.

Walker, M. and Kent, A. (2009) 'Do fans care? Assessing the influence of the corporate social responsibility on consumer attitudes in the sport industry', *Journal of Sport Management*, 23: 743–769.

INDEX